WEBER'S
NEW AMERICAN
BARBECUE™

JAMIE PURVIANCE

FOOD PHOTOGRAPHY BY
TIM TURNER

LIFESTYLE PHOTOGRAPHY BY
MICHAEL WARREN

HOUGHTON MIFFLIN HARCOURT
BOSTON · NEW YORK · 2016

CONTENTS

AMERICAN-MADE
KOREAN BARBECUE

38

SPECIAL FEATURES }

NOUVEAU 'CUE
RIBS

80

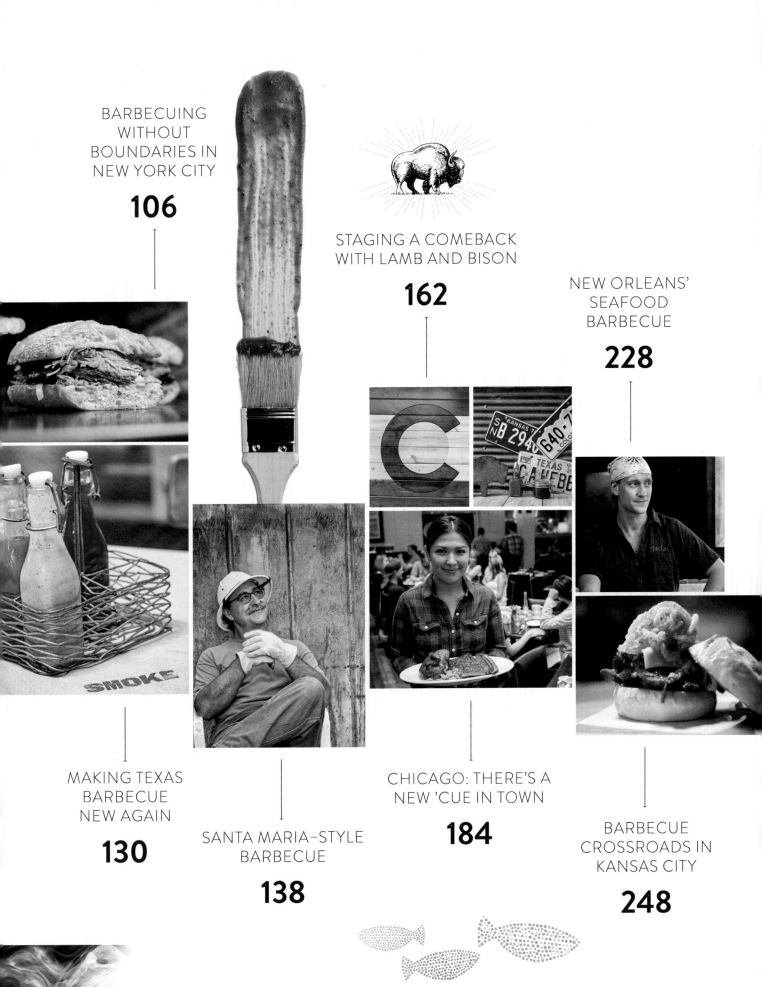

WHAT'S NEW IN BARBECUE?

Jamie Purviance

> **WHAT WAS ONCE A STYLE OF FOOD ROOTED IN THE RURAL SOUTH IS NOW ALMOST EVERYWHERE, EVEN IN BIG CITIES, AND, IN TURN, THOSE CITIES ARE INFLUENCING THE FOOD.**

Barbecue. Surely you've heard of it, but what exactly is it? I used to think I knew. It was supposed to be spice-rubbed pork ribs glistening with sauce, or tender slices of smoked brisket dripping juices on butcher paper, or succulent shreds of pork shoulder piled high on soft white buns. Those were supposed to be the epitome of barbecue—an American institution that has held tightly to strict principles since the first days of our nation. At least that is what I thought. Several years ago I accidently offended a fellow student at the Culinary Institute of America by inviting him to a weekend "barbecue" where I intended to grill hamburgers and sausages. He was raised in North Carolina with more than a little local pride, and so he responded indignantly, "That's not barbecue. Real barbecue is cooked in a pit with wood, not on a grill." Then he schooled me about serious regional differences in barbecue. Maybe you have heard of these. In the Piedmont of North Carolina, barbecue means pit-cooked and chopped pork served in a tomato-tinged vinegar sauce with slaw and hush puppies on the side. No beef is allowed. But in Texas proper, barbecue *is* beef—especially brisket and hefty beef ribs—and pit masters there are likely to protest at anyone coating it with sauce or trying to eat it with a fork. On and on my classmate went, pounding his fists on the table and telling me you can't possibly cook barbecue with gas. You have to do it like third-generation pit master Sam Jones at Skylight Inn BBQ in Ayden, North Carolina, where a billboard outside the legendary restaurant clearly states, "If it's not cooked with wood it's not BBQ." Well, okay, I assumed my red-faced classmate had sufficient credentials that I should believe him. I filed away his lesson about what "authentic" barbecue means, and for years I tended to agree with it. While writing this book, however, I felt compelled to check his facts and to dig a little deeper. Among other things, I wanted to know about the origins of American barbecue. It turns out that American barbecue's starting point was *barbacoa*, which dates to the 1500s: a framework of green branches and sticks elevated high over a fire for cooking. That's how barbecue was practiced in a region that is now the West Indies and along the southeastern coast of North America, including Florida. Just to be clear, those Indians were not cooking racks of baby back ribs or smoky briskets to be sliced for barbecue sandwiches. No, no, no. They were cooking fish, turtles, iguana, alligator, and snakes—pretty much anything they could catch and slaughter. So if you really want to talk about authentic American barbecue, maybe we should forget the pulled pork sandwiches and think instead about how to roast an alligator over a campfire.

In fact, maybe we should forget the whole question of what's authentic. Clearly, with barbecue, the food evolves over time with cultural changes. Today, brisket seems like it is permanently enshrined along with beef ribs and sausage as part of the "holy trinity" of Texas barbecue meats. Historically speaking, however, brisket is a relatively new thing, and soon it might be replaced (check out the timeline on the facing page).

What was once a style of food rooted in the rural South is now almost everywhere, even in big cities, and, in turn, those cities are influencing the food. At Hometown Bar-B-Que in Brooklyn, New York, pit master Bill Durney is a lot more creative than he ever would be in Central Texas where he did his barbecue training. On Durney's menu you will find sweet Korean sticky ribs, a Vietnamese-style lamb belly banh mi sandwich with crunchy daikon, and spicy jerk baby back ribs. Why? The people in Brooklyn, some of them from Korean, Vietnamese, and Caribbean backgrounds, like their distinctive international flavors in their barbecue.

Barbecue competitions, including the ones on reality television shows, have made barbecue a sport that has launched winners toward fame and fortune. Lee Ann Whippen was a blue-collar caterer from Virginia who smoked her way to the top at some major competitions. When a restaurateur from Chicago saw an opportunity to take barbecue upmarket, he recruited Whippen to be the executive chef at Chicago q, a fine-dining restaurant in the city's Gold Coast neighborhood. In a space that looks more like a private country club than an old-school barbecue joint, Whippen is wowing diners with her competition-style ribs, blackened alligator, and a brunch menu with eggs Benedict on prime-grade brisket. Brunch at a barbecue restaurant? Yes! Why not?

▼

▲

Doug Adams grew up near Texas barbecue country and took the food for granted until he moved to Portland, Oregon, to attend cooking school. Today this *Top Chef* finalist cooks at the high-end Imperial restaurant, where his menu draws from a wood-burning grill and tastes from his childhood. Adams' food caters to Portland's funky eclectic culture, but still he shows traces of barbecue everywhere. "I am obsessed with smoke," he says. "I try every piece of meat or produce that comes into the kitchen on the wood grill before it goes anywhere else." At first glance his dish of green beans with smoked elk tongue, kimchi, and a deep-fried egg seems to have no traditional roots at all. "Yeah, I know that dish sounds weird," admits Adams, "but to me it is so Texas. It is smoked meat and pickles. As for the egg, we deep-fry almost everything in Texas. If you break down my food, you see a lot of barbecue. As a chef I am always asking myself how can I build on barbecue but do it differently."

Traditionalists don't need to worry about these changes. Just because someone like Doug Adams or me or you asks "what if?" or "why not?" we are not threatening barbecue; we are broadening it. Gradual change has been part of its nature since the days of barbacoa.

In our food-obsessed, Internet-connected, melting-pot nation, change is happening faster than ever, and it's no coincidence that the popularity of barbecue is surging. My respect for the classic dishes is deep and permanent, and I have shared many of those recipes with you in this book. I have also shared recipes and stories inspired by the classics but freed by the creativity at play today. I hope you cook them and make them your own. Each time we bring our own styles and stories to the experience, we contribute something real to this ever-expanding phenomenon called American barbecue. So get into it. Barbecue like you mean it and ask yourself, "What's next?"

▼

"

IN OUR FOOD-OBSESSED, INTERNET-CONNECTED, MELTING-POT NATION, CHANGE IS HAPPENING FASTER THAN EVER, AND IT'S NO COINCIDENCE THAT THE POPULARITY OF BARBECUE IS SURGING.

AMERICAN BARBECUE
OVER TIME

1600s

By the 1600s settlers in the New World were using various spellings to describe the style of cooking that they had adapted from the Indians. Terms such as "borbecue" and "barbecu" were meant to signify that their ways were more civilized than the "savage" techniques they had witnessed. That's funny because the settlers' barbecues often devolved into rowdy brawls among drunken men.

1700s

Political candidates in the 1700s used barbecues as a tactic for drawing big crowds, plying undecided voters with bourbon, rum, and roasted meat. George Washington wrote in his diary that he attended six barbecues between 1769 and 1774. Later, after he had set in place the cornerstone of the United State's Capital building in 1793, he hosted a meal featuring a 500-pound barbecued ox.

1800s

During the 1800s, barbecue thrived in the South and expanded westward, too, along with the settlers. By midcentury, railroad promoters used barbecues to lure citizens into supporting railway construction: have a free meal, buy shares in a rail company. On national holidays like the Fourth of July, settlers gathered, cleared the land if needed, and pooled whatever each family had to offer—hogs, ox, venison, turkeys, and even squirrels. People ate, drank, and danced to the music of fiddlers well into the night.

The emancipation of slaves in 1865 meant that for the first time, African-American pit masters were free to run barbecue joints for their own profit. Henry Perry was born near Memphis in 1875 and worked for much of his young life in steamboat kitchens moving up and down the Mississippi River and Missouri River. In the early 1900s he moved to Kansas City and started selling smoked meat wrapped in newspaper for 25 cents a slab. Eventually he opened the first real barbecue restaurant in Kansas City, and his menu included beef, woodchuck, raccoon, and opossum. When Henry died, a former employee, Charlie Bryant, took over the restaurant and then sold it to his brother Arthur. You can go to Arthur Bryant's restaurant in Kansas City today (in a new location), but don't ask for opossum. That was old American barbecue.

1900s

In the early 1900s butchers at Central Texas meat markets bought whole forequarters of beef from local ranchers, carved off the best cuts to display in the meat case, and put the less desirable ones, like chuck and shoulder, on a smoker to prevent them from going to waste. Over time their barbecued meats proved to be more popular and profitable than fresh meats, so many butchers specialized in selling barbecue. In the 1960s, though, feedlots and refrigerated transport made beef a national industry, and meat markets could order whatever pre-butchered, shrink-wrapped cuts they wanted. Most of them chose brisket because it was so inexpensive. Today, with brisket prices much higher than they were a decade ago, some Texas pit masters predict that they might need to find something cheaper.

2000s

By the year 2000, barbecue had expanded well beyond roadside stands and restaurants. Weber had grown from a small, midwestern company to the world's largest manufacturer of barbecue grills. Today, Weber grills are sold in nearly every town in the U.S., and Americans are able to recreate many traditional barbecue dishes in their own backyards. Increasingly, barbecue cooks are riffing on tradition and shaping new, multicultural styles. See page 18 for the Top Five Barbecue Trends Today.

IT'S ALL ABOUT

FIRE

I doubt we will ever reach a consensus in America about what barbecue is and what it isn't. Fans can be downright dogmatic in their loyalties, claiming that if you are not making *their* kind of barbecue you are not making *real* barbecue. That's okay. It means we have a great diversity of styles in this country. New American barbecue encompasses all styles, with a unifying element that has been present since the days of *barbacoa*: fire. Broadly speaking, barbecue means cooking over a fire. With that in mind, if we are going to get better at barbecue, we should get better at controlling fire.

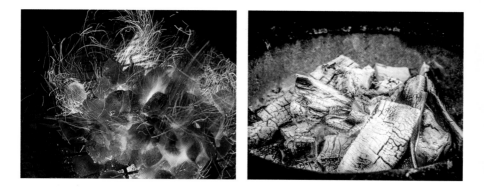

WOOD

When you introduce enough heat and oxygen to wood, it burns. Molecules in the logs get hot enough that they break apart and rearrange themselves into gases. All that activity of breaking apart and rearranging produces heat and light, or in other words, fire ... and smoke. In the early stages, while the wood is dehydrating with a lot of hissing and sizzling, the smoke is pretty dark and sooty because the wood is burning off impurities. At higher temperatures (700° to 1000°F), the wood starts to release a cleaner quality of smoke with a faint color between white and blue rippling in the air. That's "blue smoke," the kind that holds soft woodsy aromas associated with great barbecue.

WHAT IS SMOKE?

Smoke combines three types of matter in one. The smoke you see in the air is made of tiny solid particles and droplets of liquid. What you don't see are the invisible gases that are more responsible for making barbecue taste good. Those gases hold magically aromatic wood compounds that make us say *yum*.

When we barbecue we should be trying to capture those invisible gases, not so much the thick visible smoke. If you see a fire pushing dark smoke out of the vents like a freight train, the solid and liquid particles are far too big. They are piling up on the surface of the meat, probably creating a sooty taste.

If a fire has plenty of oxygen (from airflow through the vents) and the fuel is dry, temperatures rise to the point that you get lovely aromatic compounds in tiny little particles. At this point the temperature inside the fire is usually over 750°F, but that's almost impossible to measure, because we shouldn't put probes into burning embers; instead, we need to watch the color and density of the smoke.

BASICS

8

CHARCOAL

Charcoal is essentially burned wood—at least partially burned. In a process known as pyrolysis, nearly all the water, gases, and many of the organic compounds in the wood have been incinerated in the process of making charcoal. What's left then is almost pure carbon.

Hardwood lump charcoal is a perfect example. These are black, irregularly shaped lumps of thoroughly charred wood. You can still see the wood grain in some pieces. When lump charcoal is made from scrap lumber, it looks more like broken planks, only black. Either way, the wood has been burned at very high temperatures (about 1000°F) in a very-low-oxygen environment.

Today there are more than 75 types of hardwood charcoal, including many from a certain "varietal" of wood, like mesquite or hickory. Each type of wood has its own range of aromas and heating potential. For example, mesquite has more lignin (aromatic alcohols) than hickory, so it burns hotter and leaves a sharper taste in the food. When manufacturers rely on hardwood scraps from lumberyards and building supply operations, you really can't be sure of the wood's origin, and usually the aromas are generic and unimpressive.

The main reasons some cooks prefer lump charcoal are that it seems purer and more natural than briquettes, it lights easily, it burns hot, it produces a pleasant smoke, and it leaves very little ash in your cooker (because it has no fillers). Because the pieces are irregular, how and when they fall is a game of chance, and sometimes the distribution of heat shifts dramatically. One of the other challenges of cooking with lump charcoal is that it burns out pretty quickly, often within a half hour, so you need to be prepared to feed the fire continually. Otherwise, you are better off with briquettes.

Charcoal briquettes generate plenty of heat and sustain it for longer times than lump charcoal. People debate whether or not briquettes add much flavor. I believe that many of them do, which is why I use them often. The flavor, of course, depends on the type of briquettes. The biggest manufacturer in America (Kingsford) started in the late nineteenth century as a way for auto man Henry Ford to use up the scrap wood left after making Model T cars. Today, when Kingsford makes briquettes, they start with sawdust that is cooked in airtight ovens. To the crushed wood they add limestone, boric acid,

ground coal, sodium nitrate, and a binder like cornstarch. After that, the mixture is shaped into little pillows that are designed to allow air to flow easily around and between them.

With America's growing interest in natural products, some manufacturers are selling 100 percent natural briquettes, avoiding the chemicals that make the briquettes easier to light and longer lasting. The all-natural briquettes are made almost entirely with crushed hardwood charcoal held together in the familiar pillow shape with a vegetable binder.

On the opposite end of the natural spectrum, some types of charcoal are saturated with petroleum chemicals for the sake of convenience. All you need to do is drop a lit match on these briquettes and presto—you have a fire. The fact that it smells like oil may or may not be a problem for you. I know people who grew up with so much lighter fluid on charcoal that they think their food *should* taste a little like oil. As with all things in barbecue, it's a matter of personal taste. Personally, I never use briquettes made with lighter fluid. It's so easy to light them with newspaper or Weber® lighter cubes.

WOOD CHIPS

AND CHUNKS

A fire made entirely of wood in a grill requires waiting about an hour for flames to burn down to a level that's right for grilling or smoking. Cooking over embers usually works much better than cooking over wildly dancing flames, but even then, managing mercurial embers is challenging. What a lot of people do instead is to create a fire with charcoal or gas, and then supplement it with wood. The wood is typically in the form of chips or chunks. I usually use wood chips in my grills and wood chunks in my smokers. In the end they can both add the same aromas and colors to your food. When to use one or the other is largely a matter of practicality.

Wood chips burn up faster. Even when soaked in water (as they should be), they burn quicker than wood chunks. I soak my wood chips in water for at least 30 minutes, sometimes much longer. As long as they are waterlogged, the length of time doesn't really matter. Then I lift them out of the water and shake off the excess. I wouldn't want to add handfuls of water that would cool off the charcoal. I scatter the wood chips—usually two or three large handfuls at a time—over the burning charcoal to turn the grill into a smoker immediately. The chips smolder and smoke for somewhere between 20 to 30 minutes, depending on how hot the fire is and how much air is pouring through it.

Your gas grill can be a smoker, too, one that is even easier to control if it has a smoker box. This is usually a metal box with a hinged, perforated lid. In the most convenient scenario the smoker box sits right over a gas burner that you can control with its own dedicated knob. Fill the box with soaked, drained wood chips, turn the burner on high

to get the chips smoking within minutes, and then reduce the heat way down (or completely off) so that the chips smoke rather than catch fire. A nice thing about the hinged lid is that it allows you to replenish the wood chips and keep the smoke going for as long as you like. If the chips ever do catch fire, douse the flames with water from a spray bottle. That's true of flaming chips in a charcoal fire, too.

If your grill does not have a smoker box built over a dedicated burner, you can set a portable smoker box either under or on top of the cooking grate. Not surprisingly, the wood chips will light much faster when you set a box under the cooking grate and very close to one or two burners (do this *before* lighting the grill). The big limitation here is that you won't be able to replenish the chips with the box in that position. If you set a portable smoker box filled with wood chips on top of the grate, you will probably need to wait close to 30 minutes with all the burners on high and the lid closed before you get a decent amount of smoke.

To reduce this wait time, some cooks start by putting dry wood chips on the bottom of the smoker box, and then filling the rest with damp wood chips so that the dry chips light a little faster and in turn ignite the damp chips.

When you are using a smoker, you are typically cooking for several hours, and adding wood chips every half hour or so might get tedious, so this is a good case for using wood chunks instead. They generate smoke slowly and steadily for hours. You don't even need to soak them in water. You could try, but trust me; the water doesn't penetrate into the wood very far. Drop the dry chunks on the burning

charcoal. I usually start with four to six large handfuls. Sometimes one chunk is big enough for a handful. Sometimes you need three or more chunks to make a handful. The initial chunks of wood should last a few hours. After that, add a couple more handfuls at a time for a steady stream of smoke.

WOOD AS AN INGREDIENT

The barbecue world is swirling with opinions about which types of wood taste best with certain types of food. It used to be simpler. People smoked with whatever wood was plentiful and cheap. That's why hickory and pecan were so common with pork barbecue in the Carolinas. In Texas there was always post oak and mesquite nearby, so those were the types of wood pit masters used. One of the distinctive characteristics of Santa Maria–style barbecue out in California is the taste of a red oak tree that grows along the hillsides of Santa Maria County. So some regions have their rightful pairings. If you don't live in one of those regions, feel free to borrow one of their time-honored pairings or make some new ones of your own. I recommend you start with what I call "the big five." These are the woods most readily available all over the country.

APPLE
MILD

One of the mildest woods, it has a nice sweet smoke that tastes great on seafood, poultry, and pork.

CHERRY
MILD

This wood has a light fruity smoke similar to apple, but it also produces a rich, dark color that is gorgeous on barbecued chicken or pork ribs.

OAK
MODERATE

An all-purpose wood that generates a medium-strength smoke, oak goes with almost anything, and it plays well with others. Try mixing it with other woods for some aromatic blends.

HICKORY
MODERATE

This one has a nutty taste that is similar to oak but it's a bit stronger, making it a good match with pork or beef. Pecan is close in flavor to hickory, so consider using that, too.

MESQUITE
STRONG

This southwestern favorite is mighty strong, so much so that you might want to treat it like hot chile peppers. Using too much for too long would leave you with some bitter, pungent flavors. Try cutting the intensity of mesquite with something milder like apple or cherry.

BEYOND THE BIG FIVE

There are at least a dozen other wood choices. Alder wood is terrific with fish. Maple is a middle-of-the-road choice for poultry and pork. Walnut packs a punch almost as strong as mesquite, so use it sparingly and in combination with milder woods.

Whatever wood you choose, it must be seasoned, meaning the wood has dried in open air. If you buy your wood chunks or chips in a retail store, they will already be seasoned. If you want to try using wood from your backyard, stack and dry it first. Freshly cut (green) logs hold as much as 50 percent of their weight in water, so they would burn unevenly with a sooty smoke. Soft woods like pine and cedar are also problematic. They make lovely furniture, but their high sap content would make terrible barbecue, so stick to the hard (dense) woods.

HOW DO THEY } WORK?

What equipment you use to barbecue is often a matter of what you already happen to have. If your cooker can hold the temperatures you need and allow wood smoke to waft over your food, you're in business. However, each type of cooker does have its own advantages based on the way it works. Water smokers are designed to hold very low temperatures for several hours (even overnight) with little involvement required from you. A charcoal grill can do just about anything a water smoker can do (and more), but it requires frequent tending of the fire, especially for long cooking sessions. A gas grill is the easiest of these three for maintaining precise temperatures, and having the flexibility to create different zones of heat opens up a lot of possibilities. Some gas grills have built-in smoker boxes for wood chips, making it simpler than ever to barbecue.

EXHAUST DAMPER

CONVECTION HEAT

WATER PAN

LIT CHARCOAL

INTAKE DAMPER

WATER SMOKER

▼

A water smoker operates in some of the same ways as a kettle charcoal grill. Oxygen enters from below and feeds the charcoal that is raised on a grate for quick combustion. The heat radiates upwards, conducts somewhat through the cooking grates, and circulates around the cooking chamber with smoke. The big difference is that the heat is almost always low (225° to 275°F) because the amount of oxygen entering a smoker is less than what typically enters a kettle grill. The heat is also always indirect because of a water pan that sits between the charcoal and the food. The pan deflects the direct heat around the food, and the water absorbs much of the heat. The more water you pour into the pan, the more heat it absorbs. The water slowly releases heat and humidity into the cooking chamber. When you lift the lid, a lot of heat escapes, but the thermal mass of water continues to hold enough heat that the smoker can return quickly to the ideal smoking temperature.

CHARCOAL GRILL

A charcoal kettle grill is a culinary multitasker—an amazingly efficient tool for cooking many different ways, including searing, roasting, and smoking, depending on how you arrange the fire and the food in relation to one another.

In a kettle grill, the charcoal gets the oxygen it needs mostly through the damper on the bottom of the bowl. With the charcoal raised on a grate, plenty of oxygen can move under and around the individual briquettes or other pieces, causing temperatures to rise quickly. Heat radiates off the charcoal and hits the food directly, just like the sun's heat travels to earth, losing strength as it gets farther from the source. The heat also conducts through the metal cooking grate, searing whatever else is on the hot grate. And the heat circulates under the closed lid, traveling with the air that moves inside the grill. The damper on the lid allows some hot air to escape through the vents, creating a vacuum that is filled by fresh air entering at the bottom of the grill. This airflow moves heat and smoke around the food continuously in a convectional pattern. The bigger the openings in the dampers, the faster the convection happens, and the higher the temperatures climb.

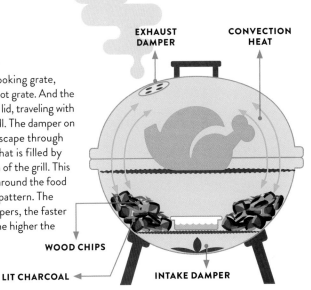

EXHAUST DAMPER

CONVECTION HEAT

WOOD CHIPS

LIT CHARCOAL

INTAKE DAMPER

GAS GRILL

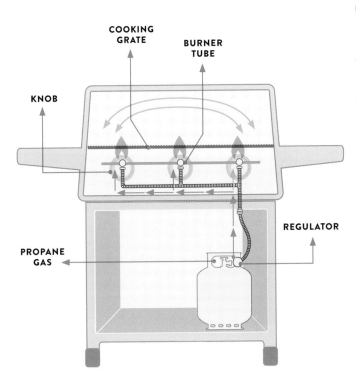

COOKING GRATE

BURNER TUBE

KNOB

REGULATOR

PROPANE GAS

A gas grill is really a horse of a different color. Its fuel is obviously very different and so is the way the fuel burns. In most cases the fuel comes in a portable tank filled with pressurized liquid propane. As you release liquid propane from the tank, it immediately vaporizes into a gas that is ignited by a spark. The spark comes from a push button igniter that makes a single loud click, or a button that operates a battery powered igniter that goes tick-tick-tick. Gas is forced through the area where the spark(s) occur and it ignites. A gas grill's regulator is that round metal device that looks like a flying saucer between the tank and the valves. Its job is to control the pressure of the gas releasing from the tank. The gas flows through a hose to valves operated by control knobs. As you turn a knob from low to medium to high, more gas is released toward the burner tubes and a blue flame above the burner becomes larger.

Metal bars above the burners radiate heat upwards to cooking grates, which transfer the heat to the food being grilled. As the food cooks, drippings fall onto hot surfaces inside the grill and vaporize into smoke. With the lid closed and air entering from the bottom of the cooking chamber, heat and smoke circulate around the food imparting that distinctive barbecued flavor. You can add wood-smoke flavor using techniques described on page 10.

Fuels such as natural gas and propane burn cleanly and completely, leaving no smoke or ash behind. Natural gas is piped from a local utility. Propane gas is compressed into a liquid that is easy to transport in tanks. When it comes to cooking, natural gas and propane deliver almost identical results, but you need a different type of grill for each type of gas. Many barbecue restaurants, including some of the most acclaimed, cook with gas-powered smokers that burn wood for flavor. The fire and flavor are easier for the cooks to control, and a similar arrangement could be easier for you, too.

▼ LIGHTING CHARCOAL

▼

A chimney starter is an upright metal cylinder with a handle on the outside and a wire rack inside. Fill the space under the wire rack with a few sheets of wadded-up newspaper or a few Weber® lighter cubes, and then fill the space above the rack with charcoal briquettes.

▼

Once the charcoal is lit, some impressive thermodynamics channel the heat evenly throughout the fuel, meaning all of the pieces burn evenly and you can start cooking with consistent temperatures all the way across your charcoal fire.

▼

When the briquettes are lightly covered with gray ash, put on two insulated barbecue mitts or gloves and grab hold of the two handles on the chimney starter. The swinging handle is there to help you lift the chimney starter and safely aim the coals just where you want them.

DIRECT AND INDIRECT HEAT

▼

People often ask me for my single most important tip about grilling and barbecue. It's a hard question to answer because most of the important tips relate to a specific type of food, like a steak or a pork shoulder or a rack of beef ribs. So the answer I usually give is something like this: If you learn how to create and control the differences between direct and indirect heat, you increase your chances of success dramatically. If you limit yourself to just one type of heat or the other, you are missing opportunities for control. A great griller masters the fire, not the other way around.

Simply put, when you are cooking right over a fire, you are using direct heat. When the fire is off to the side of the food, or the food is somehow shielded from direct heat, you are using indirect heat.

Foods that do best over direct heat are small and tender—things like hamburgers, steaks, seafood of all kinds, and vegetables. In a matter of minutes, direct heat can char the outside of the food and penetrate far enough inside that the centers are cooked, too. If you use direct

heat only with big, tough cuts of meat like a pork shoulder, the outsides will burn long before the centers are cooked, let alone tender.

An indirect fire works best for larger, tougher foods that need gentle circulating heat and longer cooking times, such as roasts, whole chickens, and ribs.

"

A GREAT GRILLER MASTERS THE FIRE, NOT THE OTHER WAY AROUND.

LIGHTING A GAS GRILL

▼

Lighting a gas grill, in most cases, is as simple as lifting the lid, turning on the gas, and igniting the burners (follow your owner's guide for lighting instructions). Here's how to do it: After you've opened the valve on your propane tank all the way (or turned on the gas at the source), wait a minute for the gas to travel through the gas line, and then turn each burner to high. Close the lid and preheat the grill to about 500°F.

BASIC }SETUPS

⊙ INDIRECT COOKING

For a charcoal grill, the lit briquettes are split apart on the charcoal grate so that you have two separate zones of direct heat on opposite sides of the food and one of indirect heat in the middle. You can use baskets to hold the briquettes or you can pour the briquettes right onto the charcoal grate in two even beds. Sometimes it helps to have a foil pan in the middle. Filling that pan about halfway with water weighs it down and provides some humidity inside the grill, which is useful for maintaining temperatures.

On a gas grill, the most common way to set up for indirect cooking is to have the outside burner(s) on and the inside burner(s) off. If you have a three-burner grill, turn all the burners on and preheat the grill for about 10 minutes. Then turn off the burner in the middle and adjust the other two burners to the level of heat you like. If you have a six-burner grill, preheat it with all six burners on for about 10 minutes. Then turn off one or two burners in the middle.

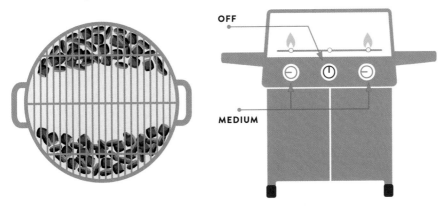

⊙ DIRECT COOKING

Set up your charcoal grill for direct cooking by spreading lit charcoal in a single layer all the way across the charcoal grate. This creates one wide zone of direct heat. If the food you're cooking is likely to flare up, it's helpful to keep a small

part of the charcoal grate clear of briquettes as a safety zone of indirect heat.

Using direct heat on a gas grill is simply a matter of cooking the food right over lit burners.

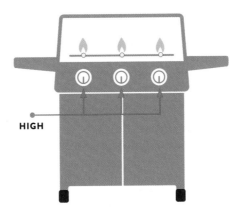

GRILL SAFETY

⊙

Please read your Owner's Guide and familiarize yourself with and follow all "dangers," "warnings," and "cautions." Also follow the grilling procedures and maintenance requirements listed in your Owner's Guide.

If you cannot locate the Owner's Guide for your grill model, please contact the manufacturer prior to use. If you have any questions concerning the "dangers," "warnings," and "cautions" contained in your Weber® gas, charcoal, or electric grill Owner's Guide, or if you do not have an Owner's Guide for your specific grill model, please visit www.weber.com to access your Owner's Guide or for the toll-free number for Weber-Stephen Products LLC Customer Service before using your grill.

SMOKER } SETUP

Smokers come in an amazing array of designs. I could show you dozens of smokers than look almost nothing like each other even though they are designed to do the same thing.

There are cinderblock pits with a wood fire on the bottom or to one side. There are barrel smokers (shaped like an oil barrel or pipeline on its side) with a firebox to one side so the fire and smoke flow horizontally over the food. There are rotisserie smokers with electric-powered Ferris wheels rotating racks of meat. There are pellet smokers in the shape of a refrigerator with a firebox to the side where an electric augur pushes tiny sawdust pellets onto a burner. There are kamado-style smokers made of ceramic material in the shape of a giant oval urn with the fire on the bottom and a plate in the middle to deflect the rising heat.

That's just an abbreviated sampling of what's out there. You could spend days looking at all the smoker options and comparing various features and costs. Whatever type of smoker you choose, the key is that you are able to gain control of how it cooks as soon as possible, rather than struggling with a lot of trial and error. That's one reason many backyard cooks start with something simple like an upright water smoker. It's inexpensive, easy to control, and very consistent from day one.

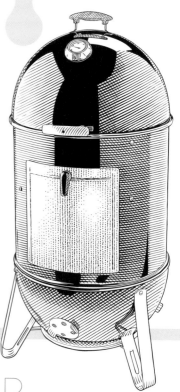

⊙ TENDING TO YOUR SMOKER

A water smoker normally maintains temperatures in the range of 200° to 275°F for several hours with no added fuel, but there are at least a few ways to fine-tune the heat:

1 The easiest way to regulate the smoker's temperature is by adjusting the vents on the dampers. The less air you allow into the smoker, the lower the temperature will go. To raise the temperature, open the vents wider.

2 You can also raise the temperature in the smoker by adding more charcoal through the access door, although this is rarely necessary for recipes that cook in less than eight hours.

3 A third way is to adjust the amount of water in the pan positioned between the fire and food. The water regulates the temperature by absorbing heat and releasing it gradually. The more water you have in the pan, the lower the temperature will be. Adding more water will lower the temperature.

1　To set up a water smoker, first separate it into it three main sections: the charcoal bowl, the cooking chamber, and the lid.

2　Lay the charcoal grate in the charcoal bowl and set the charcoal ring on top of the grate. The ring holds the charcoal in place and allows airflow through the holes for proper combustion.

3　Fill the ring about three-quarters of the way with charcoal briquettes. Fill a chimney starter with briquettes and light the charcoal in a safe place.

4　When the briquettes are lightly covered with gray ash, carefully pour the lit charcoal over the unlit charcoal.

5　Spread out the lit briquettes evenly with long-handled tongs. Over time the unlit charcoal will light and burn slowly, often extending the life of the fire for as long as eight hours without any additional fuel, although you can add that later if needed.

6　Make sure the water pan is empty and suspended inside the cooking chamber and the charcoal access door is closed. Set the cooking chamber over the charcoal bowl.

7　Immediately fill the pan about three-quarters full with water before the water pan gets too hot. Then set the two cooking grates in place inside the cooking chamber.

8　Now place the lid on top. A water smoker has vents on the bottom of the charcoal bowl and on the lid. At this point open the top vent completely and close the bottom vents about halfway. Wait until the smoker reaches the ideal smoking temperature range of 200° to 275°F.

9　Open the charcoal access door and add as many dry wood chunks as the recipe suggests. Add them either with long-handled tongs or wearing insulated barbecue mitts or gloves. Close the charcoal access door and wait a few minutes for the smoke to stream out of the vent on the lid.

TOP FIVE } BARBECUE TRENDS TODAY

1

BARBECUE IS GETTING PERSONAL

> *Regional boundaries are giving way to loose individual riffs of barbecue that show as much free-spirited creativity as they do time-honored traditions. Young chefs and backyard cooks are blending old-school techniques with fresh mixes of flavors inspired by their own imaginations to come up with recipes like pulled pork bo ssam lettuce cups and ribs with blueberry-chipotle barbecue sauce.*

2

BARBECUE IS A FULL-FLEDGED SPORT

> *In the 1980s a few Midwesterners formed a little club for people who wanted to compete at making barbecue. Bragging rights were the only prizes. Since then, the Kansas City Barbecue Society (KCBS) has grown steadily in size and stature. It now has more than 21,000 members worldwide, and it sanctions more than 500 competitions each year, with more than $4.5 million awarded in prizes during 2014 alone.*

3

BARBECUE IS COOKING WITH GAS

> In the old days, barbecue joints had a woodpile out back that was the only fuel for the pit, and a cook's primary tool was a shovel for the coals. Today, you are more likely to find barbecue chefs cooking with gas-powered, thermostat-controlled smokers with electric rotisseries turning racks of meat like a Ferris wheel. The new smokers still burn wood, but much more for flavor than heat.

4

BARBECUE IS GETTING SWEETER

> It used to be that barbecue was all about the meat, which was sometimes basted with vinegar and spices. Today restaurants typically offer four to six styles of sauce at the table, most of them heavily sweetened with sugar, molasses, honey, or agave. An average supermarket sells more than 20 kinds of barbecue sauce, and the best-selling ones are more than 50 percent corn syrup or sugar.

> Barbecue restaurants are not museums; they are businesses adapting to what matters most to customers. More and more often, menus are highlighting expensive heritage meats and organic side dishes, not to mention craft beers and dozens of bourbons and ryes. Many joints still serve barbecue on butcher paper, but there are a lot of fine dining touches out there, even pricey wine lists and valet parking.

5

BARBECUE IS MOVING UPMARKET

1

STARTERS

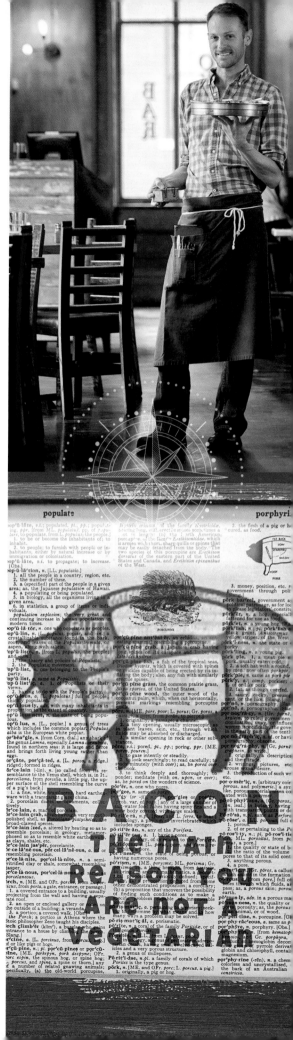

SEA BREEZE BARBECUED OYSTERS

SERVES: 4 TO 6 | **PREP TIME:** 15 MINUTES, PLUS TIME TO SHUCK THE OYSTERS
GRILLING TIME: 3 TO 4 MINUTES | **SPECIAL EQUIPMENT:** OYSTER KNIFE

2 dozen large, fresh oysters
1 large navel orange
12 fresh or frozen cranberries,
   thawed if frozen
2 tablespoons vodka
1 tablespoon fresh lime juice

Grapefruit juice is traditional in the quintessential New England cocktail; however, a new version of the Sea Breeze, with orange juice, has recently become the rage at beach resorts along the East Coast. That's something distinctive about American cuisine—it constantly morphs, with new flavors and techniques always in the offing. I've borrowed the flavors of this new take on the classic cocktail to create a fresh, summery relish for barbecued oysters. You can substitute half of a seedless grapefruit if you want the traditional flavor, but I think the orange pairs with oysters even better.

1 Grip each oyster, flat side up, in a folded kitchen towel. Find the small opening between the shells near the hinge and pry it open with an oyster knife. Try not to spill the delicious juices, known as the "oyster liquor," in the bottom shell. Cut the oyster meat loose from the top shell, and then loosen the oyster from the bottom shell by running the oyster knife carefully underneath the body. Discard the top, flatter shell, keeping the oyster and juices in the bottom, deeper shell.

2 Prepare the grill for direct cooking over high heat (450° to 550°F).

3 Use a vegetable peeler to remove two strips of zest from the orange, each 3 inches long by ½ inch wide. Peel and supreme the orange (see caption and photo below). Place the zest strips, orange supremes, cranberries, vodka, and lime juice in a blender. Cover and pulse until finely ground, almost pureed, scraping the inside of the blender jar a couple of times between pulses to achieve an even texture.

4 Spoon ½ tablespoon of the orange mixture onto each shucked oyster in its shell. Place the oysters on the cooking grate over **direct high heat**, close the lid, and grill until the juices bubble, 3 to 4 minutes. With tongs gripping one edge, transfer the oysters in their shells to a heatproof platter. Serve warm.

Supremes are more than backup singers for Diana Ross. They are also sections of citrus fruit with the membrane removed. To create orange supremes, peel the orange, removing as much of the white pith as possible. Cradle the fruit in one hand and hold it over a bowl as you use a paring knife to cut down along either side of the thin membranes between the sections, one at a time, removing the orange sections and leaving the membranes behind. Let the supremes drop into the bowl below as you make your way around the orange, removing the remaining segments.

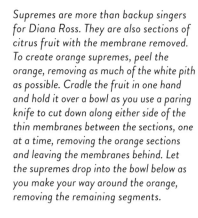

CHAR-GRILLED OYSTERS
WITH BACON-BOURBON-GINGER BUTTER

SERVES: 4 TO 6 | **PREP TIME:** 10 MINUTES, PLUS TIME TO SHUCK THE OYSTERS | **CHILLING TIME:** 2 HOURS
GRILLING TIME: 3 TO 4 MINUTES | **SPECIAL EQUIPMENT:** OYSTER KNIFE

BUTTER
1 slice bacon
½ cup (1 stick) unsalted butter, softened
1 tablespoon bourbon
2 tablespoons peeled, minced
    fresh ginger
1 teaspoon minced fresh mint leaves
¼ teaspoon kosher salt

2 dozen large, fresh oysters

This recipe comes straight out of New Orleans, where char-grilled oysters are a big deal. The flavors of bacon, bourbon, and butter are also big deals down there, so why not bring them all together in a Mardi Gras kind of moment? Once the butter has melted into the oysters, it's helpful to wear heavy-duty fire-retardant gloves for retrieving the oysters from the hot grill—or you can use long-handled tongs. Just don't lose all those buttery juices.

1 In a large skillet over medium heat on the stove, fry the bacon until crisp, 6 to 8 minutes, turning occasionally. Drain on a paper towel, reserving 1 teaspoon of the rendered fat. Finely chop the bacon and place in a bowl with the reserved 1 teaspoon rendered fat and the remaining butter ingredients. Using a fork, whisk vigorously until well blended. Scoop the butter mixture onto a sheet of wax paper, placing it on the edge closest to you. Fold the paper up and over and roll into a cylinder, smoothing as you roll. Twist the ends to seal, and wrap tightly. Chill until solid, at least 2 hours. Remove from the refrigerator 5 minutes before grilling time, and cut into ½- to 1-teaspoon chunks (depending on the size of the oysters).

2 Prepare the grill for direct cooking over medium-high heat (400° to 500°F).

3 Grip each oyster, flat side up, in a folded kitchen towel. Find the small opening between the shells near the hinge and pry it open with an oyster knife. Try not to spill the delicious juices, known as the "oyster liquor," in the bottom shell. Cut the oyster meat loose from the top shell, and then loosen the oyster from the bottom shell by running the oyster knife carefully underneath the body. Discard the top, flatter shell, keeping the oyster and juices in the bottom, deeper shell. Place a chunk of the flavored butter on top of each oyster.

4 Grill the oysters over **direct medium-high heat**, with the lid closed, until the oyster liquor starts to bubble, the butter melts, and the edges of the oysters just begin to curl, 3 to 4 minutes. With tongs gripping one edge, transfer the oysters in their shells to a heatproof platter. Serve immediately.

When you are buying oysters to grill, choose big ones that will lie flat on the bars of the grate, like the three on the left of this photo. Avoid small ones that would shrivel up quickly and wobbly ones that would spill their "liquor" in the grill, like the two on the right. Nobody likes an oyster that can't hold its liquor.

SMOKED SCALLOPS
WITH WHITE WINE BUTTER SAUCE

SERVES: 4 TO 6 | **PREP TIME:** 10 MINUTES | **GRILLING TIME:** 8 TO 14 MINUTES
SPECIAL EQUIPMENT: 1 LARGE HANDFUL PECAN WOOD CHIPS, 10-INCH CAST-IRON SKILLET

12 sea scallops, each about 1½ ounces,
   patted dry
½ teaspoon kosher salt
½ teaspoon freshly ground black pepper
1 tablespoon canola oil
6 tablespoons (¾ stick) unsalted
   butter, divided
1 tablespoon minced garlic
½ cup dry white wine, such
   as Chardonnay
2 tablespoons finely chopped fresh
   tarragon leaves
   Zest of 1 lemon

Don't hesitate to use cast-iron skillets right on the grill. It's a way of cooking that has worked wonders from the earliest days of American history, when settlers relied on skillets to cook all kinds of food over live fires. Here some smoldering pecan chips give the scallops a touch of smoke. Often I grill scallops over very high heat to sear the outsides, but in this case I prefer the silky soft texture you get from gentle roasting. With a warm, nutty-tasting butter sauce spooned on top, the results are pretty decadent.

1 Soak the wood chips in water for at least 30 minutes.

2 Prepare the grill for direct and indirect cooking over medium heat (350° to 450°F).

3 Remove and discard the small, tough side muscle that might be left on each scallop, and then season evenly with the salt and pepper. Drain and add the wood chips to the charcoal or to the smoker box of a gas grill, following manufacturer's instructions, and close the lid. When smoke appears, place a 10-inch cast-iron skillet on the cooking grate over **direct medium heat** and, without preheating the pan, swirl in the oil. Place the scallops in the skillet and cook over **direct medium heat**, with the lid closed, until lightly browned and just opaque in the center, 6 to 10 minutes, turning once. Remove the scallops from the skillet (keep the skillet on the grill) and keep them warm while preparing the sauce.

4 Add 3 tablespoons of the butter and the garlic to the skillet and cook over **direct medium heat**, with the lid open, until the butter begins to brown, stirring constantly. Pour the wine into the skillet, close the lid, and cook until reduced to about 3 tablespoons, 2 to 4 minutes, stirring occasionally.

5 Slide the skillet over **indirect medium heat** and add the remaining 3 tablespoons butter and the tarragon. Remove the skillet from the grill, spoon the sauce over the scallops, garnish with the lemon zest, and serve immediately.

Bigger is better for this recipe. Look for large sea scallops like the one on the far right. Assuming they are fresh, their texture will be superior to that of smaller scallops. They should glisten and smell sweet and their color should be somewhere between light beige and pale pink, not bright white.

SPICY SHRIMP
WITH CHARRED POBLANO ROMESCO

SERVES: 4 TO 6 | **PREP TIME:** 20 MINUTES
GRILLING TIME: 12 TO 16 MINUTES

ROMESCO

- 2 poblano chile peppers, about 8 ounces total
- ½ cup lightly packed fresh cilantro sprigs
- ¼ cup sliced almonds, toasted
- 1 small jalapeño chile pepper, seeded and chopped
- 1 tablespoon fresh lemon juice
- 1 medium garlic clove
- ¼ teaspoon freshly ground black pepper

- Extra-virgin olive oil
- Kosher salt
- 1 teaspoon smoked paprika
- 1 pound large shrimp (21/30 count), peeled and deveined, tails left on, patted dry

This green romesco sauce is less sweet and significantly spicier than a traditional roasted red pepper romesco, which is a Spanish vegetable sauce thickened with almonds. Remember that jalapeño chile peppers vary in heat from one to the next, so it is a good idea to taste them before adding them to a dish. If you like, you can even leave the jalapeño out of this recipe.

1 Prepare the grill for direct cooking over high heat (450° to 550°F).

2 Grill the poblano chiles over **direct high heat**, with the lid closed, until blackened and blistered all over, 10 to 12 minutes, turning occasionally. Place the peppers in a bowl and cover with plastic wrap to trap the steam. Let stand for about 10 minutes. Remove and discard the charred skins, stems, and seeds, and then coarsely chop the chiles.

3 In the bowl of a food processor combine the poblanos and the remaining romesco ingredients, including ¼ cup oil and ½ teaspoon salt, and process until well blended but some texture still remains. Transfer the sauce to a serving bowl.

4 In a medium bowl whisk 1 tablespoon oil, ½ teaspoon salt, and the paprika. Add the shrimp and turn to coat in the mixture. Grill the shrimp over **direct high heat**, with the lid closed, until firm to the touch and just turning opaque in the center, 2 to 4 minutes, turning once.

5 Serve the shrimp warm with the romesco sauce for dipping.

Burn, baby, burn. Grilling poblano chiles over high heat until they are blackened and blistered drives out the water and transforms their flavor into a smoky version of its former self. To loosen the skins, put the grilled chiles in a bowl, cover with plastic wrap, and let them stand for about 10 minutes. Then you can remove and discard the burnt skins easily.

HOT-SMOKED SALMON
WITH WHIPPED HORSERADISH CREAM

SERVES: 6 TO 8 | **PREP TIME:** 15 MINUTES | **DRY BRINING TIME:** 4 TO 8 HOURS | **GRILLING TIME:** 40 MINUTES TO 1½ HOURS
CHILLING TIME: 2 HOURS (OPTIONAL) | **SPECIAL EQUIPMENT:** 3 LARGE HANDFULS ALDER WOOD CHIPS

DRY BRINE
½ cup packed light brown sugar
¼ cup coarse kosher salt
1 tablespoon coarsely ground
   black pepper
1 tablespoon finely grated lemon zest

1 salmon fillet (with skin), about
   2 pounds, pin bones removed
2 tablespoons extra-virgin olive oil

HORSERADISH CREAM
½ cup chilled heavy whipping cream
1 tablespoon peeled, finely grated
   fresh horseradish or 2 teaspoons
   prepared horseradish
½ teaspoon finely grated lemon zest
⅛ teaspoon kosher salt
⅛ teaspoon freshly ground black pepper
⅛ teaspoon hot pepper sauce

2 tablespoons finely chopped
   fresh chives
   Grilled lemon slices
   Grilled baguette slices

We have all tasted thin slices of cold-smoked salmon with a texture that is fairly firm and dry because the fish is cooked at temperatures below 100°F in specialized commercial smokers. This recipe is a hot-smoked version that you can make at home. Start by soaking the salmon in a sweet, salty brine, and then smoking it with mild alder wood chips until the flesh is tender but still juicy so that it breaks apart into moist flakes. While the salmon is good eaten warm, the flavors develop even more while the fish chills in the refrigerator. Serve it at room temperature with creamy horseradish and a touch of tart lemon.

1 Combine the dry brine ingredients. Sprinkle one-third of the brine on the bottom of a large baking dish. Arrange the salmon fillet, skin side down, on top of the brine. Spread the remaining brine evenly over the salmon, pressing lightly to adhere. Cover with plastic wrap and refrigerate for 4 to 8 hours.

2 Soak the wood chips in water for at least 30 minutes.

3 Rinse the salmon under cold water to remove the brine, pat dry with paper towels, and brush both sides with the oil.

4 Prepare the grill for indirect cooking over low heat (as close to 250°F as possible).

5 Drain and add one handful of wood chips to the charcoal or to the smoker box of a gas grill, following manufacturer's instructions, and close the lid. When smoke appears, grill the salmon, skin side down, over **indirect low heat**, with the lid closed, until firm and just slightly pink all the

way to the center, 40 minutes to 1½ hours, depending on the thickness of the salmon, and watching closely to prevent overcooking. Drain and add one handful of the wood chips to the charcoal or smoker box every 20 to 30 minutes until the wood chips are gone. If using a charcoal grill, add more briquettes as necessary to maintain the heat.

6 Remove the salmon from the grill and let cool to room temperature. Cover with plastic wrap and refrigerate for at least 2 hours to allow the flavors to develop, if desired. Meanwhile, prepare the horseradish cream.

7 In the bowl of an electric mixer fitted with a whisk attachment, beat the cream until soft peaks form. Whisk in the remaining ingredients. Transfer to a serving bowl, cover, and refrigerate until ready to use.

8 Garnish the salmon with the chives and serve at room temperature with the horseradish cream, grilled lemon slices, and grilled baguette slices.

If you can, do yourself a favor and buy a piece of fresh horseradish for this recipe. Look for a blemish-free, firm root that feels heavy for its size. Clean and peel the outer layer with a vegetable peeler, and then grate the amount you need using a fine grater for a big pop of flavor. Wrap the unused portion in plastic wrap and store in the refrigerator.

SMOKED CHICKEN NACHOS
WITH CHIPOTLE CREAM AND AVOCADO

SERVES: 6 | PREP TIME: 20 MINUTES | GRILLING TIME: 32 TO 39 MINUTES | SPECIAL EQUIPMENT: 2 LARGE HANDFULS MESQUITE OR HICKORY WOOD CHIPS, LARGE GRILL-PROOF PAN OR DISPOSABLE FOIL PAN

CHIPOTLE CREAM
- 1 cup sour cream
- 1 canned chipotle chile pepper in adobo sauce, minced
- 1 tablespoon fresh lime juice
- ¼ teaspoon kosher salt

RUB
- 2 teaspoons kosher salt
- 1 teaspoon freshly ground black pepper
- 1 teaspoon ground cumin
- 1 teaspoon paprika
- ½ teaspoon ground cayenne pepper

- 4 chicken breast halves (with bone and skin), each about 8 ounces
- 12 ounces corn tortilla chips
- 14 ounces Monterey Jack cheese, coarsely grated
- 4 scallions, cut into thin slices
- 2 tablespoons finely chopped jalapeño chile peppers
- 1 large Hass avocado, cut into ½-inch cubes
  Juice of ½ lime
- ¼ cup roughly chopped fresh cilantro leaves
  Store-bought salsa (optional)

This is a fun way to use up leftover barbecued chicken or turkey. Who doesn't love some cheesy, meaty nachos with smoky sour cream and fresh avocado? It's worth smoking some spice-rubbed chicken breasts just for this recipe. Using bone-in rather than boneless chicken breasts requires a longer cooking time, but there's a dividend: the meat has more time to absorb the flavorful smoke.

1 Soak the wood chips in water for at least 30 minutes.

2 Whisk the chipotle cream ingredients, including any juices remaining from mincing the chipotle chile. Refrigerate until ready to use.

3 Prepare the grill for indirect cooking over medium heat (350° to 450°F).

4 Mix the rub ingredients. Season the chicken breasts all over and between the skin and meat with the rub.

5 Drain and add the wood chips to the charcoal or to the smoker box of a gas grill, following manufacturer's instructions, and close the lid. When smoke appears, grill the chicken, skin side down first, over **indirect medium heat**, with the lid closed, until the juices run clear and the meat is no longer pink at the bone, 25 to 30 minutes, turning once when the skin releases easily from the cooking grates. Remove the chicken from the grill and, when cool enough to handle, shred into pieces, discarding the skin and bones.

6 Increase the temperature of the grill to high heat (450° to 500°F).

7 Spread half of the tortilla chips into a large grill-proof pan. Distribute half each of the cheese, scallions, jalapeño, and chicken over the chips. Repeat with another layer.

8 Place the pan with the nachos over **indirect high heat**, close the lid, and cook until the cheese is melted and the chips are tinged golden brown, 7 to 9 minutes. Wearing insulated barbecue mitts or gloves, carefully transfer the pan to a heatproof surface. Top the nachos with the avocado and then drizzle with the chipotle cream and lime juice. Garnish with the cilantro. Serve hot with salsa, if desired.

BARBECUED BUFFALO WINGS
WITH BLUE CHEESE DIP

SERVES: 6 TO 8 | **PREP TIME:** 15 MINUTES | **GRILLING TIME:** ABOUT 20 MINUTES
SPECIAL EQUIPMENT: 1 LARGE HANDFUL MAPLE OR CHERRY WOOD CHIPS

SAUCE
- ¼ cup corn oil or peanut oil
- ¼ cup hot pepper sauce
- 2 teaspoons kosher salt
- 1 teaspoon ground white pepper
- 1 teaspoon freshly ground black pepper
- ½ teaspoon garlic powder

- 4 pounds chicken wings, wing tips removed, each split at the joint into 2 pieces

DIP
- 4 ounces crumbled blue cheese
- ½ cup sour cream
- ¼ cup mayonnaise
- 2 tablespoons fresh lemon juice
- ½ teaspoon celery seed
- ½ teaspoon kosher salt
- Hot pepper sauce

Who knew that buffalo have wings? Well, actually, these chicken wings are named for the city where they were crafted as bar food: Buffalo, New York. That story, like a lot of recipe origin stories, is disputed, but no matter how they came about, buffalo wings are fantastic at a tailgate party or wherever people appreciate spicy snacks that you can eat with your fingers.

1 Soak the wood chips in water for at least 30 minutes.

2 Prepare the grill for direct cooking over medium heat (350° to 450°F).

3 In a small saucepan combine the sauce ingredients. Cook over medium heat on the stove until warm, about 5 minutes, whisking occasionally. Set aside ¼ cup of the sauce. Pour the remaining sauce from the saucepan into a large bowl and add the wings. Turn the wings in the sauce to coat them evenly.

4 Drain and add the wood chips to the charcoal or to the smoker box of a gas grill, following manufacturer's instructions, and close the lid. When smoke appears, grill the wings over **direct medium heat**, with the lid closed, until the juices run clear, about 20 minutes, turning occasionally (don't overcook or the wings will be dry). Transfer the wings to a large, clean bowl and toss to coat with the reserved ¼ cup sauce.

5 In a medium bowl combine the dip ingredients, including a few drops of hot sauce, and mix well. Serve the dip alongside the wings with extra hot sauce, if desired.

SMOKED LOUISIANA CHICKEN WINGS
WITH CAJUN RUB

SERVES: 6 | **PREP TIME:** 15 MINUTES | **GRILLING TIME:** ABOUT 30 MINUTES
SPECIAL EQUIPMENT: 2 LARGE HANDFULS HICKORY WOOD CHIPS

RUB

1 tablespoon packed brown sugar
2 teaspoons smoked paprika
1½ teaspoons kosher salt
1 teaspoon onion powder
1 teaspoon dried oregano
¾ teaspoon garlic powder
½ teaspoon dried thyme
½ teaspoon freshly ground black pepper
½ teaspoon ground cayenne pepper

3 pounds chicken wings, wing tips
removed, each split at the joint into
2 pieces

SAUCE

¼ cup ketchup
¼ cup Louisiana-style hot sauce
2 tablespoons packed brown sugar
2 teaspoons cider vinegar
1 teaspoon hot pepper sauce
½ teaspoon Cajun spice
blend (optional)
3 tablespoons unsalted butter

Sour cream (optional)

This version of barbecued wings hails from the South, where a spicy Cajun rub meets hickory smoke and a pungent hot sauce. Serve with sour cream on the side just to take the edge off all that heat. The key to the chicken's texture is the combination of direct and indirect heat. Cooking the wings right over the fire renders out some fat and starts them on their way to being crispy. Finishing them to the side of the fire tenderizes the meat while the sauce seeps inside.

1. Soak the wood chips in water for at least 30 minutes.

2. In a large bowl combine the rub ingredients. Add the chicken wings and turn to coat. Allow the wings to stand at room temperature for about 30 minutes.

3. Prepare the grill for direct and indirect cooking over medium heat (350° to 450°F).

4. In a medium saucepan combine all the sauce ingredients, except the butter, and bring to a simmer over medium heat on the stove. Cook until slightly thickened, 3 to 4 minutes, stirring occasionally. Remove from the heat, add the butter, and whisk until the butter is melted.

5. Drain and add one handful of the wood chips to the charcoal or to the smoker box of a gas grill, following manufacturer's instructions, and close the lid. When smoke appears, grill the wings over **direct medium heat**, with the lid closed, for 5 minutes, turning once. Move the wings over **indirect medium heat** and continue grilling, with the lid closed, for 10 minutes. Drain and add the remaining wood chips to the charcoal or smoker box. Brush the wings with some of the sauce, turn, and grill until crisp, deeply browned in spots, and tender, about 15 minutes more, brushing the wings one more time with the sauce. Remove the wings from the grill and serve warm with sour cream on the side, if desired.

Los Angeles is the stage not only for the Academy Awards and a galaxy of Hollywood stars, but also for the largest community of Koreans and Korean restaurants outside of Seoul. Koreatown, or K-Town as locals know it, is a densely populated 2.7-square-mile metropolis of art deco architecture, pulsing nightlife, and a red-hot culinary scene, where dozens of restaurants serve a special brand of barbecue over sizzling tabletop grills. This is elemental live-fire cooking, with thin strips of fatty pork and marbled beef in salty-sweet marinades crackling over smoky coals. Korean barbecue has swept all the way across America in recent years, but the trend started in Los Angeles, where traditionalists and innovators alike drew on rich, cultural heritage.

Meat, particularly beef, is expensive in Korea; in Los Angeles, however, a subculture of specialists with a cult following serve Wagyu, USDA prime, and beef tongue at celebrity-heavy spots like Park's Barbeque and Genwa Korean BBQ. Brisket, short ribs, octopus, and pork belly are also popular, as are fattier cuts that are often marinated and usually enjoyed after leaner beef slices. The well-seasoned grill racks at Soot Bull Jeep are about as old school as K-town gets, and here beef bulgogi and octopus sizzle over hardwood coals—smoke permeating everything from the scissor-cut, soy-marinated kalbi (short ribs) to customers' jeans. A packed room of loyal patrons raise glasses of soju and craft beer. Equally popular are the dome-shaped grills at Honey Pig, which guarantee that no part of the pork is wasted. Rendered fat from slices of *samgyeopsal*, or pork belly, drips down to lend its rich umami to a moat of kimchi (fermented vegetables and seasonings) and bean sprouts, which are scooped up with salad and rolled in rice papers. At Sun Ha Jang, domed griddles sizzle slices of garlic and duck into cracklings, and the reserved fat is spooned over rice. Dong Il Jang puts a twist on tradition by grilling marbled beef in butter over a griddle—what L.A. food critic Jonathan Gold calls "the Korean equivalent of

Small side dishes, called *banchan*, comprised of kimchi and pickled seasonal vegetables with crunchy and acidic flavors that balance the fatty meats, are every bit as crucial to the experience as what is on the grill. It's about the subtle layering of flavors—sweet and sour with fatty, spicy, and rich. And nobody does this better than Genwa Korean BBQ, where 23 different banchan are served in a serene setting. Banchan offerings in L.A. restaurants almost always include a potato or macaroni salad, a decidedly American addition that you won't find back home in Seoul. Dipping sauces also reflect L.A.'s booming Latino population. The popular garlicky soy sauce and pickled jalapeño dip that is spooned onto meats and wrapped in lettuce is as common in L.A. Korean barbecue joints as it is in taco bars in Mexico. In fact, today, Koreatown boasts almost twice as many Latino residents as Asian, and the Latin influence is inspiring the next generation of boundary-breaking Korean-American chefs.

L.A. native son Roy Choi is a pioneer in combining Mexican street food with Korean barbecue. Choi, who grew up in Los Angeles surrounded by Latino culture, revolutionized the food truck scene in 2008 when he and his business partner launched their wildly popular Kogi BBQ taco truck specializing in Korean short rib tacos. It's a craze that rippled east and back again, bringing Detroit brothers Brian and Steven Yeun to L.A. to launch The Bun Truck in 2011, a Korean-Mediterranean taco fusion that mixes Korean barbecued pork with Greek tzatziki, Sriracha, and cucumber in a bao bun. Other American joints in the neighborhood are serving up traditional fast food with a Korean twist featuring bulgogi on burgers, Philly cheesesteaks, and pizza, while the nearby upscale French restaurant République is borrowing from Korean street food with kimchi fried rice adorned with soft-poached eggs. Koreatown, at its core, is pure Los Angeles: a melting pot of flavors, cultures, and dreams.

AMERICAN
MADE
KOREAN
BARBECUE

WARM ARTICHOKE DIP
WITH PARMESAN CRUST

SERVES: 6 | **PREP TIME:** 15 MINUTES | **GRILLING TIME:** 23 TO 30 MINUTES
SPECIAL EQUIPMENT: 1 LARGE HANDFUL APPLE WOOD CHIPS, 8-INCH CAST-IRON SKILLET

1 can (14 ounces) whole artichoke hearts packed in water, rinsed and drained, patted dry
¾ cup mayonnaise
6 ounces cream cheese, softened
4 ounces mozzarella cheese, grated
1 can (4 ounces) chopped mild green chile peppers
¼ cup sour cream
2 teaspoons minced garlic
1 teaspoon mustard powder
¼ teaspoon hot pepper sauce
¼ teaspoon freshly ground black pepper
Unsalted butter
1½ ounces Parmigiano-Reggiano® cheese, finely grated
Grilled baguette slices or crisp flat bread

Artichoke dip is a classic in steak houses and barbecue joints across the United States. Served with grilled bread slices or crisp flat bread crackers, it's a good way to start a meal, but it gets even better with the addition of a little smoke to highlight the sweet artichokes and a gratineed crust of bubbling, nutty cheese on top.

1 Soak the wood chips in water for at least 30 minutes.

2 Prepare the grill for direct and indirect cooking over medium-high heat (400° to 450°F).

3 Drain and add the wood chips to the charcoal or to the smoker box of a gas grill, following manufacturer's instructions, and close the lid. When smoke appears, grill the artichoke hearts over **direct medium-high heat**, with the lid closed, until warmed through, 3 to 5 minutes, turning once. Remove from the grill and roughly chop.

4 Combine the mayonnaise, cream cheese, mozzarella, chiles, sour cream, garlic, mustard powder, hot sauce, and pepper. Using a wooden spoon, smash the cream cheese against the inside of the bowl into a paste, and then stir the mixture until smooth. Stir in the artichoke hearts.

5 Lightly grease the inside of an 8-inch cast-iron skillet with butter. Transfer the artichoke mixture to the prepared skillet, and then distribute the Parmigiano-Reggiano® cheese evenly over the top. Cook over **indirect medium-high heat**, with the lid closed, until browned and bubbling on the surface, 20 to 25 minutes. Cool for 10 minutes before serving with grilled baguette slices or crisp flat bread.

Keep the dip on the chunky side by roughly chopping the smoked artichokes, and resist the urge to smooth the top of the dip in the skillet. The peaks and valleys will create crisp golden edges that make people flip for this dish.

NEW PIMIENTO CHEESE SPREAD

SERVES: 8 TO 10 | PREP TIME: 15 MINUTES | GRILLING TIME: ABOUT 35 MINUTES | CHILLING TIME: 2 HOURS
SPECIAL EQUIPMENT: 2 LARGE HANDFULS HICKORY WOOD CHIPS

1 red bell pepper, about 8 ounces
1 teaspoon vegetable oil
12 ounces sharp cheddar cheese, coarsely grated
½ cup mayonnaise
3 tablespoons roughly chopped sweet pickles
2 tablespoons grated yellow onion (use the large holes of a box grater)
1 teaspoon Worcestershire sauce
1 teaspoon Dijon mustard
1½ teaspoons minced canned chipotle chile peppers in adobo sauce
½ teaspoon adobo sauce from the can, or to taste (optional)
1 garlic clove, minced
Toasted bread
Celery
Carrots
Radishes

In the Carolinas, you may find an entire section of a grocery store devoted to various kinds of pimiento cheese, a spread whose main ingredients are preserved sweet red peppers (aka pimentos), shredded cheese, and mayonnaise. Here is a ramped-up recipe with contemporary flavors, including home-smoked red bell pepper to take it over the top. Not only is this a terrific party dish served with toasted bread and celery, but it is also a fine filling for grilled cheese sandwiches.

1 Soak the wood chips in water for at least 30 minutes.

2 Cut off the top and bottom ends from the pepper. Remove and discard the stem. Stand the pepper upright and cut it down one side to create one long strip. Trim and discard the ribs and seeds (see the step-by-step below). Lightly coat the pepper strip and the end pieces with the oil.

3 Prepare the grill for direct and indirect cooking over medium heat (350° to 450°F).

4 Drain and add one handful of the wood chips to the charcoal or to the smoker box of a gas grill, following manufacturer's instructions, and close the lid. When smoke appears, grill the bell pepper pieces, skin side down, over **indirect medium heat**, with the lid closed, for 10 minutes.

Drain and add the remaining wood chips to the charcoal or smoker box, and continue grilling, with the lid closed, until the skin is blistered, 18 to 20 minutes more. Move the pepper over **direct medium heat** and grill, with the lid closed, until the skin is blackened all over, 3 to 5 minutes. Place the pepper in a bowl and cover with plastic wrap to trap the steam. Let stand for about 10 minutes. Remove and discard the charred skin, and roughly chop the pepper.

5 In a food processor combine the bell pepper, cheese, mayonnaise, pickles, onion, Worcestershire sauce, mustard, chipotle chile, adobo sauce (if using), and garlic. Pulse until the mixture is combined and the pepper and pickles are finely chopped. Transfer to a bowl, cover, and refrigerate until cold, at least 2 hours. Serve cold or at room temperature with toasted bread, celery, carrots, and radishes.

Sometimes knife skills make a big difference in a recipe. By cutting a bell pepper so that it lies as flat as possible on the cooking grate, you can improve how well it caramelizes and chars, meaning you can achieve better flavors. Begin by trimming off the stem and bottom ends. Stand the pepper up and cut an opening down one side. Put the pepper on its side and position your knife inside so you can make a cut between the inner wall of the pepper and the undesirable core and seeds. Go back and trim any whitish areas off the inner wall of the pepper. Now you have lots of surface area to lie flat on the hot cooking grate.

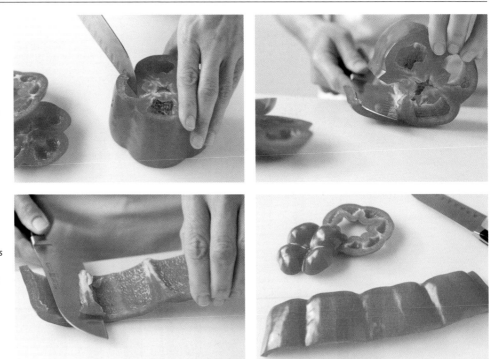

BACON-ONION-BOURBON SPREAD

SERVES: 10 TO 12 | **PREP TIME:** 20 MINUTES | **GRILLING TIME:** ABOUT 1¼ HOURS | **CHILLING TIME:** 2 HOURS TO 3 DAYS
SPECIAL EQUIPMENT: 2 LARGE HANDFULS HICKORY WOOD CHIPS, 12-INCH CAST-IRON SKILLET

This sweet and savory spread is aimed straight at the heart of barbecue fanatics who have a thing for bourbon, bacon, and brown sugar. The recipe makes about four cups of spread, but it keeps well and it is quite versatile. Serve it with a soft cheese and crostini before dinner, spread it on a sandwich, or try it as a condiment for something simple that needs oomph, like a grilled chicken breast or pork chop.

GLAZE
⅓ cup bourbon
⅓ cup pure maple syrup
3 tablespoons packed light brown sugar
2 tablespoons unsulfured molasses (not blackstrap)
2 teaspoons finely chopped fresh rosemary leaves

12 ounces sliced bacon, cut crosswise into 1-inch pieces
2 pounds yellow onions, quartered and cut into ¼-inch slices
1 pound red onions, quartered and cut into ¼-inch slices
6 garlic cloves, coarsely chopped
1 teaspoon kosher salt
½ teaspoon freshly ground black pepper
1 tablespoon brown deli mustard
Grilled baguette pieces (optional)
Brie cheese (optional)

1 Soak the wood chips in water for at least 30 minutes.

2 Prepare the grill for direct and indirect cooking over medium heat (350° to 450°F).

3 Whisk the glaze ingredients. Set aside.

4 In a 12-inch cast-iron skillet over **direct medium heat**, fry the bacon until crisp, 10 to 12 minutes, stirring frequently. Using a slotted spoon, transfer the bacon to paper towels to drain. Pour off all but 3 tablespoons of the bacon fat. Add half each of the yellow and red onions to the skillet and cook over **direct medium heat**, with the lid closed, until softened, about 5 minutes, stirring occasionally. Stir in the remaining onions, garlic, salt, and pepper. Move the skillet over **indirect medium heat**, drain and add the wood chips to the charcoal or to the smoker box of a gas grill, following manufacturer's instructions, and cook the onion mixture, with the lid closed, until very tender and beginning to brown, about 45 minutes, stirring every 10 minutes.

5 Stir the glaze into the onions. Move the skillet over **direct medium heat**, close the lid, and cook until the liquid is reduced and the bubbles begin to glisten, 10 to 15 minutes, stirring often. Remove from the grill. Coarsely chop the bacon and reserve and refrigerate 2 tablespoons for garnish. Stir the remaining bacon and the mustard into the onion mixture. Cool, cover, and refrigerate for at least 2 hours or up to 3 days. Remove from the refrigerator 1 hour before serving. Garnish with the reserved bacon, and serve on top of grilled baguette pieces with Brie, if desired.

SMOKED DEVILED EGGS

SERVES: 6 TO 12 | **PREP TIME:** 25 MINUTES | **COOKING TIME:** ABOUT 45 MINUTES | **CHILLING TIME:** ABOUT 30 MINUTES
SPECIAL EQUIPMENT: WATER SMOKER, 2 LARGE HANDFULS HICKORY WOOD CHUNKS, LARGE DISPOSABLE FOIL PAN

If you have your smoker going for a big main course, why not make an unusual appetizer by smoking some eggs on the extra cooking grate. The hickory smoke adds great flavor and color to traditional deviled eggs.

1 dozen large eggs
3 slices bacon
½ cup mayonnaise
2 tablespoons minced fresh chives
2 teaspoons Dijon mustard
½ teaspoon smoked paprika, divided
¼ teaspoon kosher salt
¼ teaspoon freshly ground black pepper

1 Prepare a water smoker for indirect cooking with very low heat (200° to 250°F). Add the wood chunks to the charcoal.

2 Place the eggs in a single layer in a large saucepan and add enough water to cover them by at least 1 inch. Place the saucepan (uncovered) over high heat on the stove and bring the water to a boil. Remove the saucepan from the heat, cover the saucepan, and let the eggs stand for 15 minutes. Drain the eggs and run cold water over them until cool to the touch. Peel the eggs and place them in a large disposable foil pan.

3 While the eggs are cooking, fry the bacon in a skillet on the stove until crisp, 7 to 10 minutes, turning occasionally. Transfer the bacon to paper towels to drain. Crumble and set aside.

4 Smoke the eggs in the foil pan over **indirect very low heat**, with the lid closed, until they develop a smoky flavor, about 45 minutes, turning periodically to coat them evenly with a smoky hue. Transfer the eggs to a bowl and refrigerate until completely chilled, about 30 minutes. Then cut each egg lengthwise in half, scoop out the yolks into a bowl, and mash with a fork. Add the mayonnaise, chives, mustard, ¼ teaspoon of the paprika, the salt, and pepper and mix until well combined. Spoon the mixture into the hollows of the egg whites and garnish with the bacon and the remaining paprika. If not serving immediately, cover and refrigerate.

SPINACH SALAD
WITH SMOKED VEGETABLES AND PIMENTÓN VINAIGRETTE

SERVES: 4 | **PREP TIME:** 15 MINUTES | **GRILLING TIME:** 25 TO 35 MINUTES
SPECIAL EQUIPMENT: 2 LARGE HANDFULS OAK WOOD CHIPS, LARGE DISPOSABLE FOIL PAN

1 can (14 ounces) garbanzo beans
(chickpeas), rinsed and drained
1 red bell pepper, about 8 ounces,
cut into ½-inch dice
6 ounces grape tomatoes
Extra-virgin olive oil

VINAIGRETTE
2 tablespoons sherry wine vinegar
1 small garlic clove, minced
½ teaspoon kosher salt
½ teaspoon smoked paprika
¼ teaspoon freshly ground black pepper

5 ounces fresh baby spinach
½ small red onion, thinly sliced
4 ounces thinly sliced Serrano ham
or prosciutto, cut crosswise into
½-inch strips
Freshly ground black pepper

This first course celebrates Spanish flavors with pimentón, or smoked paprika, garlic, and olive oil, but it is the smoked vegetables that will make it a favorite. In fact, because it only takes about 30 minutes to smoke vegetables, you may find yourself adding them to other salads. Jamón serrano is Spanish dry-cured ham similar to prosciutto, which is a good substitute, but you could use another kind of Spanish charcutería, such as lomo or chorizo. For a vegetarian salad, swap ¾ cup shredded Manchego cheese (3 ounces) for the meat.

1   Soak the wood chips in water for at least 30 minutes.

2   Prepare the grill for indirect cooking over medium-low heat (as close to 350°F as possible).

3   In a large disposable foil pan spread the garbanzo beans, bell pepper, and tomatoes into three separate sections (it's okay if they touch). Drizzle each with 1 teaspoon oil, and then mix separately to coat evenly, keeping the sections separated.

4   Drain and add the wood chips to the charcoal or to the smoker box of a gas grill, following manufacturer's instructions, and close the lid. When smoke appears, place the pan with the vegetables over **indirect medium-low heat**, close the lid, and cook until the tomatoes begin to split and the chickpeas take on a light brown patina, 25 to 35 minutes, stirring each ingredient once or twice during cooking. If the tomatoes start to collapse, remove them from the pan. Remove the pan from the grill and set aside to cool completely.

5   In a large bowl combine the vinaigrette ingredients. Slowly add ⅓ cup oil, whisking constantly to emulsify the vinaigrette. To the bowl add the spinach, onion, and the cooled garbanzo beans, bell pepper, and tomatoes; toss to combine. Divide the salad evenly among four serving plates and top with equal amounts of the ham. Finish with a grinding of pepper. Serve immediately.

Be ready for anything. Ideally all the tomatoes, garbanzo beans, and bell peppers will cook perfectly in the same amount of time, but they might not. Keeping them in separate piles allows you to remove any that are cooking faster than others.

CHARRED ICEBERG SALAD
WITH BUTTERMILK DRESSING

SERVES: 4 | **PREP TIME:** 15 MINUTES | **GRILLING TIME:** ABOUT 4 MINUTES
SPECIAL EQUIPMENT: 4 TO 6 METAL OR BAMBOO SKEWERS

Sturdy, dense iceberg lettuce holds its shape on the grill while the outer leaves char, adding an extra smoky dimension to the traditional wedge salad. The tomatoes build on the charred flavors, and their warmth is a nice contrast to the cool buttermilk dressing.

DRESSING
¼ cup buttermilk
3 tablespoons sour cream
1 tablespoon fresh lemon juice
¼ teaspoon kosher salt
¼ teaspoon freshly ground black pepper

12 ounces yellow cherry tomatoes
Extra-virgin olive oil
⅛ teaspoon kosher salt
1 medium head iceberg lettuce, outer leaves removed, cut through the core into quarters
12 baguette slices, each about ½ inch thick
4 ounces crumbled blue cheese
2 scallions (white and light green parts only), thinly sliced

1 If using bamboo skewers, soak them in water for at least 30 minutes.

2 Whisk the dressing ingredients until smooth.

3 Prepare the grill for direct cooking over medium heat (350° to 450°F).

4 Thread the tomatoes onto skewers, lightly brush with oil, and season with ⅛ teaspoon salt. Brush the cut sides of the lettuce quarters with oil, and brush the baguette slices on both sides with oil.

5 Grill the tomato skewers and lettuce quarters over **direct medium heat**, with the lid closed, until charred, about 4 minutes, turning the tomatoes as needed and the lettuce once to char the other cut side. During the last minute of grilling time, toast the baguette slices over direct heat, turning once.

6 Place the lettuce quarters on individual plates and arrange equal amounts of the tomatoes, blue cheese, and scallions around and over the lettuce. Pour as much dressing as you like over each salad and serve with the toasted baguette slices.

GRILLED BROCCOLINI
WITH BUCATINI PASTA AND LEMON BREAD CRUMBS

SERVES: 4 | **PREP TIME:** 30 MINUTES
GRILLING TIME: 3 TO 5 MINUTES

Who knew broccolini could be barbecue? Over a live fire, the outer leaves crisp and the stalks and heads char, adding a delightful smoky flavor and texture to this pasta dish, which benefits even more from a shower of toasted lemony bread crumbs. Keep an eye on the crumbs while they toast to prevent burning.

½ cup panko bread crumbs
1 teaspoon dried oregano
¼ teaspoon crushed red pepper flakes
4 ounces Pecorino Romano® cheese, finely grated
2 teaspoons finely grated lemon zest
Kosher salt
Freshly ground black pepper
Extra-virgin olive oil
1 pound broccolini, ends trimmed and stems peeled
1 pound dried bucatini pasta

1 In a medium skillet over medium heat on the stove, toast the panko, oregano, and red pepper flakes until the panko is golden, 3 to 5 minutes, stirring frequently. Transfer to a bowl and cool for 5 minutes. Add the cheese, lemon zest, ¼ teaspoon salt, and ¼ teaspoon pepper and stir to blend.

2 Prepare the grill for direct cooking over medium heat (350° to 450°F).

3 In a large bowl whisk 1 tablespoon of oil with ½ teaspoon salt, and then add the broccolini, turning to coat. Grill the broccolini over **direct medium heat**, with the lid closed, until bright green in color, charred in some spots, and crisp-tender, 3 to 5 minutes (depending on the thickness of the stalks), turning occasionally. Remove from the grill and, when cool enough to handle, cut off the florets and cut the stalks into ½-inch pieces.

4 Bring a large pot of salted water to a rolling boil. Add the pasta and cook until al dente. Drain and reserve 1 cup of the pasta water. Transfer the pasta to a serving bowl and toss with 1 tablespoon oil. Add the broccolini florets, stalk pieces, and ¾ cup of the reserved pasta water and toss to combine. If desired, add more pasta water. Distribute the bread crumbs on top. Serve warm, garnished with a generous grinding of pepper.

EGGPLANT PARMESAN
WITH TOASTED BREAD CRUMBS

SERVES: 4 TO 6 | **PREP TIME:** 25 MINUTES | **GRILLING TIME:** ABOUT 1½ HOURS
SPECIAL EQUIPMENT: PERFORATED GRILL PAN, 10-INCH CAST-IRON SKILLET OR 8-BY-8-INCH GRILL-PROOF CASSEROLE

Extra-virgin olive oil
Kosher salt
2 pounds plum tomatoes,
   each cut lengthwise in half
1½ cups chopped onion
3 garlic cloves, minced
½ teaspoon dried oregano
¼ teaspoon crushed red pepper flakes
   Freshly ground black pepper
½ cup fresh bread crumbs
4 ounces Parmigiano-Reggiano®
   cheese, finely grated (1 cup), divided
2 globe eggplants, each about
   1 pound, ends trimmed and
   cut crosswise into ½-inch slices
8 ounces fresh mozzarella cheese,
   drained and thinly sliced, divided
¼ cup chopped fresh basil leaves

This unexpected version of eggplant Parmesan gets a lot of help from the fire. Grilling the eggplant not only adds charred flavor to the gratin, it also eliminates the excess oil and fat from frying. The eggplant will continue to cook while baking in the gratin, becoming meltingly tender and rich. The results are particularly good when you barbecue this on a charcoal grill.

1 Prepare the grill for direct and indirect cooking over medium heat (350° to 450°F).

2 In a large bowl whisk 2 tablespoons oil and ½ teaspoon salt. Add the tomatoes and turn to coat. Arrange the tomatoes, cut side up, on a perforated grill pan. Place the grill pan with the tomatoes over **indirect medium heat**, close the lid, and cook until reduced slightly in size and the skins shrivel, 25 to 30 minutes. Remove from the grill and let rest until cool to the touch, about 10 minutes. Peel off and discard the skins, and then transfer the tomatoes to a food processor; process until smooth.

3 In a large saucepan over medium heat on the stove, warm 1 tablespoon oil. Add the onion and cook until soft and translucent, about 4 minutes, stirring frequently. Add the garlic, oregano, and red pepper flakes and sauté until fragrant, about 1 minute. Add the tomatoes, 1 teaspoon salt, and ½ teaspoon pepper. Simmer over medium-low heat for 5 minutes, stirring occasionally. Remove from the heat.

4 Mix the bread crumbs, 3 tablespoons oil, ½ cup of the Parmigiano-Reggiano® cheese, and ¼ teaspoon salt.

5 Brush the eggplant slices generously with oil, season evenly with ¾ teaspoon salt and ¾ teaspoon pepper, and then grill over **direct medium heat**, with the lid closed, until softened and charred, 8 to 10 minutes, turning once or twice.

6 Spoon a thin layer of the sauce into the bottom of a 10-inch cast-iron skillet. Arrange half of the eggplant slices over the sauce. Drop half of the remaining sauce by spoonfuls over each eggplant slice. Top with half of the mozzarella and the remaining ½ cup Parmigiano-Reggiano® cheese. Cover the cheese with the remaining eggplant slices in an even layer. Top with the remaining sauce and the remaining mozzarella. Spoon the bread crumbs evenly on top. Grill over **indirect medium heat**, with the lid closed, until the bread crumbs are golden, about 50 minutes. Serve warm, garnished with the basil.

SMOKED OLIVES
WITH LEMON, CHILES, AND THYME

Use whatever type olives you like to eat, or mix up a few different ones. The green ones on top are Castelvetrano (buttery and mild). The middle ones are Kalamata (with a rich, pickled flavor). And the little ones on the bottom are Picholine (with a firm texture and tart "green" taste).

SERVES: 8 (MAKES 4 CUPS) | **PREP TIME:** 10 MINUTES | **GRILLING TIME:** 45 MINUTES TO 1 HOUR
SPECIAL EQUIPMENT: 2 LARGE HANDFULS HICKORY WOOD CHIPS, LARGE DISPOSABLE FOIL PAN OR GRILL-PROOF BAKING DISH

The strong flavors of briny olives can handle the robust aromatics of a wood like hickory, but do not cook these olives longer than an hour or their consistency will turn too soft. Properly cooked, the olives make a remarkable snack or appetizer, and if you have any left, how about some smoked martinis?

4 cups assorted olives, such as Castelvetrano, Kalamata, and Picholine
½ cup extra-virgin olive oil
6 garlic cloves, each cut in half
2 red cherry chile peppers (pimiento chile peppers), each cut lengthwise into halves or quarters
Zest of 1 lemon, shaved with a vegetable peeler
4 large sprigs fresh thyme, each cut in half
4 teaspoons finely chopped fresh thyme leaves

1 Soak the wood chips in water for at least 30 minutes.

2 Prepare the grill for indirect cooking over low heat (as close to 250°F as possible).

3 In a large disposable foil pan combine all the ingredients except the finely chopped thyme.

4 Drain and add one handful of wood chips to the charcoal or to the smoker box of a gas grill, following manufacturer's instructions, and close the lid. When smoke appears, place the pan with the olives over **indirect low heat**, close the lid, and cook until the olives are fragrant but still firm, 45 minutes to 1 hour, stirring once or twice. After 20 minutes, drain and add the remaining wood chips to the charcoal or smoker box.

5 Transfer the olive mixture to a large bowl and toss with the chopped thyme. Serve warm or at room temperature.

HICKORY-ROASTED ALMONDS
WITH ROSEMARY AND SEA SALT

Presoaking almonds in water provides the necessary moisture for the hickory smoke to stick. Fresh rosemary, added after smoking, lends a beautiful, herbaceous flavor.

SERVES: 12 TO 16 (MAKES 4 CUPS) | **PREP TIME:** 15 MINUTES | **GRILLING TIME:** ABOUT 45 MINUTES
SPECIAL EQUIPMENT: 2 LARGE HANDFULS HICKORY WOOD CHIPS, CHARCOAL GRILL, PERFORATED GRILL PAN

A grill pan with holes is an excellent accessory for this recipe, as it allows you to expose all the nuts to the smoke (without any falling through the cooking grate!). Taste them after 20 minutes of roasting. If you think they are smoky enough, don't add another chunk of wood. Make sure you are using raw nuts here, since toasted ones will dry out. Cashews would work well in place of almonds.

4 cups whole raw almonds
1 tablespoon fine sea salt
2 teaspoons chipotle chile powder
2 teaspoons paprika
2 tablespoons extra-virgin olive oil
4 teaspoons finely chopped fresh rosemary leaves

1 Soak the wood chips in water for at least 30 minutes.

2 Prepare the charcoal grill for indirect cooking over low heat (as close to 250°F as possible).

3 In a medium bowl or container cover the almonds with water and let stand for 10 minutes; drain. Spread the almonds on a kitchen towel and pat until no longer wet but still damp. Place the almonds in a bowl with the salt, chile powder, and paprika. Toss to coat (the moisture will allow the spice mixture to adhere better to the almonds). Transfer the almonds to a perforated grill pan.

4 Drain and add half of the wood chips to the charcoal and put the lid on the grill. When smoke appears, place the grill pan with the almonds over **indirect low heat**, close the lid, and cook until fragrant and smoky, about 45 minutes, stirring the almonds once or twice. After 20 minutes, drain and add the remaining wood chips to the charcoal.

5 Transfer the almonds to a medium bowl and add the oil and rosemary; toss well. Serve warm or at room temperature.

2

PORK

PULLED PORK

I never thought I would find the world's greatest pulled pork sandwich on the streets of New York City, but then again, the man responsible for making it is no city slicker. Chris Lilly is a pit master from rural Alabama who, with his team, has won the American Royal Invitational in Kansas City, not to mention four Grand Championships at the Memphis in May competition. Each June he hauls his smokers to New York for The Big Apple Barbecue Block Party, a meat fest and charity fundraiser that attracts barbecue royalty from all over the country—and up to 125,000 visitors eager for the one-of-a-kind opportunity to taste dishes as fabulous as smoked lamb brisket from Tim Love in Texas, Jamaican jerk ribs from Bill Durney in Brooklyn, and, of course, Lilly's epic sandwich.

Skeptics might ask: What kind of pulled pork could possibly make it worth battling your way through such huge crowds? And isn't $12 a pretty hefty price tag for a sandwich? But just one bite of Lilly's creation tells you why he's a legend. His prowess with a live fire can transform a brawny pork shoulder into soft, moist shreds of meat mingled with outer edges of slow-smoked, seasoned bark, all with a tangy, mustard-laced snap. Put that into a soft roll and you have a lot more than a sandwich. It's a bold and savory fistful of pure happiness.

TRIMMING

An entire pork shoulder weighs in at 12 to 20 pounds, which is nothing for a pit master to smoke and serve, but probably too much meat for a backyard barbecue. Instead, get yourself the top half of the shoulder, which usually weighs 4 to 8 pounds. It goes by several names, and most of them include the term "butt," a misleading description at best because a pork butt has nothing to do with the back end of pig. Regardless of the name, look for a roast with an even thickness of well-marbled meat from edge to edge and the shoulder blade still inside, because the bone adds flavor. The finest tasting meat comes from heritage breeds such as Berkshire or Mangalitsa hogs; those breeds are what competitors often use to get blue-ribbon results.

Trim the fat down to a thickness of about ¼ inch so that it melts easily on the smoker, so the seasonings can get into the meat, and so you have a better chance of developing a gorgeous smoke ring. On the leaner side, remove as much fibrous silver skin as you can. Also remove any lymph nodes that could discolor the meat to a greenish hue. The folks at the processing plant usually remove these, but check anyway for light brownish masses, a little bigger than marbles, buried an inch or so within the meat.

DONENESS

After you have spent so many hours barbecuing a pork shoulder, all of the effort you poured into mixing a spice rub, trimming the meat, and finessing the sauce could be wasted if you under cook or overcook the shoulder. There are a few ways to know it's cooked right: the internal temperature should reach 190° to 195°F; you should be able to remove the bone easily from the meat, with the bone still looking moist (not chalky); and the meat should be so tender that you can break it apart into small pieces with just your fingers. If the meat is still quite warm, use forks or "bear claws" to tear it apart, but do wait until the shoulder has rested for at least 20 minutes. The internal temperature should come down to about 140°F. If you break it apart and see steam rising, the meat is losing precious juices to evaporation and needs to rest longer.

THE SMOKE RING

The pinkish band of color under the surface of some smoked meats strikes a thrill into the hearts of barbecue judges and backyard cooks alike. Achieving this handsome effect is a matter of encouraging the natural pink protein in the meat (called myoglobin) to react with gases carried in the smoke, specifically nitric oxide (NO) and carbon monoxide (CO). You can amplify the effect by making sure the meat is moist and cold when it first goes on the smoker, as the moisture will trap more NO and CO, and the cold temperature means you have a longer period of time for the myoglobin and gases to make their magic happen.

KANSAS CITY–STYLE PULLED PORK

SERVES: 10 TO 12 | **PREP TIME:** 30 MINUTES | **GRILLING TIME:** ABOUT 5½ HOURS | **RESTING TIME:** 1 HOUR
SPECIAL EQUIPMENT: CHARCOAL GRILL; 4 LARGE HANDFULS APPLE, CHERRY, OR HICKORY WOOD CHUNKS;
LARGE DISPOSABLE FOIL PAN; SPRAY BOTTLE FILLED WITH WATER; HEAVY-DUTY ALUMINUM FOIL; INSTANT-READ THERMOMETER

In big cities, small towns, and tiny neighborhoods across America, pulled pork appears in styles as varied and multicultural as the people living there. One style that everyone seems to like (love, actually) hails from Kansas City, where generously spiced shoulder meat is barbecued to fall-apart tenderness and coated in a sauce of sweet and spicy complexity with a touch of smokiness. That's Kansas City–style: a little bit of everything delicious.

Don't rush it. The path to great pulled pork requires a fire that burns ever so slowly at temperatures between 225° and 250°F. If you cook it hotter than that, the muscles tend to seize up and push out moisture. If the temperature is consistently just right, the collagen in the meat will melt into juicy, delicious gelatin. That's what makes barbecued meat moist. One clever way of achieving this succulence is with the "snake method" (for setup instructions, see page 76). Essentially, you create an arc of charcoal briquettes and wood along one side of the grill and light the charcoal on one end of the "snake" only. The briquettes and wood burn gradually over time, rather than all at once, so the fire never gets too high or too low and you shouldn't need to add any more fuel.

RUB
- ½ cup packed light brown sugar
- ¼ cup smoked paprika
- 4 teaspoons kosher salt
- 2½ teaspoons prepared chili powder
- 2½ teaspoons garlic powder
- 2½ teaspoons onion powder
- 1½ teaspoons coarsely ground black pepper
- ½–1 teaspoon ground cayenne pepper

- 1 boneless pork shoulder roast (Boston butt), 4 to 5 pounds, trimmed of excess fat and silver skin, rolled and tied

SAUCE
- 3 slices bacon
- ½ medium yellow onion, finely diced
- 3 garlic cloves, minced
- ½ cup ketchup
- ½ cup light corn syrup
- ½ cup cider vinegar
- ¼ cup tomato paste
- ¼ cup prepared chili powder
- 2 tablespoons packed light brown sugar
- 1 tablespoon unsulfured molasses (not blackstrap)
- 1 tablespoon liquid smoke
- 1 tablespoon Worcestershire sauce
- 1 teaspoon celery salt
- ½ teaspoon kosher salt

1 Mix the rub ingredients, and then season the roast all over with the rub. Allow the roast to stand at room temperature for 30 minutes before grilling.

2 Prepare the charcoal grill for indirect cooking over very low heat (225° to 250°F) using the snake method (see photo at left and setup instructions on page 76). When the temperature of the grill reaches

225°F, grill the roast, fat side down, over ***indirect very low heat***, with the lid closed, for 4 hours, adjusting the top vent so the temperature of the grill stays as close to 225°F as possible. At the start of every hour, after the first hour, lightly spray the roast with water.

3 Meanwhile, make the sauce. In a medium, heavy-bottomed saucepan over medium heat on the stove, fry the bacon until browned and most of the fat is rendered out. Using a slotted spoon, remove the bacon. Leave 2 to 3 tablespoons of bacon fat in the pan. Eat the bacon or save for another use. Add the onion and cook until soft and translucent, 3 to 4 minutes, stirring occasionally. Add the garlic and cook for 1 minute, stirring occasionally to prevent it from burning. Whisk in the

remaining sauce ingredients, bring to a simmer over medium heat, and cook for 10 to 15 minutes, stirring occasionally. Set aside to cool. Once the sauce has cooled, pour into a blender and blend until smooth. Separate the sauce into two containers. One half will be used for basting the roast before wrapping it in foil. The other half will be mixed with the pulled pork.

4 After 4 hours, use an instant-read thermometer to check the internal temperature of the roast. If it has not reached 160°F, continue cooking until it does. Once the roast has reached 160°F, remove it from the grill. Put the lid back on the grill to prevent heat loss.

5 On a large work surface, crisscross two sheets of heavy-duty aluminum foil, each

about 3 feet long. Place the roast in the center of the foil, fat side up. Lightly brush the roast all over with the sauce. Bring the ends of the inner sheet together, folding on top of the roast. Then bring the ends of the outer sheet together, wrapping the roast tightly to trap the steam. Return the roast to the grill and cook over ***indirect very low heat***, with the lid closed, until the internal temperature reaches 190° to 195°F, about 1½ hours. Remove from the grill and let rest, still in the foil, for 1 hour.

6 Unwrap the roast and, when cool enough to handle, pull the meat apart to shred it. Discard any large pieces of fat and sinew. Moisten the meat with as much sauce as you like. Serve immediately.

SMOKED PULLED PORK SHOULDER
WITH VINEGARY SLAW

SERVES: 12 | **PREP TIME:** 40 MINUTES | **COOKING TIME:** 8 TO 10 HOURS
SPECIAL EQUIPMENT: WATER SMOKER; 6 LARGE HANDFULS APPLE, CHERRY, OR HICKORY
WOOD CHUNKS; INSTANT-READ THERMOMETER

*In the Carolinas a lot of people are partial to a vinegary slaw with pulled pork.
The sharp, tangy flavors and crisp, fresh textures play balancing roles against the
rich, slow-cooked meat. The slaw here has all the right hallmarks but it also has a
little twist to make it a bit different. You will find thinly sliced celery and chopped
fresh dill tossed with the standard ingredients. Save time by using a mandolin
or other shredder for the cabbage, but don't skimp on the time the slaw sits in
the fridge. It needs several hours to become almost pickled.*

PUSHING THROUGH "THE STALL"

When you cook a big piece of meat like a pork shoulder, internal temperatures rise to about
150°F, and then curiously they stall or plateau for a while, sometimes hours, freaking out
backyard cooks. Don't freak. The reason for the stall is that the meat is cooling on the surface
as juices are evaporating. Just as sweat cools us when we get too hot, evaporating juices cool
meat on a smoker and prevent internal temperatures from climbing until the surface of the meat
dries out. You can wait patiently for all the moisture to evaporate or push through the stall by
wrapping the meat in foil to trap the heat and moisture.

SLAW

- ¾ cup distilled white vinegar
- ⅓ cup granulated sugar
- 2 tablespoons finely chopped fresh dill
- 2 teaspoons kosher salt
- ½ teaspoon freshly ground black pepper
- 1 head green cabbage, about 1½ pounds, cored and shredded
- 3 large ribs celery, very thinly sliced
- 2 medium carrots, peeled and grated through the large holes of a box grater
- 1–2 tablespoons minced jalapeño or serrano chile pepper

RUB

2 teaspoons paprika

2 teaspoons kosher salt

2 teaspoons freshly ground
black pepper

1 teaspoon ground cumin

½ teaspoon granulated onion

1 bone-in pork shoulder roast (Boston
butt), about 6 pounds, trimmed of
excess fat and silver skin

SAUCE

2 cups distilled white vinegar

1 cup ketchup

¼ cup packed light brown sugar

1 tablespoon Worcestershire sauce

2 teaspoons kosher salt

½ teaspoon ground cayenne pepper

12 hamburger buns, split

1 In a large bowl whisk the vinegar, sugar, dill, salt, and pepper. Add the remaining slaw ingredients. Toss well, cover, and refrigerate until ready to serve.

2 In a small bowl combine the rub ingredients, and then massage the rub all over the roast.

3 Prepare the smoker for indirect cooking with very low heat (200° to 250°F). When the temperature reaches 225°F, add the wood chunks to the charcoal. Cook the roast, fat side down, over *indirect very low heat*, with the lid closed, until the internal temperature registers 190° to 195°F (not touching the bone) and the meat is so tender that it pulls apart easily, 8 to 10 hours. Check the smoker every hour and maintain an even heat. You may need to close some vents (partially) to lower the temperature or open some vents to raise the temperature.

Also, you may need to add water to the water pan halfway through the cooking time, which will lower the temperature.

4 Meanwhile, make the sauce. In a medium saucepan combine the sauce ingredients. Bring to a boil over medium-high heat on the stove and cook until the sugar is dissolved and the sauce is reduced to a ketchup-like consistency, 8 to 10 minutes. Remove from the heat and let cool.

5 Remove the roast from the smoker and let rest for 10 minutes. Remove the bone (it should come out cleanly) and, when cool enough to handle, pull the meat apart to shred it. Discard any clumps of fat and sinew. Moisten the meat with as much of the sauce as you like. Pile the pulled pork on buns and top with the slaw, adding mayonnaise or mustard, if desired.

PORK SHOULDER
WITH SWEET CAROLINA MUSTARD SAUCE

SERVES: 12 TO 16 | **PREP TIME:** 1 HOUR | **COOKING TIME:** 9 TO 11 HOURS | **RESTING TIME:** 1 TO 2 HOURS
SPECIAL EQUIPMENT: INJECTOR; WATER SMOKER; 6 LARGE HANDFULS HICKORY WOOD CHUNKS; SPRAY BOTTLE; LARGE DISPOSABLE FOIL PAN; HEAVY-DUTY ALUMINUM FOIL; INSTANT-READ THERMOMETER; DRY, INSULATED COOLER; BEAR CLAWS (OPTIONAL)

If your pulled pork aspirations include competition-worthy results, here are some tips to point you toward perfection.

1 Start with a large roast—8 to 9 pounds of nicely marbled pork shoulder. A heritage breed of pork like Berkshire of Mangalitsa will give you excellent flavor, but even standard supermarket pork will barbecue better if the cut is bigger. The meat has to be able to stay on the smoker long enough to melt the connective tissue. If the roast is too small, it is likely to dry out before the connective tissue dissolves into succulent juices.

2 Give special attention to the "money muscle," a tube-shaped section of meat opposite the bone that has superior pork flavor and soft but not mushy texture. For competitions, some pit masters make a shallow cut to separate this muscle a little bit from the rest of the shoulder, exposing more surface area to smoke and making it easier to find after the shoulder is cooked. They inject the muscle carefully, puncturing it as few times as possible. Finally, they slice little medallions from it, rather than pulling/shredding the meat.

3 Inject the meat evenly with some fruit juice. This is not so much for flavor as it is for extra moisture. The meat will be on the smoker for so long that it is bound to lose at least one-third of its moisture. The more you have at the start, the more you can afford to lose. Alternatively, you could brine the meat for 24 hours in a solution of 2 cups kosher salt dissolved in a gallon of water.

INJECTION
- 1 cup unsweetened apple juice
- ½ cup (1 stick) unsalted butter
- 1 tablespoon Worcestershire sauce
- 1 tablespoon kosher salt

RUB
- 2 tablespoons kosher salt
- 2 tablespoons packed light brown sugar
- 2 tablespoons prepared chili powder
- 1 tablespoon paprika
- 2 teaspoons granulated onion
- 1 teaspoon ground cumin
- 1 teaspoon freshly ground black pepper

- 1 bone-in pork shoulder roast, 8 to 9 pounds, trimmed of excess fat and silver skin
- ½ cup unsweetened apple juice

SAUCE
- 1 cup yellow mustard
- ¼ cup unsweetened apple or white grape juice
- 2 tablespoons packed light brown sugar
- 2 tablespoons honey
- 2 tablespoons unsulfured molasses (not blackstrap)
- 1½ teaspoons granulated garlic
- 1½ teaspoons granulated onion
- 1½ teaspoons prepared chili powder
- 1½ teaspoons freshly ground black pepper
- ½ teaspoon sweet cocoa powder

1 In a small saucepan mix the injection ingredients. Bring to a simmer over medium heat on the stove and cook until the butter is melted. Allow the injection to cool.

2   In a small bowl mix the rub ingredients. Set aside 2 tablespoons of the rub for seasoning the pork later.

3   Inject the meat all over with the injection mixture, including the "money muscle."

4   Season the roast evenly with the rub left in the small bowl. Allow the roast to stand at room temperature while you prepare the smoker.

5   Prepare the smoker for indirect cooking with very low heat (200° to 250°F). When the temperature of the smoker reaches 225°F, add the wood chunks to the charcoal. Set the roast on the cooking grate, fat side down, close the lid, and cook over **indirect very low heat** until the surface is dark brown all over, 7 to 8 hours, maintaining the temperature of the grill between 225° and 250°F throughout that time.

6   Fill a spray bottle with ½ cup apple juice.

7   Remove the roast from the smoker, spray it all over with juice, season evenly with the reserved 2 tablespoons rub, and place it, fat side down, in a large disposable foil pan. Cover the pan tightly with heavy-duty aluminum foil, crimping the edges.

8   Return the roast in the covered foil pan to the smoker and continue cooking until the internal temperature registers 190° to 195°F (not touching the bone) and the meat is so tender that it pulls apart easily, 2 to 3 hours more. Check on the smoker every hour to maintain even heat. You may need to partially close some vents to lower the heat or open some vents to raise the heat. Also, you may have to add water to the water pan (this will lower the heat).

9   Set the roast, still wrapped in the pan, in a dry, insulated cooler and let rest for 1 to 2 hours. Meanwhile, make the sauce.

10 In a saucepan whisk the sauce ingredients until smooth. Place the saucepan on the stove over medium heat and bring to a simmer. Simmer for about 5 minutes, stirring often to prevent it from burning on the bottom. Remove from the heat.

11 Remove the roast from the pan. Remove and discard the bone from the roast (it should come cleanly out of the meat). Find the "money muscle" and cut it away from the rest of the roast. Cut the money muscle crosswise into ½-inch slices. Pull apart the remaining meat using bear claws or two forks. Discard any clumps of fat and sinew. Pour the sauce over the meat and toss to coat evenly. Serve warm.

LEFTOVERS?

A big bone-in pork shoulder weighing 8 to 9 pounds makes a lot of pulled pork—enough for at least a dozen people. If you are not serving a big crowd all at once and you plan to have leftovers, make a double batch of the mustard sauce. Use half of it to sauce the meat right after it has been pulled. Use the other half as a sauce for these fried patties of pulled pork.

For every 4 cups of leftover meat, mix in 1 cup panko bread crumbs and 2 lightly beaten eggs. Shape into 12 patties, each about 3 inches wide and ¾ each thick. Pour enough oil into a large skillet to come ¼ inch up the side. Heat the oil over medium heat, and then fry the patties (in batches) until golden brown and warm throughout, about 2 minutes per side, turning once or twice. Serve the patties warm with extra sauce and a fresh salad.

ROTISSERIE LECHÓN ASADO

SERVES: 6 TO 8 | **PREP TIME:** 20 MINUTES | **MARINATING TIME:** 8 TO 24 HOURS | **GRILLING TIME:** 2¼ TO 2¾ HOURS
SPECIAL EQUIPMENT: 2 LARGE HANDFULS HICKORY WOOD CHIPS, LARGE DISPOSABLE FOIL PAN, BUTCHER'S TWINE, ROTISSERIE, INSTANT-READ THERMOMETER

MARINADE

1½ cups fresh orange juice
½ cup fresh lemon juice
½ cup extra-virgin olive oil
1 medium yellow onion, finely chopped in a food processor
20 garlic cloves, peeled, finely chopped in a food processor
1 tablespoon dried oregano
1 tablespoon kosher salt

1 boneless pork shoulder roast (Boston butt), 5 to 6 pounds, trimmed of excess fat and silver skin
1½ teaspoons kosher salt
1 teaspoon freshly ground black pepper
1–2 tablespoons chopped fresh oregano leaves

When you roast this Cuban-style pork shoulder on a rotisserie that spins over a smoky fire, you can expect the internal juices to baste the meat from within while the aromas of wood seep into the savory crust. Take the pork off the grill when it reaches about 170°F internally. At this temperature, it will be tender yet firm enough to slice.

1 Soak the wood chips in water for at least 30 minutes.

2 In a large bowl combine the marinade ingredients. Make small slits all over the roast. Add the roast to the bowl with the marinade, and spread the marinade all over it. Cover and refrigerate for 8 to 24 hours, turning occasionally.

3 Prepare the grill for indirect cooking over medium-low heat (300° to 350°F). Place a large disposable foil pan in the center of the charcoal grate between the two piles of charcoal or in the middle of the cooking grates of a gas grill.

4 Remove the roast from the bowl, reserve the marinade, and allow the roast to stand at room temperature for 30 minutes before grilling. Cover and refrigerate the marinade until needed in step 6. Season the roast with the salt and pepper. Using butcher's twine, tie the roast to make the shape as uniform as possible. Slide one pronged fork onto the spit, with the tines facing inward, about 10 inches from the end of the spit. Secure the fork, but do not tighten it yet. Slide the spit through the roast as close to the center as possible, and then gently push the meat into the fork tines so that they are deep inside. Add the other pronged fork to the spit with the tines facing inward, and then push firmly into the meat. Secure the fork, but don't tighten it yet. Place the spit into the rotisserie motor and center the roast over the foil pan. Tighten the forks.

5 Drain and add the wood chips to the charcoal or to the smoker box of a gas grill, following manufacturer's instructions. Close the lid and turn on the rotisserie motor. Grill the roast over **indirect medium-low heat**, with the lid closed, until an instant-read thermometer inserted into the thickest part of the roast registers 170°F, 2¼ to 2¾ hours. If using a charcoal grill, add more briquettes as necessary to maintain the temperature of the grill.

6 Meanwhile, in a medium saucepan over medium-high heat on the stove, bring the marinade to a boil. Continue cooking at a low to medium boil until slightly reduced, about 5 minutes. This salty-sweet juice becomes the sauce for the roast. Pour the marinade through a fine-mesh strainer into a medium bowl and discard the solids. Let stand for about 5 minutes to allow the oil to rise to the surface. Skim off and discard as much of the oil as you desire. Cover and refrigerate until just before serving.

7 Wearing insulated barbecue mitts or gloves, carefully remove the spit from the grill. Gently loosen the forks and slide the roast off the spit. Transfer to a cutting board and let rest for 20 to 30 minutes. Cut the roast into slices and garnish with the oregano. Just before serving, gently reheat the sauce and serve it alongside the meat.

Trussing the roast with twine will give the meat a uniform shape that allows you to secure it with all the tines of the rotisserie forks and to cook it more evenly.

SLOW-ROASTED PORK BO SSAM
WITH CARROT-SCALLION-GINGER SLAW AND CHILI SAUCE

SERVES: 6 TO 8 | **PREP TIME:** 45 MINUTES | **DRY BRINING TIME:** 24 HOURS | **GRILLING TIME:** 4 TO 4¾ HOURS
SPECIAL EQUIPMENT: 2 LARGE, HEAVY-DUTY DISPOSABLE FOIL PANS

DRY BRINE
½ cup granulated sugar
½ cup kosher salt

1 boneless pork shoulder roast (Boston butt), 4 to 4½ pounds, trimmed of excess fat and silver skin
1½ cups basmati rice

SLAW
10 scallions (white and light green parts only), thinly sliced
1 carrot, 4 to 5 ounces, coarsely grated
½ cup roughly chopped fresh cilantro leaves
2 tablespoons peeled, finely grated fresh ginger with juices
2 tablespoons vegetable oil
1 tablespoon unseasoned rice vinegar
1 tablespoon soy sauce

SAUCE
3 tablespoons sweet chili sauce
2 tablespoons black bean garlic sauce
2 tablespoons vegetable oil
2 tablespoons unseasoned rice vinegar
1 teaspoon toasted sesame oil

¼ cup packed light brown sugar
1–2 heads butter lettuce, leaves separated

The hardest part about this recipe for Korean-style barbecued pork is resisting the glorious aromas while the meat roasts over the fire for more than four hours. It's well worth the wait because the pork will develop a caramelized crust, thanks in part to a dry brine of sugar and salt that draws out some moisture that is then reabsorbed into the meat with seasoning. A last-minute crisping of the meat in a hot pan creates glistening edges for nice bits of crackling texture.

1 Twenty-four hours before grilling, dry brine the roast. In a large bowl mix the sugar and salt. Place the roast in the bowl and rub the dry brine on all sides and crevices of the meat. Cover the bowl with plastic wrap and refrigerate for 24 hours.

2 Prepare the grill for indirect cooking over medium-low heat (as close to 300°F as possible).

3 Remove the roast from the bowl and place it in a large, heavy-duty disposable aluminum foil pan. Gently pat off any excess dry brine and juices with a paper towel. Cook the roast over ***indirect medium-low heat***, with the grill lid closed, until the meat is very tender and beginning to fall apart, 4 to 4¾ hours, turning the roast and basting with any pan juices every hour (there may only be a very small amount of juices to baste with). Remove the pan from the grill and transfer the roast to a cutting board. Discard the foil pan.

4 During the last hour of grilling time, cook the rice according to package instructions. In a medium bowl mix the slaw ingredients. In a small bowl whisk the sauce ingredients.

5 Increase the temperature of the grill for indirect cooking over high heat (450° to 550°F).

6 Using two forks, shred the pork, discarding any large pieces of fat and sinew. Spread the pork in an even layer in the second large, heavy-duty disposable foil pan. Sprinkle the brown sugar over the pork, and then grill over ***indirect high heat***, with the lid closed, until slightly browned and caramelized in spots, 5 to 8 minutes, stirring occasionally. Transfer the pork to a serving bowl.

7 To assemble, spoon the rice and pork into a lettuce leaf, but do not overfill. Top with a spoonful of slaw and a drizzle of sauce. Roll up and eat.

PULLED PORK BREAKFAST BURRITOS
WITH EGGS AND CHEESE

SERVES: 6
PREP TIME: 25 MINUTES

2 tablespoons extra-virgin olive oil, divided

1¼ pounds leftover pulled pork (already tossed with sauce)

2 canned chipotle chile peppers in adobo sauce, minced

3 tablespoons adobo sauce (from the can)

1 white onion, thinly sliced

1 green bell pepper, thinly sliced

2 garlic cloves, minced

8 large eggs

¾ teaspoon kosher salt

¼ teaspoon freshly ground black pepper

2 tablespoons unsalted butter

6 burrito-size tortillas

8 ounces Monterey Jack cheese, grated

¼ cup finely chopped fresh cilantro leaves

Shredded lettuce

Avocado slices

Store-bought salsa (optional)

Sour cream (optional)

At the end of slow days, barbecue restaurants all over Texas and the Southwest have leftover 'cue. Many places use their remaining pulled pork and other meats in clever ways, from salads to pastas, but one of my favorite ways is in breakfast burritos. What makes these so special is that you reheat the meat with chipotle chiles in adobo sauce, giving it a new layer of spiciness while you crisp up the edges.

1 In a large skillet over medium-high heat on the stove, warm 1 tablespoon of the oil. Add the pork, chipotle chile peppers, and adobo sauce and cook until the pork is crispy and hot, 7 to 9 minutes, stirring occasionally. Reduce the heat to low and keep warm.

2 In a large, nonstick skillet over medium-high heat on the stove, warm the remaining 1 tablespoon oil. Add the onion, bell pepper, and garlic. Cook until softened and the onion just starts to brown, 8 to 9 minutes, stirring occasionally. Stir the mixture into the skillet with the pulled pork and keep warm.

3 Clean the nonstick skillet and return it to the stove over medium heat. Whisk the eggs, salt, and pepper. Melt the butter in the skillet and, when the foam subsides, add the eggs. Cook the eggs, scraping the bottom of the skillet occasionally with a flexible, heatproof spatula, until just set, 2 to 3 minutes, or to your desired doneness.

4 Warm the tortillas according to package directions. Place the tortillas on plates and divide the pork, eggs, cheese, and cilantro evenly among them. Top with lettuce and avocado. Roll up the tortillas, folding in the ends to hold in the filling. Serve with salsa and sour cream, if desired.

MEMPHIS PULLED PORK SPAGHETTI

The unusual sauce here picks up sweet, mild chile flavors from cubanelle peppers, also known as "Cuban peppers," which are light greenish in color and tapered in their shape. If you can't find cubanelles, use Anaheim chile peppers instead, although the Anaheim peppers will taste a little hotter.

SERVES: 8 TO 10 (MAKES 2½ QUARTS SAUCE)
PREP TIME: 15 MINUTES, PLUS 35 MINUTES FOR THE SAUCE

Barbecue purists from the Carolinas may be shocked and dismayed to see the object of their great respect, pulled pork, in the company of anything so foreign and unrelated as spaghetti, but that's the way barbecue goes. Several restaurants in Memphis, Tennessee, are mixing soft and warm noodles with pulled pork and coating them with something that straddles the line between tomato sauce and barbecue sauce.

SAUCE

¼ cup extra-virgin olive oil
1 cup chopped red onion
2 medium cubanelle or Anaheim chile peppers, 3 to 4 ounces each, stemmed, cored, and chopped
4 teaspoons minced garlic
2 cans (each 28 ounces) crushed tomatoes in juice
¼ cup unsulfured molasses (not blackstrap)
1 tablespoon mustard powder
1 teaspoon ground cinnamon
1 teaspoon kosher salt
½ teaspoon freshly ground black pepper
1½ pounds leftover smoked pulled pork, chopped

2 pounds dried spaghetti pasta
Chopped fresh Italian parsley leaves
Crushed red pepper flakes

1 In a large saucepan over medium heat on the stove, warm the oil. Add the onion and chile peppers and cook until softened, about 4 minutes, stirring often. Stir in the garlic and cook until aromatic, about 20 seconds.

2 Add the tomatoes, molasses, mustard powder, cinnamon, salt, and pepper. Bring the sauce to a low boil, and then reduce the heat to low; simmer, uncovered, until thickened to a marinara-sauce consistency, about 20 minutes, stirring occasionally.

3 Add the pulled pork to the tomato sauce. Simmer about 10 minutes to warm through and blend the flavors. While the sauce is simmering, cook the pasta according to package instructions. Drain the pasta, transfer to a large serving bowl, and then pour 6 cups of the sauce over the pasta, mixing gently to coat.

4 Serve the pasta in shallow bowls and garnish each with more sauce (about ¼ cup), parsley, red pepper flakes, and slices of crusty, grilled bread, if desired.

CHICKEN-FRIED PORK RIBS

Start with the meatiest ribs you can find. After you've dipped each rib in the egg mixture, allow the excess to drip back into the dish before coating with the cornmeal mixture. An excessively wet rib does not fry well. Also, have the ribs at room temperature to help keep the oil's temperature even.

SERVES: 8 | **PREP TIME:** 25 MINUTES
SPECIAL EQUIPMENT: DEEP-FRY THERMOMETER

In some Georgia barbecue joints, cooks have figured out how to combine chicken-fried steak and smoked ribs. (Finally!) If you want to try this at home, make sure the ribs have no sauce on them, or even any assertive rub, just the tender meat clinging to the bones. Coated with cornmeal-laced batter, the ribs fry up with a satisfying little crunch. Serve the ribs with Peachy Dipping Sauce—the recipe can be found on page 279.

2 cups unbleached all-purpose flour, divided
4 large eggs, at room temperature
¼ cup whole milk
⅓ cup yellow cornmeal
2 teaspoons paprika
1 teaspoon kosher salt
1 teaspoon freshly ground black pepper
Peanut oil
2 racks leftover smoked baby back ribs, cut into individual ribs, at room temperature
Pickled jalapeño rings (optional)

1 Set out two shallow bowls and one deep bowl. Put 1 cup of the flour in the first shallow bowl. In the deep bowl whisk the eggs and milk until uniform and smooth. In the second shallow bowl combine the remaining 1 cup flour, cornmeal, paprika, salt, and pepper. Set the bowls in this order near the stove, with the second shallow bowl nearest to the frying pot.

2 Pour enough oil into a large, deep pot to come 2 inches up the side. Attach a deep-fry thermometer to the side of the pot. Heat the oil over medium heat on the stove until the temperature on the thermometer registers 350°F.

3 Dip a rib into the flour, coating it lightly. Shake off any excess, and then dip in the egg mixture, coating well. Again, shake off any excess, and then dip into the cornmeal mixture, coating evenly. Set aside. After you've coated four or five ribs, slip them into the hot oil and fry until crisp and golden, 5 to 6 minutes, turning once or twice and adjusting the heat to keep the oil's temperature constant. Transfer the finished ribs to a wire rack set over a sheet pan. Bring the oil's temperature back to 350°F and continue dipping and frying the remaining ribs in batches to prevent sogginess and overcrowding.

4 Serve the crispy ribs immediately, garnished with sliced pickled jalapeño rings, if desired.

LESSONS FROM THE LEGENDS
BABY BACK RIBS

Writing this book, I must have eaten my weight in baby back ribs. My first belt-busting research trip was to Pappy's Smokehouse in St. Louis, where pit master Mike Emerson cooks about a ton of dry-rubbed ribs every day over apple and cherry wood. At Pappy's they have adopted the Memphis style of barbecuing ribs without sauce, although customers can choose from a few squeeze bottles of sauce on the tables. Just across town, a few miles from St. Louis's graceful arch alongside the Mississippi River, chef Skip Steele, who used to cook at Pappy's, makes ribs with a different twist. For one thing, he finishes his racks with an apricot glaze and caramelizes the sugars into the

meat with a ferocious blowtorch. What he achieves is a thin sheet of glistening, candy-like flavor that helps his barbecue stand out in the crowd.

This kind of distinction is the case in dozens of other cities and small towns I visited, especially outside big bastions of American barbecue like Memphis, Kansas City, the Carolinas, and Texas. Traditionalists and innovators are barbecuing ribs in the same zip code but with different approaches, meaning that while long-standing traditions remain intact, there is plenty of room for the next wave of clever ideas.

CHOOSING THE RIGHT RACKS

1

Choose the meatiest ribs you can find. If you see any bones peeking through the meat (as in the photo above), it's a bad sign. We call those racks "shiners," and it means a butcher has cut the meat too close to the bone. Racks that weigh 2½ to 3 pounds usually have plenty of meat.

2

Choose racks with plenty of fat. Ideally the fat will be evenly distributed throughout the meat. Big clumps of jiggly fat lying on top should be trimmed off and discarded, as they do you no good. On the other hand, thin streaks of fat woven within the meat pack flavor and richness.

3

If you are fortunate you will find a strip of loin meat that runs horizontally on the meaty side of a rack. When the meat is fully cooked, you can pull off the whole strip and eat it by itself, and it's wonderful.

PULLING THE MEMBRANE

On the bone side of each rack is a thin, slick membrane that has a leathery texture when it's cooked; many pros remove it if the butcher hasn't done so already. To remove the membrane, start by finding a straight bone near the middle of the rack. Slide a dull knife or your fingertips under the membrane at both the top and bottom of the bone and work your fingers under the membrane until they meet at the middle of the bone. You can now get a couple of fingers under the membrane and pull it straight up while holding the rest of the rack down with your other hand. The membrane often tears off in one whole sheet, but sometimes it requires a few separate pulls.

SMART SEASONING

The standard way to season ribs is to sprinkle a mixture of dried spices over both sides, especially the meaty side because it is most of what people eat. Some barbecue gurus like to add moisture to this step because they know that smoke dissolves into damp surfaces, so adding moisture improves the look of their smoke rings. A wet paste of dried spices with mustard or Worcestershire sauce is a clever way to get smokier ribs.

RIB FUNDAMENTALS

INDIRECT HEAT. The traditional way to barbecue baby back ribs is with indirect heat. That means the fire burns off to the side(s) of the racks on a gas or charcoal grill. On a smoker, a shield or water pan deflects the fire. A few barbecue joints, like Rendezvous in Memphis, cook ribs over direct heat, but I find it makes the meat dry.

BONE SIDE DOWN. Even though indirect heat circulates around all sides of the racks, the heat coming from the fire below is a little hotter. So start the racks bone side down to protect the meat on top from cooking too quickly. You need to give the connective tissue (collagen) in the meat enough time to melt slowly. That's when ribs taste juicy. Near the end of cooking, turn the rack over to collect juices that you use for basting.

SPRAY THE MEAT. Over time the surface of the meat will darken into a rich mahogany crust, but to prevent the crust from burning, especially on the ends, spray the meat on both sides with water. Be careful not to use so much water that you rinse away the spice rub.

ARE THEY DONE?

One way to check whether your ribs have reached the desired point of tenderness, without being mushy, is to push the tips of two exposed bones in opposite directions. The meat in between should begin to tear. The other way is with the bend (or bounce) test: Lift a rack at one end and let it bend (or bounce) in the air. If the meat in the middle tears open, it's done.

PULLING CLEAN OFF THE BONE

Some folks like ribs to be so tender you could eat them without teeth, but most aficionados like a little chewiness in the meat. In fact, while I was training to be a KCBS certified barbecue judge, I was taught that if the meat slips off the bone with little effort, it's overdone. It should come clean off the bone, but only after you have taken a strong bite. At least that's what the pros say. You eat your ribs however you like.

One of the many unsubstantiated stories in barbecue folklore tells of a technique developed in Texas for steaming meat in foil after it has been smoked. The steam tenderizes the meat, achieving the kind of tenderness that barbecue masters in other parts of the country can supposedly achieve without "the Texas crutch." Well, nowadays almost every barbecue team, countless barbecue restaurants, and cookbook authors like me use it ... because it works.

THE TEXAS CRUTCH

To try it yourself, brush smoked ribs (after they have achieved a dark brown crust) with juice, beer, or barbecue sauce, and wrap each rack individually in heavy-duty aluminum foil, not the thin foil that could easily tear and leak. You must have a tight, unbroken seal to create enough steam.

Be careful not to cook the ribs too long in the foil. If you do, the precious crust on the surface will get soggy and the meat will turn both dry and mushy. Thirty minutes to one hour in foil is plenty of time. If the surface of the meat looks a little too wet coming out of the foil, set the ribs back over the heat without foil for 20 minutes or so to reestablish a crust.

BASIC BABY BACKS

SERVES: 4 | **PREP TIME:** 15 MINUTES | **GRILLING TIME:** 2 TO 2¼ HOURS | **SPECIAL EQUIPMENT:** 3 LARGE HANDFULS HICKORY WOOD CHIPS, GAS GRILL WITH AT LEAST 3 BURNERS, METAL SMOKER BOX, SPRAY BOTTLE FILLED WITH WATER

PASTE

2 tablespoons yellow mustard
2 tablespoons Worcestershire sauce
2 teaspoons kosher salt
2 teaspoons packed light brown sugar
2 teaspoons prepared chili powder
1 teaspoon garlic powder
1 teaspoon freshly ground black pepper

2 racks baby back ribs, each 2½ to 3 pounds
1 cup store-bought barbecue sauce

1 Soak the wood chips in water for at least 30 minutes.

2 Mix the paste ingredients, and then spread evenly all over the racks, spreading most of it on the meaty side.

3 Before lighting the gas grill, drain and add the wood chips to a metal smoker box. Set the smoker box under the cooking grate and over a burner on one side of the grill. Prepare the grill for indirect cooking over high heat (450° to 550°F), heating the wood chips in the smoker box. When the wood begins to smoke, lower the temperature of the grill to low heat, as close to 300°F as possible.

4 Lay the racks, bone side down and flat, on the cooking grates over *indirect low heat*. Close the lid and cook for 1 hour, maintaining the temperature of the grill as close to 300°F as possible. You may need to turn off one of the burners temporarily, especially on hot days. The wood chips should smoke for about 30 minutes. If they catch fire, spray a little water over the smoker box.

5 After the first hour of cooking, lightly spray the racks with water and swap their positions for even cooking. After 1½ hours of cooking, brush the racks on both sides with about half of the barbecue sauce. Continue cooking, bone side down, over *indirect low heat*, with the lid closed, until some of the meat has shrunk back from the ends of most of the bones by ¼ inch or more. They are completely done when you lift a rack at one end with tongs, bone side up, and the rack bends so much in the middle that the meats begins to tear easily. This may take 30 to 40 minutes more.

6 Remove the racks from the grill and, just before serving, lightly brush with more sauce. Cut the racks between the bones into individual ribs and serve warm.

TAMING THE FLAMES

Sometimes wood chips in a smoker box will dry out and catch fire. Don't panic. A few squeezes from a spray bottle filled with water will tame the flames.

BABY BACK RIBS
WITH SWEET AND SPICY BARBECUE SAUCE

SERVES: 4 | **PREP TIME:** 20 MINUTES | **GRILLING TIME:** ABOUT 3 HOURS
SPECIAL EQUIPMENT: CHARCOAL GRILL; 4 TO 5 LARGE HANDFULS APPLE, CHERRY, OR HICKORY WOOD CHUNKS; LARGE
DISPOSABLE FOIL PAN; SPRAY BOTTLE FILLED WITH WATER; HEAVY-DUTY ALUMINUM FOIL

One recent barbecue innovation is a low-maintenance way of sustaining a low temperature and steady smoke for hours and hours in a kettle grill. It's called the "snake method" because charcoal briquettes are arranged in the shape of a snake that bends around the perimeter of the grill. The fire burns slowly from one end to the other, never getting too hot and never needing more fuel. Here is how to do it.

Start by forming two rows of briquettes around the perimeter on about half of the charcoal grate. The longer the snake, the longer with fire will last. The briquettes need to be neatly packed and touching. Stack another two rows on top of the first two so that now you have a charcoal configuration that is two briquettes wide and two briquettes high. Arrange the wood chunks in a row over one end (the end where you will start the fire burning).

In a chimney starter light 10 to 12 briquettes. Meanwhile, place a disposable foil pan on the charcoal grate beside the snake and fill the pan about three-quarters full with water. When the briquettes are ashed over, pile them carefully, using tongs, over one end of the snake. Make sure the bottom of the grill is swept clean of ash and the bottom vent is wide open so the fire gets plenty of air.

Set the cooking grate in place, close the lid, and adjust the damper on the lid so the vent is about halfway open. Preheat the grill until the temperature falls between 250° and 300°F. Then lay your ribs over indirect heat, bone side down, so that no part of any rack is directly above the snake. Use the damper on the lid to control the airflow and temperature of the fire. Sit back and let the snake do its thing.

RUB

- 1 tablespoon packed light brown sugar
- 1 tablespoon smoked paprika
- 1 tablespoon granulated onion
- 1 tablespoon prepared chili powder
- 1 tablespoon kosher salt
- 2 teaspoons freshly ground black pepper

- 2 racks baby back ribs, each 2½ to 3 pounds
- 2 tablespoons extra-virgin olive oil

SAUCE

- ¾ cup ketchup
- ½ cup water
- ¼ cup packed light brown sugar
- ¼ cup unsulfured molasses (not blackstrap)
- 1 tablespoon Worcestershire sauce
- 1 tablespoon prepared chili powder
- 1 teaspoon kosher salt
- ½ teaspoon freshly ground black pepper

1   Mix the rub ingredients. Using a dull knife, slide the tip under the membrane in the middle of the back of each rack of ribs. Lift and pull off each membrane (see how-to, page 73). Brush the racks with the oil and season them all over with the rub, putting more of the rub on the meaty side of the racks. Allow the racks to stand at room temperature while you prepare the grill.

2   Prepare the charcoal grill for indirect cooking over low heat (250° to 300°F) using the snake method (see photo and setup instructions at left).

3   Meanwhile, in a medium saucepan combine the sauce ingredients and bring to a gentle boil over medium-high heat on the stove, stirring frequently. Reduce the heat to medium-low and simmer until the sauce thickens slightly to a light syrupy consistency, 5 to 10 minutes, stirring occasionally.

4   Lay the racks on the cooking grate, bone side down and positioned over the foil pan. Close the lid and grill the racks over *indirect low heat* for 1 hour, maintaining the temperature of the grill between 250° and 300°F by opening the vents wider to increase heat or partially closing the vents to decrease heat, checking the temperature frequently.

5   After the first hour of cooking time, lightly spray the racks with water and swap their positions for even cooking. Continue cooking over *indirect low heat* for another hour.

6   After the second hour of cooking, transfer the racks from the grill to a large rimmed baking sheet. Close the grill lid to maintain the temperature. Brush the racks on both sides with some of the sauce, and then wrap each rack individually in heavy-duty aluminum foil. Return the racks to the grill, bone side down and positioned over the foil pan, and continue cooking over *indirect low heat* for 45 minutes.

7   After 45 minutes of cooking in the foil, remove the racks from the grill to check for doneness. Close the grill lid to maintain the temperature. Unwrap the racks and check to see if the meat has shrunk back from the ends of most of the bones by ¼ inch or more. If it has not, continue to cook the racks in the foil until it does, 10 to 15 minutes more. Remove the racks from the foil and lightly brush both sides with some of the sauce.

8   Return the racks to the grill, bone side down and positioned over the foil pan, and cook over *indirect low heat* until the sauce has set into the meat, about 10 minutes. Just before serving, lightly brush with another layer of sauce. Cut the racks into individual ribs and serve warm.

PB AND J RIBS

SERVES: 6 TO 8 | **PREP TIME:** 30 MINUTES | **COOKING TIME:** ABOUT 3 HOURS
SPECIAL EQUIPMENT: WATER SMOKER, 4 LARGE HANDFULS APPLE/CHERRY WOOD CHUNKS

The ideas behind my recipes sometimes come from scattered experiences in my past. Here is one example. Long before I was a cookbook author, I was a young schoolteacher in San Francisco with so many classes to manage and papers to grade that I often missed lunch. I kept a loaf of bread along with jars of peanut butter and jelly in my desk to make sandwiches I could scarf down while covering recess. As unsophisticated as those sandwiches were, they sustained me through unpredictable days trying to steer a rowdy group of adolescents. Later I taught at a school in Jakarta, Indonesia, where I was amazed by myriad ways of making peanut dipping sauces for skewered meats and seafood called satay. Maybe peanut butter doesn't have to be so childish after all, I thought.

Those taste memories have stayed with me through my career in barbecue. As I was working on this book, I was searching for ways of presenting familiar foods in unexpected ways. I hit on this: synthesizing pieces of my childhood and early adulthood with my relatively new fascination with barbecue. Does it work? I think so. The raspberry glaze is reminiscent of the fruity sweetness in some barbecue sauces today, taking the edge off the spiciness in the dry rub, and the salty, creamy qualities of the peanut sauce add however much nutty richness you feel like spreading on top. At the very least the recipe is a good example of how barbecue continues to evolve. Sometimes as cooks we look to the past for something new.

RUB
- 2 tablespoons prepared chili powder
- 2 tablespoons paprika
- 2 tablespoons packed light brown sugar
- 1 tablespoon granulated onion
- 1 tablespoon kosher salt
- 1 tablespoon freshly ground black pepper

- 4 racks baby back ribs, each 2½ to 3 pounds

GLAZE
- 1 cup raspberry preserves
- ½ cup unsweetened apple juice
- 2 tablespoons balsamic vinegar

SAUCE
- 1 cup creamy peanut butter
- ¾–1 cup unsweetened apple juice, divided
- 2 tablespoons cider vinegar

1   Mix the rub ingredients. Using a dull knife, slide the tip under the membrane in the middle of the back of each rack of ribs. Lift and pull off each membrane (see how-to, page 73). Season the racks evenly with the rub, putting more of the rub on the meaty side. Allow the racks to stand at room temperature while you prepare the smoker.

2   Prepare the smoker for indirect cooking with very low heat (250° to 300°F), filling the water pan halfway to three-quarters of the way with water.

3   Add the wood chunks to the charcoal and close the lid. When smoke appears, place the racks, bone side down, over ***indirect very low heat***. Put the lid on the smoker, and then close the top vent about halfway. Cook the racks for 2½ hours, maintaining the temperature of the smoker between 250° and 300°F. Meanwhile, make the glaze and sauce.

4   In a saucepan mix the glaze ingredients. Bring to a simmer over medium heat on the stove and cook for 3 to 5 minutes, stirring occasionally. Remove from the heat.

5   In another saucepan combine the peanut butter, ½ cup of the apple juice, and the vinegar. Heat slowly over medium heat on the stove until the sauce is smooth, about 2 minutes, whisking constantly. Remove from the heat.

6   After 2½ hours, lightly brush the racks on both sides with the glaze. Continue to cook for 30 minutes more.

7   After 3 hours total cooking time, the meat will have shrunk back from most of the bones by ¼ inch or more. If it has not, continue cooking until it does. They are done when you lift a rack at one end with tongs, bone side up, and the rack bends so much in the middle that the meat tears easily. If the meat does not tear easily, continue to cook until it does. Another way to test for doneness is to push two adjacent rib bones in opposite directions. When the racks are fully cooked, the meat between the bones should tear easily (but should not be mushy either).

8   Return the saucepan with the peanut sauce over medium heat. Add ¼ to ½ cup of the remaining apple juice and warm for a few minutes, stirring occasionally. Lightly brush the racks with more glaze, and then cut the racks into individual ribs. Serve warm with the peanut sauce.

NOUVEAU 'CUE
RIBS

12 BONES

The folks at 12 Bones Smokehouse (Asheville, NC) are famous for their wild ways with ribs. The flavor combinations change daily and are posted on a chalkboard next to the counter, and they always include a few conservative preparations like plain brown sugar or Memphis-style dry rub. The real draws, though, are the edgier offerings like sweet butterscotch or extra-hot pineapple habanero. 12 Bones has earned the most notoriety for their blueberry-chipotle ribs, which have a sweet, fruity hit upon first bite and a mellow, smoky heat that shines through underneath—a totally unexpected but delightful combination.

≡ SOUTHERN STYLE ≡

DEEP IN THE SOUTH, WHERE TRADITIONS RUN WIDE AND DEEP, BARBECUED RIBS HAVE BEEN COOKED THE SAME WAYS FOR GENERATIONS. MANY PIT MASTERS SEASON THEIRS WITH NOTHING MORE THAN SALT AND PEPPER, ALLOWING THE SMOKE OF THE PIT TO PLAY A LEADING ROLE. OTHERS START WITH A PAPRIKA- AND SPICE-LACED RUB OR FINISH THEIR RACKS WITH A SWEET, TANGY BARBECUE SAUCE. DINERS CAN CHOOSE BETWEEN "DRY" (NO SAUCE) OR "WET" (PLENTY OF SAUCE) RIBS, BUT THE TASTE OF THE MEAT IS FAMILIAR TO ANYONE WHO HAS EATEN SOUTHERN-STYLE BARBECUE.

THESE DAYS, THOUGH, MORE AND MORE COOKS ARE STARTING TO LOOK AT THESE BIG SLABS OF BONE AND MEAT AS PLATFORMS FOR EXPERIMENTATION. THESE SO-CALLED "NOUVEAU 'CUE" PIT MASTERS—COOKS WHO TAKE THEIR CRAFT SERIOUSLY BUT DON'T FEEL PARTICULARLY CONSTRAINED BY TRADITIONAL RECIPES AND STYLES—ARE BRINGING A NEW, BOLD SET OF IDEAS.

HEIRLOOM MARKET BBQ
ATLANTA, GA

At Heirloom Market BBq (Atlanta, GA), Southern barbecue classics get fused with spicy Korean flavors, reflecting the backgrounds of co-owners Cody Taylor, a self-described "hillbilly chef," and Jiyeon Lee, a former South Korean pop star who moved to the United States to pursue a culinary career. They smear their ribs with gochujang hot pepper paste, and then coat them with a sweet Georgia-style dry rub that's laced with paprika, garlic, onion, and—for a little kick— Korean red pepper flakes. If you like, you can even top those ribs with a Korean "sweet heat" barbecue sauce, which has a base of gochujang paste blended with lemon-lime soda.

SOUTHERN SOUL BARBEQUE
St. Simons Island, Georgia

Sweet heat is also the order of the day at Southern Soul Barbeque (St. Simons Island, GA), and co-owner and pit master Harrison Sapp doesn't feel hemmed in by old Georgia standards. A self-taught cook, he sprinkles his St. Louis–cut ribs with a sugar-laced rub. Midway through, he takes them off the pit, drizzles them with tupelo honey, and rubs on a generous layer of brown sugar.

After a few more hours in the smoke, the ribs are finished on a hot grill with a little more honey, resulting in beautiful, mahogany-hued slabs with an almost candy-like crust. That sweetness is complemented nicely by the restaurant's Hot Georgia Soul sauce laced with Sriracha. Who knew that one of Thailand's trendiest sauces would find a welcome home on the coast of Georgia.

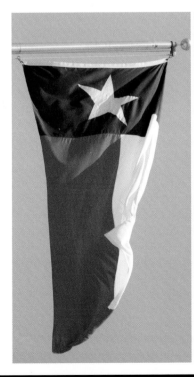

PORK RIBS AREN'T THE ONLY RIBS GETTING A TWIST. BEEF IS THE STAR OF THE SHOW IN TEXAS, AND AT THE GRANARY 'CUE & BREW (SAN ANTONIO, TX), THE BEEF RIBS GET A TREATMENT MORE OFTEN ASSOCIATED WITH NEW YORK DELIS THAN TEXAS BARBECUE JOINTS. TO START, A FULL SHORT RIB PLATE IS BRINED WITH PASTRAMI SPICES, AND THEN SMOKED AND TRIMMED DOWN TO INDIVIDUAL RIBS. BY DAY, THE SHORT RIB PASTRAMI IS SERVED ON PAPER-LINED TRAYS WITH PICKLES AND A DRAMATIC SMEAR OF YELLOW BEER MUSTARD. AT NIGHT IT GETS THE WHITE-PLATE TREATMENT COMPLETE WITH SAUERKRAUT AIOLI AND MICRO-GREEN GARNISH. IT'S A DARING BLEND OF TRADITIONAL BARBECUE AND CONTEMPORARY FLAVORS AND A SHINING EXAMPLE OF HOW RIBS CAN BE A SPRINGBOARD FOR BARBECUE INNOVATION.

LESSONS FROM THE LEGENDS
SPARERIBS

If Webster published a dictionary of America barbecue, you would find Mike Mills listed first under the definition of legend. In the early 1990s his Apple City Barbecue team won a jaw-dropping 32 Grand Championships. The team retired in 1994 after their fourth World Championship and third Grand World Championship at Memphis in May. They also won the Grand Championship at the Jack Daniel's World Invitational Barbecue Cooking Contest in 1992.

Today Mills oversees 17th Street Barbecue, with two locations in southern Illinois, and two versions of the restaurant in Las Vegas. He is a partner in Blue Smoke, a pioneer of upscale urban barbecue in New York City, and, with his daughter, Amy, he has a best-selling cookbook and a consulting company for the barbecue industry.

I asked Mike for his long perspective about the barbecue world today. "I've seen it evolve from a hole in the ground or a shack in the back to fancy restaurants with today's motorized stainless steel pits. I've watched many regional styles merge and evolve into something else entirely ... I think that overall the quality of barbecue today is better than it has ever been, but some places have lost their way. Trying to be so different, they lost some of that old-time flavor. I think barbecue should be about the meat. Nowadays, seasonings and sauces get too much of the attention. I don't care for all those thick, sweet sauces that sit on top of meat like toothpaste."

THE HOLLYWOOD CUT

In barbecue competitions, one way to impress the judges is to give them as much meat as possible on each rib. To do this at home, sacrifice and discard every other bone so that each bone you serve has twice as much meat as usual.

TRIMMING

A full rack of spareribs has 13 ribs holding together meat that is tougher and fattier than what you get on baby back ribs. Weighing 5 to 6 pounds, the rack includes a flap of meat (called the "skirt") hanging off the middle of the bone side and also a triangular section (called the "point") at one end. To make the St. Louis–style cut, trim off both of those chewy sections, and then remove the cartilaginous section of meat (the "rib tips") that extends below the bones. Find the joint just below the longest rib at one end. Cut through that joint with a sharp, heavy knife and lot of pressure, and run your knife under the bottom of the bones, creating a straight-sided rectangle weighing 3 to 4 pounds. Now peel off the membrane clinging to the bones and trim off the obvious areas of silver skin and excess fat.

ALOHA SPARERIBS
WITH COCONUT-GINGER GLAZE

SERVES: 4 TO 6 | **PREP TIME:** 20 MINUTES | **GRILLING TIME:** 2¼ TO 2½ HOURS | **SPECIAL EQUIPMENT:** 3 LARGE HANDFULS APPLE, CHERRY, OR HICKORY WOOD CHIPS; GAS GRILL WITH AT LEAST 3 BURNERS; METAL SMOKER BOX

Easy does it. That's the right mantra some days. It doesn't get much easier than barbecuing ribs on a gas grill that can hold temperatures steady for as long as you like.

If you have a smoker box, great. Before you fire up the grill, fill the box with soaked and drained wood chips, and then set the box under the cooking grate, right over a burner or two, so the chips will smoke easily.

For this recipe, don't even bother with peeling the membrane off the ribs. The membrane on spareribs is not as tough as it is on baby back ribs. Just season the ribs with a mellow mix of spices and let them cook in the aromatic smoke. After about an hour, baste them with a coconut-ginger glaze that keeps them moist and evokes a Hawaiian vacation.

RUB

- 2 tablespoons curry powder
- 2 teaspoons granulated garlic
- 2 teaspoons granulated onion
- 2 teaspoons paprika
- 2 teaspoons kosher salt
- 2 teaspoons freshly ground black pepper

- 2 racks St. Louis–style spareribs, each 2½ to 3 pounds

GLAZE

- 1 tablespoon toasted sesame oil
- 1 tablespoon peeled, grated fresh ginger
- 1 teaspoon crushed red pepper flakes
- 1 cup unsweetened coconut milk, stirred
- ¼ cup soy sauce
- 2 tablespoons packed light brown sugar Grated zest and juice of 1 lime

1 Soak the wood chips in water for at least 30 minutes.

2 Combine the rub ingredients. Season the racks all over with the rub, putting more on the meaty side. Refrigerate the racks until ready to grill.

3 In a medium saucepan combine the oil, ginger, and red pepper flakes. Warm over medium heat on the stove just until the ginger sizzles, about 30 seconds, stirring once or twice (do not burn the oil or it will be bitter). Add the remaining glaze ingredients, mix well, and bring to a simmer. Simmer for about 3 minutes. Remove the saucepan from the heat.

4 Before lighting the gas grill, drain and add the wood chips to a metal smoker box. Set the smoker box under the cooking grate and over a burner on one side of the grill. Prepare the grill for indirect cooking over high heat (450° to 550°F), heating the wood chips in the smoker box. When the wood begins to smoke, lower the temperature of the grill to low heat, as close to 300°F as possible.

5 Lay the racks, bone side down and flat, on the cooking grates over **indirect low heat**. Close the lid and cook for 1 hour, maintaining the temperature of the grill as close to 300°F as possible. You may need to turn off one of the burners temporarily, especially on hot days. The wood chips should smoke for about 30 minutes. If they catch fire, spray a little water over the smoker box.

6 After the first hour of cooking, baste the racks on both sides with glaze and swap their positions for even cooking. Continue cooking, bone side down, over **indirect low heat** for 1 hour more, basting the racks on both sides every 30 minutes.

7 Now that the racks have cooked for 2 hours at 300°F they should be close to done. They are completely done when you lift a rack at one end with tongs, bone side up, and the rack bends so much in the middle that the meat begins to tear easily. This may take 15 to 30 minutes more.

8 Remove the racks from the grill, let rest for 5 to 10 minutes, and then cut between the bones into individual ribs. Serve warm.

ROTISSERIE SPARERIBS
WITH ROOT BEER–BOURBON GLAZE

SERVES: 4 TO 6 | **PREP TIME:** 30 MINUTES | **GRILLING TIME:** 2 TO 2½ HOURS
SPECIAL EQUIPMENT: 2 LARGE HANDFULS PECAN, APPLE, OR HICKORY WOOD CHIPS;
ROTISSERIE; LARGE DISPOSABLE FOIL PAN

*Ribs on the rotisserie? You bet! The rotisserie works wonders when you are
cooking just one or two racks. The even heat and slow rotation of the ribs allow
for a nice bark on the outside and tender, moist meat within. The key is to skewer
the ribs in an "S" shape that exposes as much meat as possible to the circulating
heat. Use a ring of aluminum foil in the center to keep a space between the racks
so they develop as much bark as possible and so it is easier to brush on the
sticky glaze.*

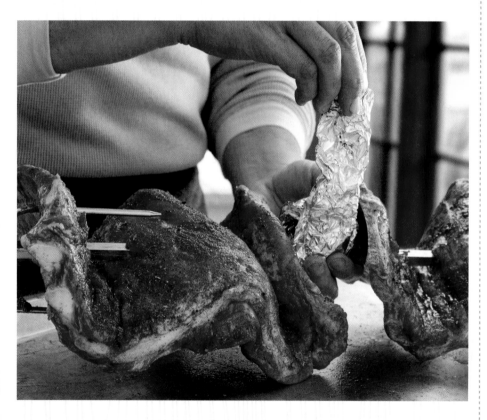

RUB
- 2 tablespoons packed light brown sugar
- 1 tablespoon kosher salt
- 1 tablespoon prepared chili powder
- 2 teaspoons paprika
- 1 teaspoon garlic powder
- 1 teaspoon ground cumin
- 1 teaspoon freshly ground black pepper
- ½ teaspoon ground allspice
- ½ teaspoon mustard powder

- 2 racks St. Louis–style spareribs,
  each 3 to 3¼ pounds

GLAZE
- 2 cups root beer (not diet)
- 1 cup bourbon
- ⅓ cup packed light brown sugar
- 1 cinnamon stick
- 1 bay leaf
- ¼ cup cider vinegar
- 1 teaspoon vanilla extract
- ½ teaspoon kosher salt
- 1 tablespoon grated orange zest
- ½ teaspoon hot pepper sauce

- 1 large orange, cut into wedges

1   Soak the wood chips in water for at least 30 minutes.

2   Combine the rub ingredients. Using a dull knife, slide the tip under the membrane covering the back of each rack of ribs. Lift and loosen the membrane until you can pry it up, then grab a corner of it with a paper towel and pull it off. Season the racks all over with the rub, putting more of it on the meaty side. Allow the racks to stand at room temperature for 1 hour before grilling.

3   Prepare the grill for indirect cooking over medium-low heat (about 300°F). Place a large disposable foil pan in the center of the charcoal grate between the two piles of charcoal or in the middle of the cooking grates of a gas grill.

4   In a saucepan over medium-high heat on the stove, bring the root beer, bourbon, brown sugar, cinnamon stick, bay leaf, vinegar, vanilla extract, and salt to a boil. Cook until the mixture is reduced to about ½ cup, 20 to 25 minutes, stirring occasionally. Remove from the heat, discard the cinnamon stick and bay leaf, and stir in the orange zest and hot sauce.

5   Place one pronged fork onto the rotisserie spit with the tines facing inward, about 10 inches from the end of the spit. Secure the fork, but do not tighten it yet. Thread one rack of ribs onto the spit in an "S" shape by pushing the pointed end through the meat every three or four ribs and making sure that one end is secured by the tines of the fork. Form a thin snake out of foil and wrap it into a ring around the spit where the two racks will come together to prevent them from leaning against each other as they cook. Thread the second rack onto the spit in an "S" shape like the first one, and then slide the second pronged fork onto the spit with the tines facing inward. Push the fork through the rack and secure it, but don't tighten it yet. Wearing insulated barbecue mitts or gloves, place the pointed end of the spit into the rotisserie motor. If necessary, adjust the racks so that they are centered on the spit over the foil pan. Tighten the forks.

6   Drain and add half of the wood chips to the charcoal or to the smoker box of a gas grill, following manufacturer's instructions, and close the lid. Turn on the rotisserie motor and cook the racks over **indirect medium-low**

heat for 1 hour, maintaining the temperature of the grill as close to 300°F as possible. Drain and add the remaining handful of wood chips to the charcoal or smoker box, and continue cooking until the meat starts to shrink away from the ends of the bones, about 45 minutes. Brush the racks with half of the glaze and continue to cook and glaze until the meat has shrunk back from the ends of most of the bones by ½ inch or more, about 15 minutes. At this point, check to see if the ribs are done. If the ribs are not done, glaze them and continue cooking for another 15 to 30 minutes.

7   Turn off the rotisserie motor and, wearing insulated barbecue mitts or gloves, carefully remove the spit from the grill. Gently loosen the forks and slide the ribs off the spit. Transfer to a cutting board, brush the remaining glaze on both sides, cover loosely with foil, and let rest for 10 minutes. Cut the racks between the bones into individual ribs, and squeeze the orange wedges over the ribs. Serve immediately.

CHERRY-SMOKED SPARERIBS
WITH CRANBERRY-GINGER BARBECUE SAUCE

SERVES: 6 TO 8 | **PREP TIME:** 30 MINUTES | **COOKING TIME:** ABOUT 3½ HOURS | **SPECIAL EQUIPMENT:** WATER SMOKER, 2 LARGE HANDFULS CHERRY WOOD CHUNKS, 2 LARGE HANDFULS PECAN WOOD CHUNKS, SPRAY BOTTLE, HEAVY-DUTY ALUMINUM FOIL

Awesome spareribs call for a series of coordinated and interdependent steps that add up to more than the sum of their parts. First you buy thick meaty ribs and slather them with a thin coat of mustard to help the spice rub hold on. The rub in this case is based on turbinado (raw) sugar, which I like because it is sweet but not easily burnt. You then smoke the racks with pecan and cherry wood for two hours. The pecan is used mostly for its nutty flavor, and the cherry is used mostly for the dark color it creates in the ribs. Next you spray the ribs with apple juice, reseason them with the rub, and wrap them in foil to cook in their juices during the final 1½ hours on the smoker. When they are fully cooked, you brush them with a glistening sauce—in this case, something a bit unusual that initially tastes sweet and then finishes with a tinge of ginger. It may not be as unusual as the blueberry-chipotle sauce that pit masters serve at the wildly popular 12 Bones Smokehouse in Asheville, North Carolina, but it is a sure sign of new and evolving American barbecue sauces.

RUB
- ¼ cup turbinado sugar
- 2 tablespoons paprika
- 2 tablespoons prepared chili powder
- 4 teaspoons granulated onion
- 4 teaspoons kosher salt
- 2 teaspoons ground ginger
- 2 teaspoons freshly ground black pepper

- ½ cup prepared yellow mustard
- 4 racks meaty spareribs, each about 3 pounds, membrane removed

SAUCE
- 1 cup ketchup
- 1 can (8 ounces) jellied cranberry sauce
- ½ cup unsweetened apple juice
- ⅓ cup cider vinegar
- ⅓ cup honey
- 2 tablespoons unsulfured molasses (not blackstrap)
- 1 tablespoon Worcestershire sauce
- 1 teaspoon prepared chili powder
- 1 teaspoon ground ginger
- ¼ teaspoon freshly ground black pepper

- ½ cup unsweetened apple juice
  Sea salt (optional)

1. In a small bowl mix the rub ingredients. Reserve 3 tablespoons of the rub for seasoning the racks later. Spread the mustard evenly over both sides of the racks. Use the rub in the small bowl to season the racks on both sides, especially the meaty side. Allow the racks to stand at room temperature while you prepare the smoker.

2. Prepare the smoker for indirect cooking with very low heat (250° to 275°F). Fill the water pan halfway to three-quarters of the way with water.

3   Add half of the wood chunks to the charcoal. When smoke appears, place two racks on the bottom cooking grate and two racks on the top cooking grate, bone side down. Cook over *indirect very low heat*, with the lid closed, for 1 hour. After 1 hour, add the remaining wood chunks to the charcoal. Cook for 1 hour more. Meanwhile, prepare the sauce.

4   In a small saucepan whisk the sauce ingredients. Bring to a simmer over medium heat on the stove and cook until slightly thickened, about 5 minutes, stirring occasionally. Remove from the heat.

5   Pour the apple juice into a spray bottle. Cut four long sheets of heavy-duty aluminum foil, each about 4 feet long.

6   After 2 hours of cooking (when the color of the racks is dark brown), remove the racks from the smoker. Lay each rack on one end of a sheet of foil, spray both sides with apple juice, and season with the reserved rub. Fold over the other end of each sheet of foil to enclose the rack and seal the ends on all sides to trap the steam.

7   Return the wrapped racks to the smoker and cook, bone side up, over *indirect very low heat*, with the lid closed, for about 1 hour.

8   Remove the racks from the smoker and take them out of the foil. Discard the foil. Brush the racks evenly on both sides with some of the sauce, return to the smoker, and cook, bone side down, over *indirect very low heat*, until the sauce has cooked into the meat a bit, 15 to 30 minutes. To check for doneness, slide a toothpick into the meat between the bones. It should slip in and out with little resistance.

9   Just before serving, lightly brush the racks with sauce. Cut the racks into individual ribs (Hollywood style, if you wish, see page 82) and serve warm with any extra sauce on the side. If desired, as a final step, season the meaty side of the ribs with a little bit of salt to boost the flavors.

DONENESS

With spareribs, get them tender but not too tender. When you slide a sharp toothpick through the meat between the bones, it should move in and out easily; however, if you pull the bones apart, some meat should still cling to the bones. If all the meat slips off the bones, the ribs are overcooked.

BARBECUED CHAR SIU

SERVES: 6 | **PREP TIME:** 15 MINUTES | **MARINATING TIME:** 24 TO 48 HOURS | **GRILLING TIME:** 45 MINUTES TO 1 HOUR
SPECIAL EQUIPMENT: CHARCOAL GRILL, 2 LARGE HANDFULS APPLE OR CHERRY WOOD CHIPS, INSTANT-READ THERMOMETER

MARINADE
½ cup hoisin sauce
½ cup bourbon
¼ cup soy sauce
¼ cup honey
2 tablespoons toasted sesame oil
2 tablespoons peeled, minced fresh ginger
1 tablespoon minced garlic
2 teaspoons Chinese five spice
½ teaspoon ground white pepper

1 boneless pork loin roast, about 3 pounds
Ramen (optional)
Sliced scallions (optional)

In Chinatown neighborhoods all over America, the enticing aroma of char siu—or Cantonese roasted pork—wafts down the narrow streets from the old-school restaurants, some of them still using charcoal for the way the wood aromas mingle with the flavors of a sweet and salty marinade. Thin slices of char siu are wonderful in a bowl of ramen.

1   In a large bowl whisk the marinade ingredients. Pour off and reserve ½ cup of the marinade for basting the roast. Place the roast in a large, resealable plastic bag and pour in the remaining marinade. Press the air out of the bag and seal tightly. Turn the bag to distribute the marinade, place in a bowl, and refrigerate for at least 24 hours or up to 48 hours, turning occasionally.

2   Remove the roast from the bag and discard the marinade in the bag. Allow the roast to stand at room temperature for 30 minutes before grilling.

3   Soak the wood chips in water for at least 30 minutes.

4   Prepare the charcoal grill for indirect cooking over medium heat (350° to 450°F).

5   Drain and add the wood chips to the charcoal. Grill the roast over *indirect medium heat*, with the lid closed, until an instant-read thermometer inserted into the center of the roast registers 150°F, 45 minutes to 1 hour, basting occasionally with the reserved ½ cup marinade. Do not baste during the final 15 minutes of cooking time. Remove from the grill and let rest for 10 minutes (the internal temperature will rise 5 to 10 degrees during this time). Cut into ¼-inch-thick slices. Serve warm with ramen and sliced scallions, if desired.

The outside of the roast will develop a lovely, savory crust thanks to the marinade of hoisin sauce, bourbon, soy sauce, and honey. In restaurants, char siu is often much redder in color, not from smoke but from red food coloring. Let the meat rest properly before you slice into it. If you see steam coming off the slices, let the meat rest longer; the steam is moisture you are losing.

PORK LOIN SPIEDIES

SERVES: 6 | PREP TIME: 10 MINUTES | MARINATING TIME: 2 HOURS | GRILLING TIME: 9 TO 11 MINUTES
SPECIAL EQUIPMENT: 6 LONG BAMBOO SKEWERS, 1 LARGE HANDFUL HICKORY WOOD CHIPS, INSTANT-READ THERMOMETER

MARINADE

- 1 cup extra-virgin olive oil
- ¼ cup red wine vinegar
- ¼ cup fresh lemon juice
- ¼ cup finely chopped fresh mint leaves
- ¼ cup finely chopped fresh Italian parsley leaves
- 2 tablespoons finely chopped fresh dill
- 2 teaspoons minced garlic
- 2 teaspoons kosher salt
- 1½ teaspoons fennel seed
- ½ teaspoon freshly ground black pepper

- 1½ pounds trimmed pork loin, cut into 1½-inch chunks
- 6 Italian or French sandwich rolls, cut lengthwise in half but not all the way through

A spiedie is a type of hoagie hailing from Binghamton, New York, and now enjoyed across the central part of the state. Cubes of meat are marinated with a combination of Italian seasonings and mint, and then cooked and arranged, skewer and all, in a long roll or slice of Italian bread without much more fuss or fandango. Have a big bag of potato chips on hand!

1 In a large bowl whisk the marinade ingredients. Reserve ¼ cup plus 2 tablespoons of the marinade to drizzle over the cooked pork. Place the pork chunks in the large bowl with the remaining marinade, cover, and refrigerate for 2 hours, stirring once.

2 Soak the skewers and wood chips (separately) in water for at least 30 minutes.

3 Prepare the grill for direct cooking over medium heat (350° to 450°F).

4 Thread the pork cubes onto the skewers. Discard the marinade. Drain and add the wood chips to the charcoal or to the smoker box of a gas grill, following manufacturer's instructions, and close the lid. When smoke appears, grill the skewers over **direct medium heat**, with the lid closed, until the meat is evenly seared and cooked to an internal temperature of 145°F, 9 to 11 minutes, turning occasionally. During the last minute of grilling time, toast the rolls, cut side down, over direct heat.

5 To serve this dish in its authentic style, place a skewer on each roll and, using the roll as a potholder to grasp the meat, twist and pull out the skewer, leaving the pork cubes in a neat line right down the middle of the roll. Drizzle each spiedie with 1 tablespoon of the reserved marinade and serve right away.

PORK LOIN SANDWICHES
WITH GREEN CHILES, GRUYÈRE, AND GRILLED ONIONS

SERVES: 4 | **PREP TIME:** 20 MINUTES | **MARINATING TIME:** 30 TO 45 MINUTES | **GRILLING TIME:** 10 TO 12 MINUTES
SPECIAL EQUIPMENT: 1 LARGE HANDFUL CHERRY WOOD CHIPS, CAST-IRON SKILLET OR GRILL PRESS

MARINADE

¼ cup extra-virgin olive oil
2 tablespoons cider vinegar
1 teaspoon prepared chili powder
¾ teaspoons kosher salt
¼ teaspoon freshly ground black pepper
¼ teaspoon garlic powder

4 boneless pork loin chops, each 4 to 5 ounces and about ½ inch thick
½ cup mayonnaise
3 tablespoons store-bought barbecue sauce
1 red onion, about 8 ounces, cut into 4 slices, each about ⅓ inch thick
4 crusty rolls, split
8 thin slices Gruyère cheese
1 can (7 ounces) whole mild green chile peppers, drained, opened flat, and seeds removed

There seems to be no end to the growing popularity of pressed sandwiches, including Cubans and panini. Here is a new version that stacks smoked pork with grilled onions, cheese, and chiles. If you like, you could add some whole cilantro leaves in there. You could also use pickled jalapeño slices instead of the milder green chiles. I like Portuguese or ciabatta rolls for this recipe; both have a nice crust and enough density to stand up to all the meaty juices.

1 Soak the wood chips in water for at least 30 minutes.

2 In a medium bowl combine the marinade ingredients. Place the pork chops in the marinade, turn to coat evenly, and allow to stand at room temperature for 30 to 45 minutes.

3 Prepare the grill for direct and indirect cooking over medium heat (350° to 450°F).

4 Mix the mayonnaise and barbecue sauce. Set aside until ready to use.

5 Drain and add the wood chips to the charcoal or to the smoker box of a gas grill, following manufacturer's instructions, and close the lid. When smoke appears, grill the chops and onion slices over **direct medium heat**, with the lid closed, until the chops are almost fully cooked and the onions are charred, 6 to 8 minutes, turning once or twice. Remove from the grill.

6 Spread the cut side of the rolls with the mayonnaise mixture. Place the bottom halves of the rolls on a baking sheet and top each with 1 cheese slice, 1 pork chop, 1 onion slice that has been separated into rings, 1 green chile pepper, another slice of cheese, and the top half of the roll. Press the top of the roll firmly with your hand to compress the sandwich (try not to break the bread).

7 Place the sandwiches over **indirect medium heat** and, using a spatula, cast-iron skillet, or grill press, press them down, one at a time. Close the lid and grill for 2 minutes. Turn the sandwiches over, press them down again, close the lid, and grill until the bread is toasted and the cheese is melted, about 2 minutes more. Remove the sandwiches from the grill, wrap each in parchment paper, cut in half, and skewer with toothpicks, if desired. Serve immediately.

Use your hand to press the sandwiches before they go on the grill, and then press them again into the hot cooking grate using a spatula, cast-iron skillet, or a heavy grill press like the one shown here.

ROSEMARY-LEMON PORK CHOPS
WITH EMBER-SMOKED BUTTER

SERVES: 4 | **PREP TIME:** 25 MINUTES | **MARINATING TIME:** 2 TO 4 HOURS | **GRILLING TIME:** 6 TO 8 MINUTES
CHILLING TIME: ABOUT 1 HOUR | **SPECIAL EQUIPMENT:** CHARCOAL GRILL, ALL-NATURAL LUMP CHARCOAL

MARINADE

¼ cup extra-virgin olive oil
 Grated zest and juice of 1 lemon
2 tablespoons finely chopped fresh
 rosemary leaves
1 tablespoon country-style
 Dijon mustard
1 tablespoon minced garlic

 Kosher salt
 Freshly ground black pepper
4 boneless or bone-in pork chops,
 each about 8 ounces and 1 inch thick

BUTTER

6 tablespoons (¾ stick) unsalted
 butter, softened
 Grated zest of 1 lemon
2 teaspoons finely chopped fresh
 rosemary leaves
1 teaspoon country-style Dijon mustard
1 teaspoon minced garlic

It's time to play with fire. The idea of setting a charcoal ember on a slice of seasoned butter right before serving the marinated pork chops is much more than a show-stopping scene. Yes, the butter will smoke viciously and melt over the sides of chops. Yes, your guests will gasp with delight. But the real excitement is in the flavor that the infused butter adds to the chops. Of course, you should only use 100% natural lump charcoal for this technique.

1 Mix the marinade ingredients, including 1¼ teaspoons salt and ½ teaspoon pepper. Coat the pork chops on all sides with the marinade, place in a bowl, cover, and refrigerate for 2 to 4 hours. Meanwhile, make the butter.

2 In a medium bowl mash the butter ingredients, including ½ teaspoon salt and ¼ teaspoon pepper, with the back of a fork. Form the mixture into a log, 3 to 4 inches long. Set the log in the bowl, cover, and refrigerate for at least 1 hour.

3 Prepare the charcoal grill with all-natural lump charcoal for direct cooking over medium-high heat (400° to 450°F).

4 Lift the pork chops from the bowl, allowing the excess marinade to drip off, and discard the marinade. Grill the chops over **direct medium-high heat**, with the lid closed, until still slightly pink in the center, 6 to 8 minutes, turning once. Transfer to a metal tray and let rest for 3 to 5 minutes. Cut the butter lengthwise into four long pieces and set each one on top of a pork chop. Using long-handled tongs, lift a large ember, about the size of an orange, from the bed of charcoal and very carefully set the burning ember on top of each piece of butter for 1 to 2 seconds. The butter will smoke and melt. Return the burning ember to the grill. Serve the pork chops right away.

PORK CHOPS
WITH SWEET SOY GLAZE AND SCALLION-SESAME RICE

SERVES: 6 | **PREP TIME:** 15 MINUTES
MARINATING TIME: 30 MINUTES | **GRILLING TIME:** ABOUT 8 MINUTES

MARINADE

- 2 tablespoons soy sauce
- 2 tablespoons Asian rice wine, dry sherry, or lemon juice
- 2 tablespoons water
- ½ teaspoon hot chili-garlic sauce, such as Sriracha

- 6 boneless pork loin chops, each about 5 ounces and ¾ inch thick

GLAZE

- 2 tablespoons soy sauce
- 1 tablespoon honey
- 1 tablespoon ketchup
- 1 tablespoon Asian rice wine, dry sherry, or lemon juice
- 2 teaspoons hoisin sauce
- ½ teaspoon hot chili-garlic sauce, such as Sriracha
- ¼ teaspoon Chinese five spice
- ⅛ teaspoon granulated garlic
- ⅛ teaspoon onion powder

- 2 teaspoons sesame seeds
- 2 cups water
- 1 cup long-grain rice
  Kosher salt
  Vegetable oil
- ½ teaspoon freshly ground black pepper
- 2 scallions, white and light green parts minced, dark green tops thinly sliced, divided

This recipe emerges from ancient traditions of Korean barbecue, where marinades and glazes are often used together for flavors that are big, bold, and complex, yet so quick and simple to execute. Grilled over charcoal, this is Asian-American barbecue in minutes.

1 Prepare the grill for direct cooking over medium heat (350° to 450°F).

2 Whisk the marinade ingredients. Place the pork chops in a large, resealable plastic bag and pour in the marinade. Press the air out of the bag and seal tightly. Turn the bag to distribute the marinade, and set aside at room temperature for 30 minutes, turning the bag once or twice.

3 Combine the glaze ingredients. Reserve half of the glaze to use on the grilled chops.

4 Meanwhile, heat a medium saucepan over medium heat on the stove. Add the sesame seeds and toast until light golden, 2 to 3 minutes, stirring often. Transfer the seeds to a plate. Add the water, rice, and ½ teaspoon salt to the same saucepan and bring to a boil over high heat. Reduce the heat to low, cover tightly, and cook until the rice is tender and the liquid is absorbed, 15 to 18 minutes. Remove from the heat and set the covered saucepan aside. The rice will stay warm for 15 minutes.

5 Remove the chops from the bag, shaking off the excess marinade. Discard the marinade. Generously brush the chops on both sides with oil, season evenly with ¾ teaspoon salt and the pepper, and then grill over **direct medium heat**, with the lid closed, until browned on both sides, about 6 minutes, turning once. Brush the tops of the chops with the glaze and continue grilling, with the lid closed, until the meat is still slightly pink in the center, about 2 minutes more. Remove from the grill.

6 Stir the white and light green parts of the scallions and the sesame seeds into the rice, fluffing with a fork. Spoon the reserved glaze over the pork chops and top with the dark green scallion tops. Serve warm.

SMOKED PORK TENDERLOINS
WITH BLACKBERRY-SAGE SAUCE

SERVES: 6 | **PREP TIME:** 30 MINUTES | **GRILLING TIME:** 15 TO 20 MINUTES
SPECIAL EQUIPMENT: 1 SMALL HANDFUL APPLE OR PECAN WOOD CHIPS, INSTANT-READ THERMOMETER

SAUCE

- 1 tablespoon unsalted butter
- 2 tablespoons finely chopped shallot
- 12 ounces fresh blackberries (2⅔ cups), divided
- ¼ cup honey
- 2 tablespoons ketchup
- 2 tablespoons balsamic vinegar
- 2 teaspoons minced fresh sage leaves
- 1 teaspoon Worcestershire sauce
- ½ teaspoon freshly ground black pepper
- ⅛ teaspoon kosher salt

RUB

- 2 teaspoons packed brown sugar
- 1 teaspoon kosher salt
- 1 teaspoon mustard powder
- 1 teaspoon paprika
- ½ teaspoon granulated onion
- ½ teaspoon granulated garlic
- ½ teaspoon freshly ground black pepper

- 2 pork tenderloins, each about 1¼ pounds, trimmed of excess fat and silver skin
- 2 teaspoons canola oil

Vaguely familiar and different at the same time, this recipe works because of the way that smoked pork plays so well with sweet, fruity sauces. What a sauce this one is! I think it's one of the best in the book. You might want to strain out the blackberry seeds from the puree before you mix in the whole blackberries. Don't worry about eating pork that looks a little pink in the middle. The USDA has declared it safe at 145°F, when it is still nice and juicy.

1 Soak the wood chips in water for at least 30 minutes.

2 In a small saucepan over medium heat on the stove, melt the butter. Add the shallot and cook until lightly browned, about 2 minutes, stirring often. Add 2 cups of the berries, the honey, ketchup, vinegar, sage, Worcestershire sauce, pepper, and salt. Bring to a boil, and then reduce the heat to medium-low. Cook the sauce at a steady simmer until the juices have thickened slightly, about 10 minutes, stirring often and mashing some of the berries to release their juice. Remove from the heat. Puree the sauce in a blender (in batches) with a small opening in the lid to let the steam escape, and return to the saucepan. You should have about 1 cup of sauce. Stir in the remaining ⅔ cup berries. Let the sauce cool until tepid and slightly thickened.

3 Combine the rub ingredients, mashing well with a fork to mix thoroughly. Brush the tenderloins with the oil and season evenly with the rub. Allow the tenderloins to stand at room temperature for 15 to 30 minutes before grilling.

4 Prepare the grill for direct cooking over medium heat (350° to 450°F).

5 Drain and add the wood chips to the charcoal or to the smoker box of a gas grill, following manufacturer's instructions, and close the lid. When smoke appears, grill the tenderloins over **direct medium heat**, with the lid closed, until the outsides are evenly seared and the internal temperature reaches 145°F, 15 to 20 minutes, turning every 5 minutes. Remove from the grill and let rest for 5 minutes (the internal temperature will rise 5 to 10 degrees during this time). Cut the tenderloins crosswise into ½-inch slices. Serve warm with the sauce.

BACON-WRAPPED PORK TENDERLOINS
WITH CIDER-BALSAMIC REDUCTION

SERVES: 8 | **PREP TIME:** 20 MINUTES, PLUS ABOUT 30 MINUTES FOR THE REDUCTION | **GRILLING TIME:** 40 TO 45 MINUTES
SPECIAL EQUIPMENT: 2 LARGE HANDFULS APPLE WOOD CHIPS, LARGE DISPOSABLE FOIL PAN, INSTANT-READ THERMOMETER

RUB
1 tablespoon packed brown sugar
1 teaspoon smoked paprika
½ teaspoon prepared chili powder
1 teaspoon kosher salt
½ teaspoon freshly ground black pepper

2 pork tenderloins, each about
 1¼ pounds, trimmed of excess fat
 and silver skin
1 pound bacon (not thick cut)

REDUCTION
3 cups apple cider
½ cup balsamic vinegar
¼ cup plus 2 tablespoons unsulfured
 molasses (not blackstrap)
1 cinnamon stick
⅛ teaspoon ground allspice
¾ cup heavy whipping cream
 Kosher salt
 Freshly ground black pepper

This tenderloin is my ode to the pork farmers of Iowa, who produce some exceptionally flavorful meat. I'd like to sit all of them down at one long table that stretches across Iowa pastures and feed them spice-rubbed tenderloins wrapped in blankets of bacon, smoked over apple wood, and served with a sweet and creamy apple cider reduction. For the easiest wrapping, be sure to use regular bacon rather than the thick-cut variety.

1 Soak the wood chips in water for at least 30 minutes.

2 Combine the rub ingredients, and then season the tenderloins evenly with the rub.

3 On a work surface lay out half of the bacon in one layer, with each slice slightly overlapping the next (just barely overlap the bacon so it cooks evenly. You may not need the full pound of bacon). Place one of the tenderloins on top of the bacon. The length of the tenderloin should be perpendicular to the strips of bacon. Roll it up jelly roll style, and when the bacon just overlaps itself going around the tenderloin, use a sharp knife to cut off any extra. Repeat with the remaining bacon and tenderloin. Allow the tenderloins to stand at room temperature for 30 minutes before grilling.

4 Place a large disposable foil pan underneath the cooking grate to catch the bacon drippings. You may have to smash the foil pan a bit, but that's okay. Or, if you are using a charcoal grill, place the foil pan on the charcoal grate between the two piles of charcoal. Then prepare the grill for indirect cooking over medium heat (350° to 450°F).

5 Drain and add half of the wood chips to the charcoal or to the smoker box of a gas grill, following manufacturer's instructions, and close the lid. When smoke appears, cook the tenderloins, bacon seam side down, over **indirect medium heat**, centered over the drip pan, with the lid closed, for 20 minutes. Turn the tenderloins over, drain and add the remaining wood chips to the charcoal or smoker box, close the lid, and cook for 15 minutes. Turn the tenderloins over once more and continue grilling until an instant-read thermometer inserted into the center of the meat registers 145°F, 5 to 10 minutes more. Remove the tenderloins from the grill, tent with foil, and let rest for 5 minutes (the internal temperature will rise 5 to 10 degrees during this time).

6 While the tenderloins cook, prepare the reduction. In a medium saucepan over high heat on the stove, combine the cider, vinegar, molasses, cinnamon stick, and allspice. Bring to a boil and cook until thick enough to coat the back of a spoon, 25 to 30 minutes. Remove and discard the cinnamon stick. Stir in the heavy cream, season with salt and pepper, and cook 1 minute more.

7 Cut the tenderloins crosswise into slices and serve warm with the reduction.

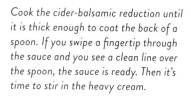

Cook the cider-balsamic reduction until it is thick enough to coat the back of a spoon. If you swipe a fingertip through the sauce and you see a clean line over the spoon, the sauce is ready. Then it's time to stir in the heavy cream.

DOUBLE-SMOKED HAM
WITH STRAWBERRY-MANGO SALSA

SERVES: 8 TO 10 | **PREP TIME:** 30 MINUTES | **GRILLING TIME:** 1¾ TO 2 HOURS
SPECIAL EQUIPMENT: 4 LARGE HANDFULS APPLE, CHERRY, OR HICKORY WOOD CHIPS;
2 LARGE DISPOSABLE FOIL PANS; INSTANT-READ THERMOMETER

1 bone-in smoked ham shank, about 7 pounds

SALSA
2 mangoes, each about 12 ounces, peeled and cut into ½-inch dice
12 ounces fresh strawberries, hulled and cut into ½-inch dice
2 tablespoons minced scallion (white and light green parts only)
2 tablespoons fresh lime juice
2 tablespoons finely chopped fresh mint leaves
1½ tablespoons agave nectar or honey
1 tablespoon rice vinegar
1 tablespoon minced jalapeño chile pepper
1½ teaspoons peeled, finely grated fresh ginger

GLAZE
⅓ cup strawberry preserves
2 tablespoons whole-grain mustard

Here is a fairly easy ham recipe that feeds a crowd with juicy, smoked meat and a colorful strawberry and mango salsa with accents of mint, ginger, and jalapeño. Try it as a festive main course for an Easter dinner. The quality of ham is crucial. Avoid any that have been pumped with solutions; the label should read just "ham," with no "natural juices" or other additives. The shank end is fattier (better) than the butt end and is easier to carve because it has just one straight bone, as opposed to the convoluted pelvic bone of the butt end.

1 Allow the ham to stand at room temperature for 30 to 40 minutes before grilling.

2 Soak the wood chips in water for at least 30 minutes.

3 Prepare the grill for indirect cooking over medium-low heat (about 350°F).

4 Place one large disposable foil pan inside of the other to create a single pan of double thickness. Score the ham in a large crisscross pattern about ½ inch deep on all sides, except the cut side, and place it, cut side down, in the foil pans.

5 Drain and add half of the wood chips to the charcoal or to the smoker box of a gas grill, following manufacturer's instructions, and close the lid. When smoke appears, place the pan with the ham over **indirect medium-low heat**, close the lid, and cook until an instant-read thermometer inserted into the thickest part of the ham (not touching the bone) registers 120°F, 1¼ to 1½ hours, checking periodically to be sure the ham is not browning too quickly. If it is getting too dark, tent lightly with foil. After the first 30 minutes of cooking time, drain and add the remaining wood chips to the charcoal or smoker box.

6 Meanwhile, in a medium bowl combine the salsa ingredients. Let stand at room temperature until ready to serve.

7 In a small bowl whisk the glaze ingredients, breaking up the preserves. Remove the foil tent, if using, and brush half of the glaze on the top and sides of the ham; cook for 15 minutes. Then brush the ham with the remaining glaze and continue cooking until an instant-read thermometer inserted in the thickest part of the ham (not touching the bone) registers 135° to 140°F, 10 to 15 minutes more. If the glaze gets too dark, cover the ham loosely with aluminum foil for the remainder of the cooking time. Remove from the grill, tent loosely with foil, and let rest for 15 to 45 minutes (the internal temperature will rise 5 to 10 degrees during this time).

8 Carve the ham and serve warm with the salsa.

By scoring a ham, you expose more of the rind to the heat and smoke in your grill. This simple step is how you develop gloriously sweet, crispy edges where the glaze seeps into the creases. Run the tip of sharp knife about ½ inch deep into the rind, making long crosshatch slits about 1 inch apart.

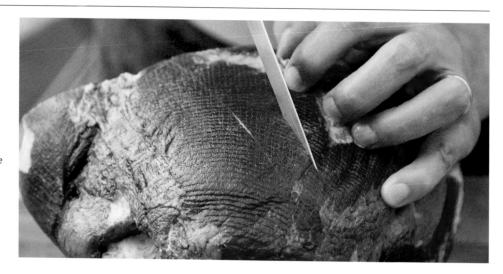

BARBECUING
without boundaries
IN NEW YORK CITY

Barbecue is a food and preparation method that has long been identified with the American South, but that doesn't keep Northerners from trying. Honest attempts at barbecue can now be found all over the country. Many are still in the copycat phase—find a style or styles and make an attempt at replication—but in New York City there's a shift toward a flavor all their own.

Twenty years ago, barbecue was just getting its legs in New York. Virgil's Real Barbecue opened in Times Square and the Brother Jimmy's BBQ chain began their expansion across the city with menus that read like a culinary grab bag—Carolina pork, Texas brisket, and Memphis ribs. A little later, Blue Smoke upped the game in quality, but it was still working from a borrowed menu. Pearson's Texas Barbecue was the only game in town with a real focus, but the final version was gone in 2005 before their brisket ever really got its time in the spotlight. The barbecue cupboard

That void was soon filled by Fette Sau, in the Williamsburg neighborhood of Brooklyn, and Hill Country Barbecue Market, in Lower Manhattan. These were the first of the meat market–style barbecue joints, where smoked meats are chosen individually and served on butcher paper. With their connection to Kreuz Market, Hill Country is all Texas style, and, while Fette Sau branded itself as uniquely Brooklyn, it feels more like a mash-up of Kansas City and Texas. Now, a new breed of joints is taking their New York barbecue to another level.

At Hometown Bar-B-Que in Brooklyn, pit master Billy Durney sports a Texas tattoo on his calf, homage to where he did some barbecue training at Louie Mueller Barbecue in Taylor, Texas. As expected from such tutelage, his brisket and beef ribs are on point, but the menu ranges far beyond those two Texas classics. You'll also find sweet Korean sticky ribs, a Vietnamese-style lamb belly banh mi with the added crunch of daikon, and spicy/sweet jerk baby back ribs. "All of these are using southern techniques of smoking, then I'm manipulating the flavors after they come off the smoker," says Durney. It's like a barbecue world tour under one roof, but it's not just a facsimile of other traditions.

It would be remiss not to mention the groundbreaking but now defunct Fatty 'Cue that came to Brooklyn in 2010. It may have been the first barbecue joint in New York to bring flavors unique to the city. Beef brisket was served with kimchi and bao buns, lamb ribs were marinated with fermented shrimp before being smoked, and big pork spareribs—fragrant with fish sauce and sweet from a palm sugar glaze—got their spice from Indonesian long peppers. It may have been a restaurant ahead of its time (it closed in 2014), but those dishes laid a foundation that allowed others in the city to be more

Similar Asian flavors can be found at Fletcher's Brooklyn Barbecue, where a menu mainstay is pork char siu; pork shoulder steaks marinated in a Chinese-style sauce and then smoked. Instead of cooking the pork to the point where it can be pulled, at Fletcher's they slice it thinly, like a brisket. The result is smoky, tangy, salty, and sweet—more interesting than most versions of simple pulled pork.

In discussing contemporary versus traditional barbecue, we shouldn't forget pastrami. It's New York's original indigenous barbecue. To make it, beef belly or brisket is cured, rubbed with black pepper and coriander, and then smoked and steamed until tender. It's usually found between two slices of rye, but Danny Bowien of Mission Chinese Food in Manhattan slams it into a completely unfamiliar context. His house-made pastrami is cubed and fried with celery, peanuts, potatoes, and Tianjin chiles in his now famous Kung Pao pastrami dish. Even with all the strong flavors competing on your tongue, the smoke of the pastrami comes through full force. That bold smokiness can also be found elsewhere on the adventurous menu—in a whole smoked pork jowl, and in smoked prime rib served in New York fashion with a king crab leg garnish. As Billy Durney puts it so well, "The beauty of cooking barbecue in New York is that we don't have any of our grandfathers' stipulations of

COUNTRY-STYLE PORK RIBS
WITH LOUISIANA HOT SAUCE

SERVES: 6 TO 8 | **PREP TIME:** 30 MINUTES | **GRILLING TIME:** ABOUT 1 HOUR
SPECIAL EQUIPMENT: 2 LARGE HANDFULS PEACH OR HICKORY WOOD CHIPS

RUB
1 tablespoon paprika
1 tablespoon packed brown sugar
1 teaspoon garlic powder
1 teaspoon kosher salt
½ teaspoon dried thyme
½ teaspoon dried oregano
½ teaspoon celery salt
½ teaspoon onion powder
½ teaspoon mustard powder

3½–4 pounds boneless country-style pork ribs
2 tablespoons Worcestershire sauce

SAUCE
6 tablespoons (¾ stick) unsalted butter, divided
1 onion, about 9 ounces, finely chopped
¼ cup finely chopped green bell pepper
¾ cup Louisiana-style hot sauce
3 tablespoons packed brown sugar
1½ tablespoons fresh lemon juice
1½ tablespoons paprika
1½ teaspoons hot pepper sauce
1½ teaspoons onion powder
1½ teaspoons garlic powder
½ teaspoons freshly ground black pepper

¼ cup ketchup
2 tablespoons fresh orange juice

Country-style pork ribs aren't really ribs at all. They are normally cut from the shoulder (fairly close to baby back ribs) and sometimes they don't even contain bones. Really, they are more like pork chops than anything else. That's why they are sometimes called blade chops or blade steaks. Whatever the name, they are meaty and delicious when you smoke them gently over indirect heat and then char them for five minutes or so right before serving them with a lip-smacking barbecue sauce.

1 Soak the wood chips in water for at least 30 minutes.

2 Combine the rub ingredients. Brush the ribs with the Worcestershire sauce and season evenly with the rub. Allow the ribs to stand at room temperature for 15 to 30 minutes before grilling.

3 Prepare the grill for indirect cooking over medium-low heat (300° to 350°F).

4 In a medium saucepan over medium heat on the stove, melt 1½ tablespoons of the butter. Add the onion and bell pepper and cook until slightly softened, about 4 minutes, stirring occasionally. Add the Louisiana-style hot sauce, brown sugar, lemon juice, paprika, hot pepper sauce, onion powder, garlic powder, and pepper. Bring to a simmer and cook for 3 minutes more, stirring occasionally. Remove from the heat and whisk in the remaining butter, whisking until melted. Reserve ¾ cup of the sauce to serve with the ribs.

5 Drain and add half of the wood chips to the charcoal or to the smoker box of a gas grill, following manufacturer's instructions, and close the lid. When smoke appears, place the ribs over **indirect medium-low heat**, close the lid, and cook for 30 minutes. Turn the ribs over, brush generously with some of the sauce, drain and add the remaining wood chips to the charcoal or smoker box, close the lid, and continue cooking for 15 minutes. Turn the ribs over, brush generously with more of the sauce, and grill until the ribs are fully cooked and nicely glazed, about 10 minutes more.

6 Raise the temperature of the grill to medium-high heat (425° to 450°F). Grill the glazed ribs over **direct medium-high heat**, with the lid closed, until nicely browned and marked by the grill, 5 to 7 minutes, turning once or twice.

7 In a saucepan over medium-low heat on the stove, warm the reserved ¾ cup sauce with the ketchup and orange juice. Serve the ribs warm with the sauce on the side.

GARLIC- AND LEMON-BRINED BACON

SERVES: 12 | **PREP TIME:** 15 MINUTES | **COOLING TIME:** 4 TO 6 HOURS FOR THE BRINE AND 1 TO 2 HOURS FOR THE BACON
BRINING TIME: 48 HOURS | **DRYING TIME:** 12 HOURS | **COOKING TIME:** 2 TO 3 HOURS | **SPECIAL EQUIPMENT:** WATER SMOKER,
3 LARGE HANDFULS PECAN OR APPLE WOOD CHUNKS, INSTANT-READ THERMOMETER

BRINE

3½ quarts water
2 cups granulated sugar
1 cup kosher salt
   Zest of 4 lemons, zest removed with
   a vegetable peeler in long, wide strips
2 heads of garlic, smashed and peeled
2 tablespoons black peppercorns
1½ teaspoons pink curing salt
2 bay leaves

2 pieces boneless pork belly, each
   about 2 pounds, rind removed
2 tablespoons dried sage
1 teaspoon crushed red pepper flakes

Bacon continues to be all the rage with chefs and backyard smokers. Making your own takes two days of brining, half a day of drying the meat in the refrigerator, and about 3 hours of smoking, but the DIY approach allows you to customize the flavors. Here I've blurred the lines of tradition by packing the brine with garlic and lemon, and I've coated the meat with sage and red pepper flakes, so the bacon has an Italian-American character that I think you will love.

1 In a large, nonreactive pot combine the brine ingredients. Bring just to a simmer over medium-high heat on the stove, stirring a few times at first until the sugar dissolves and all the salt dissolves. Cool to room temperature, 4 to 6 hours.

2 Submerge the pork belly in the brine, cover, and refrigerate for 48 hours, turning the meat occasionally.

3 Remove the pork belly from the pot and blot dry with paper towels. Discard the brine. Season the meat side of the pork belly with the sage and red pepper flakes. Place on a wire rack set inside a large, rimmed sheet pan and refrigerate, uncovered, for 12 hours.

4 Prepare the smoker for indirect cooking with very low heat (225° to 250°F). Fill the water pan three-fourths of the way with water.

5 Add the wood chunks to the charcoal. Transfer the pork belly from the wire rack to the smoker and cook over **indirect very low heat**, with the lid closed, until an instant-read thermometer inserted into the thickest part of the meat registers 150°F, 2 to 3 hours.

6 Remove the bacon pieces from the smoker and cool to room temperature, 1 to 2 hours. Wrap tightly in plastic wrap and store in the refrigerator for up to 1 week; or store in the freezer for up to 3 months. To serve, slice crosswise into strips about ⅛ inch thick and cook on a rack set inside a baking sheet or fry in a skillet.

You will need a couple pieces of pork belly, preferably from the center of the belly where the meat is relatively even in thickness. Sometimes the most reliable places to find them are Chinese food markets. After the bellies are brined and dried to firm up the texture of that fatty meat, coat them with spices and smoke them at very low temperatures.

BOSTON BACON FATTIES

SERVES: 8 | **PREP TIME:** 30 MINUTES | **GRILLING TIME:** 1½ TO 2 HOURS
SPECIAL EQUIPMENT: 1 LARGE HANDFUL HICKORY WOOD CHIPS, INSTANT-READ THERMOMETER

- 2 pounds sweet Italian sausage, casings removed
- 1 ounce Parmigiano-Reggiano® cheese, finely grated
- 32 slices thick-cut bacon, about 3 pounds
- ½ cup packed, drained marinated artichoke hearts, chopped
- ½ cup packed, drained marinated sun-dried tomatoes, chopped
- ½ cup roasted red bell pepper (from a jar), chopped

In the BBQ world, a basic (or naked) fatty is a roll of sausage that is smoked and sliced like meat loaf, but barbecuers don't always leave well enough alone, so there are versions filled with sautéed onions, cheese, and even hot dogs. Many cooks like to make even more extravagant fatties by wrapping them in a bacon weave, which I think is an excellent idea. To give this version a touch of Boston's North End, I stuffed it with ingredients you would find on an Italian antipasto plate. Keep the fire low so the bacon gets crisp without burning.

1 Soak the wood chips in water for at least 30 minutes.

2 Prepare the grill for indirect cooking over low heat (250° to 350°F).

3 Mix the sausage and cheese thoroughly but gently. Divide the meat into two equal portions.

4 Lay a large sheet of wax paper on a work surface. On the wax paper, using half of the bacon slices (eight slices going in one direction and eight in the other), weave a tight square, as if you are making a lattice piecrust. The finished size should be about 11 by 11 inches (don't be afraid to stretch the bacon strips a little to fit).

5 Lay a large sheet of wax paper on another work surface. Press one of the meat portions into an 8-inch square. About 2 inches from the side nearest you, arrange half of the artichokes, half of the sun-dried tomatoes, and half of the bell peppers in parallel, horizontal lines, leaving

about 1 inch at each end. Roll up the sausage tightly around the fillings, and then pinch the ends to seal everything in. This should look like a small meat loaf. Place this meat loaf at the edge of the bacon weave closest to you. Using the wax paper underneath the bacon to help, roll the bacon blanket around the sausage, tucking the ends in as you go. Set aside, seam side down. Repeat with the remaining ingredients, making a second wrapped fatty.

6 Drain and add the wood chips to the charcoal or to the smoker box of a gas grill, following manufacturer's instructions, and close the lid. When smoke appears, grill the fatties over **indirect low heat**, with the lid closed, until an instant-read thermometer inserted into the thickest part of the meat registers 155°F, 1½ to 2 hours. Remove from the grill and let rest for 10 minutes (the internal temperature will rise 5 to 10 degrees during this time). Cut into 1-inch-thick slices and serve right away.

1 *Working on a piece of wax paper, create a bacon weave. Keep the bacon slices tight. The finished size should be about 11 by 11 inches.*

2 *Arrange the artichokes, tomatoes, and bell peppers in a horizontal line on the sausage square. Leave room, about 1 inch, on either side.*

3 *Roll up the sausage around the filling, and pinch the edges to seal everything in.*

4 *Place the sausage roll on the bacon weave, and roll it up.*

PIZZAS
WITH PROSCIUTTO, PARMESAN, AND PROVOLONE

SERVES: 6 TO 8 (MAKES TWO 12-INCH PIZZAS) | **PREP TIME:** 25 MINUTES | **RISING TIME:** 1¼ TO 1½ HOURS
GRILLING TIME: 6 TO 9 MINUTES PER PIZZA | **SPECIAL EQUIPMENT:** NONSTICK ALUMINUM FOIL

DOUGH

- 1 cup warm water (105° to 115°F)
- 1 tablespoon extra-virgin olive oil
- 1¾ teaspoons kosher salt
- 1½ teaspoons rapid-rise instant yeast (do not use the entire packet)
- 3 cups unbleached all-purpose flour, plus more as needed

- Extra-virgin olive oil
- 1 garlic clove, minced
- 4 ounces aged, sharp provolone cheese, coarsely grated, divided
- 1 red onion, 6 to 7 ounces, thinly sliced, divided
- 4 ounces thinly sliced prosciutto, divided
- 4 ounces Parmigiano-Reggiano® cheese, finely grated (1 cup), divided
- 2 ounces fresh baby arugula, divided

When I was a young chef fresh out of cooking school, I ate one of the most memorable meals of my life at a restaurant in Providence, Rhode Island. At Al Forno, pioneering chefs Johanne Killeen and George Germon elevated humble pizzas to remarkable expressions of art, jostling them over hardwood charcoal fires so the smoke drifted into the blistered crust and bubbling toppings. When you do this at home, have all your supplies within reach, because the thin crust cooks quickly over a live fire.

1 In a large bowl combine the water, oil, salt, and yeast. Mix in about 2¾ cups flour to make a stiff dough that cannot be stirred. Turn the dough out onto a floured work surface and knead by hand, working in the final ¼ cup flour, or more as needed, until the dough is smooth, supple, and slightly tacky, about 6 minutes.

2 Coat a medium bowl with oil. Shape the dough into a ball, place in the bowl, and turn to coat with the oil. Cover the bowl tightly with plastic wrap. Let stand in a warm, draft-free area until the dough is doubled in volume, 1¼ to 1½ hours; or refrigerate the dough for 6 to 8 hours. Return to room temperature before using.

3 Prepare the grill for direct cooking over medium heat (350° to 450°F).

4 In a small bowl whisk ¼ cup oil and the garlic.

5 Divide the dough into two equal balls. On an oiled square of nonstick aluminum foil, using your hands, stretch out one ball of dough to a 12-inch round. Brush the top side of the dough with olive oil.

6 Lay the dough on the cooking grate with the foil side facing up. Grab one corner of the foil with tongs and peel it off. Cook the dough over **direct medium heat**, with the lid closed, until the underside is golden, 2 to 3 minutes. Transfer the crust to the back of a baking sheet with the grilled side facing up. Brush with 1 tablespoon of the garlic oil, leaving a ½-inch border. Top with half of the provolone and half of the onion. Drape half of the prosciutto over and around the onion, and top with ¼ cup of the Parmigiano-Reggiano® cheese, half of the arugula, and another ¼ cup Parmigiano-Reggiano cheese. Return the pizza to the grill, close the lid, and continue grilling until the arugula wilts, the cheese melts, and the crust is crisp and golden brown, 4 to 6 minutes more. Transfer to a cutting board, drizzle with 1 tablespoon of the garlic oil, cut into wedges, and serve warm. Make another pizza with the remaining ingredients.

THREE-CHEESE PIZZAS
WITH SAUSAGE, MUSHROOMS, AND PEPPERS

SERVES: 6 TO 8 (MAKES TWO 12-INCH PIZZAS) | **PREP TIME:** 40 MINUTES | **RISING TIME:** 1¼ TO 1½ HOURS
GRILLING TIME: 13 TO 16 MINUTES, PLUS 12 TO 15 MINUTES PER PIZZA
SPECIAL EQUIPMENT: PIZZA STONE, PIZZA PEEL (OPTIONAL), PERFORATED GRILL PAN, SILICONE PASTRY BRUSH

DOUGH
1 cup warm water (105° to 115°F)
1 tablespoon extra-virgin olive oil
1¾ teaspoons kosher salt
1½ teaspoons rapid-rise instant yeast
(do not use the entire packet)
3 cups unbleached all-purpose flour,
plus more as needed

Extra-virgin olive oil
1 red bell pepper, about 8 ounces
8 ounces cremini mushrooms, cut
into quarters
Kosher salt
Freshly ground black pepper
12 ounces crumbled Italian sausage
4 ounces Pecorino Romano® cheese,
finely grated (1 cup), divided
4 ounces Fontina cheese, coarsely
grated (1 cup), divided
½ small yellow onion, thinly sliced
crosswise, divided
8 ounces fresh mozzarella cheese, well
drained, thinly sliced, divided
4 teaspoons fresh thyme leaves, divided
Crushed red pepper flakes

There is something both ancient and modern about baking a freshly made pizza in a wood-burning oven. You can replicate this on your grill by preheating a pizza stone for a full 10 minutes right on the cooking grate. A really hot stone will expand the air bubbles inside the dough, giving you a soft, cloud-like interior above a crisp, toasted exterior.

1 In a large bowl combine the water, oil, salt, and yeast. Mix in about 2¾ cups flour to make a stiff dough that cannot be stirred. Turn the dough out onto a floured work surface and knead by hand, working in the final ¼ cup flour, or more as needed, until the dough is smooth, supple, and slightly tacky, about 6 minutes.

2 Coat a medium bowl with oil. Shape the dough into a ball, place in the bowl, and turn to coat with the oil. Cover the bowl tightly with plastic wrap. Let stand in a warm, draft-free area until the dough is doubled in volume, 1¼ to 1½ hours; or refrigerate the dough for 6 to 8 hours. Return to room temperature before using.

3 Prepare the grill for direct cooking over medium heat (350° to 450°F) and preheat a perforated grill pan for 10 minutes.

4 Grill the bell pepper over **direct medium heat**, with the lid closed, until blackened and blistered all over, 10 to 12 minutes, turning occasionally. Place the pepper in a bowl and cover with plastic wrap to trap the steam. Let stand for about 10 minutes. Remove and discard the charred skin, stem, and seeds, and cut the bell pepper into ¼-inch strips.

5 Brush the mushrooms with oil, season with ¼ teaspoon salt and ¼ teaspoon pepper, and then arrange in a single layer on the grill pan. Grill over **direct medium heat**, with the lid closed, until golden brown, 3 to 4 minutes, stirring once or twice. Transfer to a plate.

6 In a medium skillet over medium heat on the stove, warm 1 tablespoon oil. Add the sausage and sauté until cooked through, 6 to 8 minutes, stirring frequently. Using a slotted spoon, transfer the sausage to a plate lined with paper towels.

7 Prepare the grill for indirect cooking over high heat (500° to 550°F) and preheat the pizza stone for about 10 minutes, following manufacturer's instructions.

8 Divide the dough into two equal balls. On a lightly floured work surface, using a rolling pin or your hands, roll or stretch out one ball of dough to a 12-inch round. Liberally dust a pizza peel or a rimless baking sheet with flour. Transfer the dough round to the pizza peel. Top the dough with ¼ cup of the Pecorino and ¼ cup of the Fontina, leaving a ½-inch border. Spread half of the onion, bell peppers, mushrooms, and sausage over the cheese. Distribute half of the mozzarella over and between the toppings, and ¼ cup Fontina and ¼ cup Pecorino over the pizza. Season with 2 teaspoons of the thyme, a pinch of salt, and a pinch of black pepper.

9 Carefully slide the pizza onto the preheated pizza stone. Grill over **indirect high heat**, with the lid closed, until the crust is golden and crisp and the cheese is melted, 12 to 15 minutes. Transfer to a cutting board, top with red pepper flakes, cut into wedges, and serve warm.

10 Use a silicone pastry brush to brush off any flour left on the pizza stone. Close the lid and reheat the pizza stone for 10 minutes. Make another pizza with the remaining ingredients.

3

RED MEAT

BACON CHEESEBURGERS
WITH KENTUCKY BOURBON SAUCE

SERVES: 4 | PREP TIME: 20 MINUTES, PLUS ABOUT 35 MINUTES FOR THE SAUCE | GRILLING TIME: 8 TO 10 MINUTES
SPECIAL EQUIPMENT: 2 LARGE HANDFULS HICKORY OR MESQUITE WOOD CHIPS

SAUCE
- 2 teaspoons vegetable oil
- 2 slices bacon, cut into ½-inch-wide strips
- 1 yellow onion, about 5 ounces, finely chopped
- 1 garlic clove, minced
- ¼ cup bourbon
- 1 cup ketchup
- ¼ cup water
- 3 tablespoons cider vinegar
- 3 tablespoons unsulfured molasses (not blackstrap)
- 2 tablespoons dark steak sauce
- 1 tablespoon spicy brown mustard
- 1 teaspoon liquid smoke
- ½ teaspoon hot pepper sauce

- 8 slices bacon
- 1½ pounds ground chuck (80% lean)
- 1 teaspoon kosher salt
- ½ teaspoon freshly ground black pepper
- 4 ounces smoked cheddar cheese, grated
- 4 hamburger buns, split
- 4 leaves romaine lettuce, shredded
- 8 slices ripe tomato

Like all of America's iconic foods, cheeseburgers can be either inspired or insipid depending on how they are made. For me, the surest way to elevate an ordinary cheeseburger to greatness is to grill it with wood. Anyone with a quarter of a taste bud will notice the difference when the comforting smells of smoldering wood chips have seeped into these burgers. Since they don't spend a lot of time on the grill, be sure to use a stronger-flavored wood like hickory or mesquite, and let it build up a good head of smoke before you add the patties.

1 Soak the wood chips in water for at least 30 minutes.

2 In a heavy, medium saucepan over medium heat on the stove, warm the oil. Add the bacon strips and fry until browned and crisp, 3 to 5 minutes. Using a slotted spoon, transfer the bacon to paper towels to drain and cool, leaving the drippings in the saucepan.

3 Add the onion to the saucepan, reduce the heat to medium-low, and cook until soft and golden brown, 8 to 10 minutes, stirring occasionally. Stir in the garlic and cook until fragrant, about 1 minute. Add the bourbon, increase the heat to medium-high, and boil to reduce slightly, about 1 minute. Add the remaining sauce ingredients and bring to a boil over medium-high heat. Reduce the heat to low and simmer, uncovered, until the mixture thickens and is reduced to about 2 cups, about 20 minutes, stirring occasionally. Turn off the heat and stir in the fried and cooled bacon. Cover and keep warm.

4 Meanwhile, in a skillet over medium heat on the stove, fry the eight bacon slices until browned and crisp, 8 to 10 minutes, turning occasionally. Transfer the bacon to paper towels to drain.

5 Mix the ground chuck, salt, and pepper, and then gently form four patties of equal size, each about ¾ inch thick. With your thumb or the back of a spoon, make a shallow indentation about 1 inch wide in the center of the patties to prevent them from forming a dome as they cook. Refrigerate the patties until ready to grill.

6 Prepare the grill for direct cooking over medium-high heat (about 400°F).

7 Drain and add the wood chips to the charcoal or to the smoker box of a gas grill, following manufacturer's instructions, and close the lid. When smoke appears, grill the patties over **direct medium-high heat**, with the lid closed, until cooked to medium doneness (160°F), 8 to 10 minutes, turning once. During the last minute of grilling time, place one-quarter of the cheese on each patty to melt, and toast the buns, cut side down, over direct heat.

8 Build each burger on a bun with lettuce, tomato slices, a patty, bacon slices, and sauce. Serve warm.

Don't do this! Smashing patties with a spatula may make them flatter, but it also pushes juices and fat out, triggering flare-ups. If you like flat patties, use your thumb or the back of a spoon to make a shallow well in the center of the raw patties before you put them on the cooking grate. As they cook, that well will fill in and flatten out nicely.

TRIPLE BEER BURGERS

SERVES: 4 | **PREP TIME:** 20 MINUTES, PLUS ABOUT 20 MINUTES FOR THE SAUCE
GRILLING TIME: 24 TO 31 MINUTES | **SPECIAL EQUIPMENT:** LARGE DISPOSABLE FOIL PAN

One of the secrets of making especially juicy burgers is adding a little beer to the raw meat. If you use too much, the patties get too wet to develop a good crust and they tend to fall apart, but just a little full-bodied beer helps in a big way.

1 garlic clove, minced
   Extra-virgin olive oil
1 cup ketchup
1 cup plus 2 tablespoons IPA or
   dark ale, divided
2 tablespoons cider vinegar
1 tablespoon packed brown sugar
3 teaspoons Worcestershire
   sauce, divided
   Kosher salt
1 medium yellow onion, cut crosswise
   into ⅓-inch slices
1 tablespoon Dijon mustard
1½ pounds ground chuck (80% lean)
1 teaspoon smoked paprika
¼ teaspoon freshly ground black pepper
4 pretzel rolls, split
4 leaves Boston lettuce

1 In a saucepan over medium heat on the stove, sauté the garlic in 1 tablespoon oil until fragrant, about 1 minute. Add the ketchup, ½ cup of the beer, the vinegar, brown sugar, 2 teaspoons of the Worcestershire sauce, and ½ teaspoon salt and bring to a gentle boil. Reduce the heat to low and simmer until the sauce is the consistency of ketchup, 15 to 20 minutes, stirring often. Let cool.

2 Prepare the grill for direct cooking over medium-high heat (400° to 500°F).

3 Brush the onion with oil, and then grill over ***direct medium-high heat***, with the lid closed, until lightly charred, about 6 minutes, turning once. In a large disposable foil pan mix ½ cup of the beer, the mustard, and 1 teaspoon salt. Add the onions to the beer mixture. Grill over ***direct medium-high heat***, with the lid closed, until most of the liquid is evaporated and the onion is soft, 10 to 15 minutes, stirring occasionally. Remove from the grill.

4 Mix the ground chuck, paprika, pepper, 1½ teaspoons salt, the remaining 2 tablespoons beer and 1 teaspoon Worcestershire sauce, and then gently form four patties of equal size, each about ¾ inch thick. With your thumb or the back of a spoon, make a shallow indentation about 1 inch wide in the center of the patties to prevent them from forming a dome as they cook.

5 Grill the patties over ***direct medium-high heat***, with the lid closed, until cooked to medium doneness (160°F), 8 to 10 minutes, turning once. During the last 30 seconds to 1 minute of grilling time, toast the rolls, cut side down, over direct heat.

6 Build each burger on a roll with lettuce, a patty, onions, and sauce. Serve warm.

GASTROPUB LAMB BURGERS

SERVES: 4 | **PREP TIME:** 20 MINUTES
GRILLING TIME: 7 TO 9 MINUTES

These burgers strut with a little upscale swagger on account of ground lamb, a mixed olive tapenade with gourmet oomph, and big slabs of summer's best tomatoes. The brioche bun adds another elegant element, but any rich, eggy bread, such as challah, would be great.

1¼ pounds ground lamb, preferably from the shoulder
3 garlic cloves, minced
2 tablespoons finely chopped fresh Italian parsley leaves
½ teaspoon dried oregano
　Kosher salt
　Freshly ground black pepper

TAPENADE
½ cup pitted mild green olives, such as Picholine, drained
½ cup pitted brine-cured black olives, such as Kalamata, drained
2 tablespoons extra-virgin olive oil
1 tablespoon red or white wine vinegar
　Finely grated zest of 1 orange
2 garlic cloves, thinly sliced

4 brioche buns, split
8 slices ripe tomato, each about ¼ inch thick

1 Combine the lamb, garlic, parsley, oregano, ¼ teaspoon salt, and ¼ teaspoon pepper. Mix well, and then gently form four patties of equal size, each about ¾ inch thick. With your thumb or the back of a spoon, make a shallow indentation about 1 inch wide in the center of the patties to prevent them from forming a dome as they cook. Refrigerate the patties until ready to grill.

2 In a food processor combine the tapenade ingredients. Pulse on and off until minced and well blended, scraping down the inside of the bowl several times.

3 Prepare the grill for direct cooking over medium-high heat (400° to 500°F).

4 Lightly season the patties on both sides with salt and pepper, and then grill over **direct medium-high heat**, with the lid closed, until cooked to medium doneness (160°F), 7 to 9 minutes, turning once. During the last 30 seconds to 1 minute of grilling time, toast the buns, cut side down, over direct heat. Remove from the grill and let the patties rest for 2 to 3 minutes.

5 Build each burger on a bun with a patty, tapenade, and tomato slices. Serve warm.

GROUND RIB EYE STEAK SLIDERS
WITH CARAMELIZED ONIONS AND TOMATO-BACON JAM

SERVES: 6 (MAKES 12 SLIDERS | PREP TIME: 20 MINUTES, PLUS ABOUT 55 MINUTES FOR THE JAM
AND 25 TO 35 MINUTES FOR THE ONIONS | GRILLING TIME: ABOUT 4 MINUTES

JAM

- 8 ounces smoked bacon, cut into
  ¼-inch strips
- 1 sweet yellow onion,
  8 to 10 ounces, chopped
- 1½ pounds plum tomatoes, chopped
- 3 tablespoons packed light brown sugar
- 2 tablespoons cider vinegar
- 1 tablespoon hot pepper sauce
  or Sriracha

  Kosher salt
  Freshly ground black pepper
- 2 tablespoons extra-virgin olive oil
- 2 sweet yellow onions, about
  1½ pounds total, each cut in half
  and thinly sliced
- 2 pounds ground rib eye steak
- 1 tablespoon Worcestershire sauce
- 12 slider buns, split

Grinding up rib eye steaks might sound like a crazy splurge, and I'll admit that it is not essential for an everyday burger, but it sure does improve the rich, meaty flavors in these little sliders. If you don't have a meat grinder, ask your butcher to grind the meat for you. This business of using freshly ground beef from one or more special cuts of meat is a burgeoning trend in the world of gourmet burgers.

1 In a large skillet over medium heat on the stove, fry the bacon until browned and crisp, 5 to 7 minutes, turning occasionally. Using a slotted spoon, transfer the bacon to a large, heavy saucepan. Set aside. Drain off all but 1 tablespoon fat from the skillet. Add the chopped onion and sauté until softened but not colored, 3 to 4 minutes, stirring occasionally. Transfer the onion and the remaining jam ingredients, including 1 teaspoon salt and ½ teaspoon pepper, to the saucepan with the bacon. Bring to a boil over medium-high heat and cook until the sugar dissolves, stirring frequently. Reduce the heat to medium-low and simmer, partially covered, until most of the juices are absorbed and the mixture is thickened to a moist, jam-like consistency, 40 to 45 minutes, stirring frequently.

2 In another large skillet over medium heat on the stove, warm the oil. Add the onions and 1 teaspoon salt and cook until the onions begin to turn light golden, 10 to 15 minutes, stirring occasionally. Reduce the heat to medium-low and cook until the onions are deep golden brown and caramelized, 15 to 20 minutes more, stirring frequently. Remove from the heat and stir in ¼ teaspoon pepper.

3 Prepare the grill for direct and indirect cooking over high heat (450° to 550°F).

4 Mix the ground rib eye steak, Worcestershire sauce, 1 teaspoon salt, and ¾ teaspoon pepper, and then gently form 12 patties of equal size, each about 2 inches in diameter and ½ inch thick.

5 Grill the patties over **direct high heat**, with the lid closed, until cooked to medium doneness (160°F), about 4 minutes, turning once when the patties release easily from the cooking grate without sticking (if flare-ups occur, move the patties temporarily over indirect heat). During the last 30 seconds to 1 minute of grilling time, toast the buns, cut side down, over direct heat.

6 Build each slider on a bun with a patty, onions, and jam. Serve warm.

These decadent sliders benefit from caramel-lacquered onions and this sweet, smoky condiment that simmers down to a moist, jam-like consistency. The recipe may make more jam than you need for the sliders, but that's a good thing—it's also delicious served with cheese or spread on crostini. The jam may be refrigerated for up to 1 week.

COWBOY STEAKS
WITH SMOKED SHALLOT BUTTER

SERVES: 4 TO 6 | **PREP TIME:** 15 MINUTES | **GRILLING TIME:** ABOUT 1 HOUR
SPECIAL EQUIPMENT: 2 LARGE HANDFULS MESQUITE WOOD CHIPS, SMALL DISPOSABLE FOIL PAN

BUTTER

1 shallot, about 1 ounce, peeled and
   cut lengthwise into quarters
1 teaspoon extra-virgin olive oil
¼ teaspoon smoked paprika
¼ cup (½ stick) unsalted butter, softened
1 tablespoon finely chopped fresh
   Italian parsley leaves
2 teaspoons dry sherry (optional)
1 teaspoon freshly grated lemon zest

   Kosher salt
   Freshly ground black pepper
2 bone-in rib eye cowboy steaks, each
   about 2 pounds and 2 inches thick
   Extra-virgin olive oil
½ teaspoon garlic powder

To make manly carnivores sing for joy like Maria prancing through the Alps in The Sound of Music, *serve them marbled bone-in rib eye steaks (aka cowboy steaks) that come with their own handles. The handles are not really for picking up the steaks, but the bones do protect and flavor the meat alongside it, making those parts often the juiciest and tastiest of all. Season these thick steaks well and let them stand at room temperature long enough so that the salt can draw out moisture and the meat can reabsorb those juices with the seasonings. That usually takes 30 to 40 minutes.*

1 Soak the wood chips in water for at least 30 minutes.

2 Prepare the grill for direct and indirect cooking over medium-high heat (about 450°F).

3 In a small disposable foil pan combine the shallot quarters, oil, and paprika. Drain and add one handful of the wood chips to the charcoal or to the smoker box of a gas grill, following manufacturer's instructions, and close the lid. When smoke appears, place the foil pan with the shallot over **indirect medium-high heat**, close the lid, and cook until the shallot is tender, about 40 minutes. Transfer to a cutting board and let cool for 10 minutes. Mince the shallot, transfer to a small bowl, and add the remaining butter ingredients, including ½ teaspoon salt and ¼ teaspoon pepper, mixing thoroughly. Refrigerate, covered, until firm. Remove from the refrigerator about 10 minutes before serving.

4 Lightly brush both sides of the steaks with oil and season evenly with 2 teaspoons salt, ½ teaspoon pepper, and the garlic powder. Allow the steaks to stand at room temperature for 30 to 40 minutes before grilling.

5 Drain and add the remaining wood chips to the charcoal or smoker box. When smoke appears, sear the steaks over **direct medium-high heat**, with the lid closed, for 6 to 8 minutes, turning once. Then move the steaks over **indirect medium-high heat**, close the lid, and continue cooking to your desired doneness, 12 to 14 minutes more for medium rare. Remove from the grill and let rest for 3 to 5 minutes. Serve warm, topped with the butter.

For a great steak to reach the level of a feast, it needs something special like the sweet succulence of this smoky shallot butter. Cook a quartered shallot in mesquite smoke until tender and golden. Mince the shallot and blend with softened butter, parsley, lemon zest, and maybe a little sherry.

MESQUITE T-BONES
WITH SMOKED TOMATO SALSA

SERVES: 4 TO 6 | **PREP TIME:** 15 MINUTES
GRILLING TIME: 36 TO 55 MINUTES | **SPECIAL EQUIPMENT:** 2 LARGE HANDFULS MESQUITE WOOD CHIPS

6 medium plum tomatoes

RUB
2 teaspoons freshly ground black pepper
½ teaspoon ground cumin
½ teaspoon paprika
¼ teaspoon onion powder
¼ teaspoon garlic powder

Kosher salt
2 T-bone steaks, each 1½ to 2 pounds and about 1½ inches thick
3 tablespoons minced shallot
1½ tablespoons fresh lemon juice
1 tablespoon extra-virgin olive oil
1½ teaspoons chopped fresh thyme leaves
1 teaspoon minced garlic
¼ teaspoon ancho chile powder, or to taste

These thick T-bones call for a more interactive method of grilling than just turning them once over the flames, especially if you are cooking over charcoal, where the fire is inherently uneven. Turning the steaks every minute (or even more often) helps to cook them more evenly and more quickly. When you flip steaks often, both sides stay hot throughout the grilling time, meaning the meat reaches the desired doneness faster.

1 Soak the wood chips in water for at least 30 minutes.

2 Prepare the grill for indirect cooking over low heat (250° to 350°F).

3 Drain and add one handful of the wood chips to the charcoal or to the smoker box of a gas grill, following manufacturer's instructions, and close the lid. When smoke appears, grill the tomatoes over **indirect low heat**, with the lid closed, until the skins are wrinkled, 20 to 35 minutes, depending on the size and ripeness of the tomatoes (do not turn). Don't worry if the skins split. Very carefully transfer them to a large cutting board. Increase the temperature of the grill and prepare it for direct cooking over medium heat (350° to 450°F).

4 Roughly chop the tomatoes, skin and all, and remove any tough cores. Scrape them into a fine-mesh strainer set over a bowl and drain well.

5 Mix the rub ingredients, including 1 teaspoon salt. Season the steaks all over with the rub, including the sides, and refrigerate until ready to grill.

6 Drain and add the remaining wood chips to the charcoal or smoker box. When smoke appears, grill the steaks over **direct medium heat**, with the lid closed, until cooked to your desired doneness, 16 to 20 minutes for medium rare, turning often. Transfer to a cutting board and let rest for 5 minutes.

7 Place the well-drained tomatoes in a serving bowl (discard their juice or save for another use). Stir in the shallot, lemon juice, oil, thyme, garlic, chile powder, and ½ teaspoon salt. Carve the steaks and serve warm with the smoked tomato salsa.

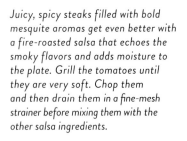

Juicy, spicy steaks filled with bold mesquite aromas get even better with a fire-roasted salsa that echoes the smoky flavors and adds moisture to the plate. Grill the tomatoes until they are very soft. Chop them and then drain them in a fine-mesh strainer before mixing them with the other salsa ingredients.

MAKING
TEXAS
BARBECUE NEW AGAIN

★

If your definition of barbecue is a limited one, a few hours talking with chef Tim Byres will have you questioning your beliefs. His menus at two Smoke restaurants in the Dallas area highlight the diversity of wood as a cooking fuel like few others. Byres' creativity in coaxing the flavors of smoke and fire into meats and vegetables is unmatched by most chefs, and he's not done yet.

A vast hearth kitchen is the focal point of the newest Smoke restaurant in Plano. Chops, steaks, fish, and fowl cover the wood grill while whole chickens hang overhead gathering the smoke on its way up. Flames rise and flicker in a dance with the cast of grill cooks who flip meat and prepare sauces in pans set directly onto wood coals. Food runners bump into customers who stand gazing into the open kitchen with mouthwatering anticipation. It's not your normal fine dining experience, and it's not your "normal" barbecue, especially in Dallas, and that's just what Byres was hoping for.

Byres reflects on his decision to create a unique vibe in Dallas along with a new way of honoring American foodways. "To be a great restaurant it seemed like you needed to have expensive stemware, linen napkins in the bathroom, and an elite squad of valet attendants. That's when I decided to step out of the box." He had worked in the five-star kitchens of Stephan Pyles and John Tesar, but fine dining had left him unfulfilled. He hit the ceiling of haute cuisine and it hurt. He had wandered too far from the gratifying days of his youth cooking outside. The first Smoke restaurant was Byres' attempt at finding his culinary soul again. He committed to getting reacquainted with firewood cooking, which he calls "the origin of American foodways."

> ## "I ENJOY BARBECUE AND I ENJOY THE IDEA OF IT, BUT I ENJOY THE COMMUNITY OF IT MOST."

As you'd expect from the name, Smoke features barbecue in the strictest sense of that word. Smoked brisket, the signature of Texas, is on the menu along with spareribs and pulled pork, but there's a lot more. Byres smokes his owns hams, homemade sausages, and thick-sliced bacon. Pork jowl also gets the low smoke treatment before making it onto a platter with sweet chiles and half-sour pickles. Byres is no one-trick pony.

The signature at Smoke in Dallas has become The Big Rib. It's a gargantuan beef short rib barely clinging to a bone the size of an adult forearm. Most Texas barbecue joints would insist on leaving such a cut unadorned, but Byres brings a multifaceted chef's mentality of

layering flavors. That means a healthy spoonful of chimichurri sauce, raw sliced shallots, and cilantro. "You balance the char with sweet, acidic, and raw," he explains. The combination is stunning on the palate and, if you close your eyes, you can see its origins in the traditional Texas barbecue garnish of dill pickle chips and raw onion.

At festivals these days, Byres has moved on to meat swords. These are sticks of rebar mounted to the edges of his aptly named "meat sword box." Raw meats—cabrito and flank steak work especially well—are affixed to the swords, which hang at an angle over

the fire. They cook slowly over the far away heat source, but are flavored by the smoke in a way similar to an indirect smoker. It's hard to say which category the meat sword box fits in, but Byres says that's the beauty. "It's really direct and indirect heat cooking, but how direct or indirect? That's the swing." He says the more important thing about the meat swords is that they bring people together. "I enjoy barbecue and I enjoy the idea of it, but I enjoy the community of it most." In a festival setting, people gather around to gawk at the spectacle of meat on metal sticks, but they stick around to share the food with friends and strangers alike.

Back at Smoke in Plano, the restaurant is quickly becoming known for one item that is about as direct-heat you can get. The enormous tomahawk rib eye is called the Eisenhower steak. It gets heavily seasoned, then grilled dirty, which means directly on the hot coals, just like the 34th president preferred it. The crust is stout, while the meat within remains ridiculously juicy. The plating and presenting at the table on a board the size of a small coffee table becomes a bit of performance art. It's just the latest in Byres' ever-expanding barbecue repertoire.

When pressed about what genre of barbecue he'll tackle next, Byres is unsure. "I don't know what next year's plan will be, but we need to come up with something fun and different." For him, that is the nature of barbecue. It has always been ripe for reinterpretation.

COAL-COOKED STRIP STEAKS
WITH BALSAMIC GLAZE

SERVES: 4 | PREP TIME: 15 MINUTES | GRILLING TIME: 6 TO 7 MINUTES
SPECIAL EQUIPMENT: CHARCOAL GRILL, ALL-NATURAL LUMP CHARCOAL

GLAZE
⅔ cup balsamic vinegar
2 teaspoons packed light brown sugar
1 garlic clove, smashed and peeled

RUB
2 teaspoons kosher salt
2 teaspoons freshly ground black pepper
1 teaspoon mustard powder
½ teaspoon crushed red pepper flakes

4 New York strip steaks, each
10 to 12 ounces and 1 inch thick,
trimmed of nearly all fat around
the perimeter
Kosher salt

As if the pyrotechnics of traditional grilling aren't exciting enough, cooking right on live coals is a thrilling showstopper. This method requires a charcoal grill, and while it may seem daunting to cook without the cooking grate, it is actually quite fun.

1 In a small saucepan over medium-high heat on the stove, bring the glaze ingredients to a boil. Reduce the heat and simmer until the glaze is reduced by about half, 3 to 5 minutes, watching carefully that it does not boil and burn. Remove from the heat and let cool and thicken slightly. Discard the garlic.

2 Combine the rub ingredients, and then season the steaks evenly with the rub. (Do not brush the steaks with oil; this will cause flare-ups.) Allow the steaks to stand at room temperature for 15 to 30 minutes before cooking.

3 Set the cooking grate aside; you will not be using it for this recipe. Make sure that the bottom vent on the grill is open. Place a chimney starter on the charcoal grate, and pack and fill it over the brim with all-natural lump charcoal (do not use briquettes). You need enough charcoal that, when ashed over, it will fill two-thirds of the

charcoal grate. Place newspaper or paraffin cubes underneath the chimney starter (do not use lighter fluid), ignite it, and let the charcoal burn until lightly covered with white ash. Wearing insulated barbecue mitts or gloves, turn the coals out onto the charcoal grate. Break apart the larger pieces of charcoal to create a relatively even bed of coals. Using a sheet pan, fan any loose ashes from the coals.

4 Place the steaks directly on the coals. Put the lid on the grill, open the top vent on the lid, and cook until the steaks are browned and have reached your desired doneness, 6 to 7 minutes for medium rare, turning once and using a spatula to knock off any coals that may cling to the meat. Remove from the grill and let rest for 5 minutes. Just before serving, season the steaks with salt and drizzle with the glaze. Serve right away.

Use boneless steaks at least one inch thick for this method, and trim off nearly all the fat around the perimeter, as the extra fat will cause serious flare-ups.

Lump charcoal is the only choice with direct coal cooking because it is completely natural.

Use long-handled tongs to smash very large chunks of charcoal into smaller pieces; you want the bed of coals to be as even as possible with a minimum of peaks and valleys.

Before adding the steaks, fan any loose ashes off the coals with a metal sheet pan.

Surprisingly, the meat does not always get a deep, dark char from direct coal cooking. With the meat right on the coals, there is not as much air to promote browning.

As you turn each steak or remove it from the grill, use a spatula to knock off any charcoal pieces clinging to the meat.

REVERSE-SEAR NEW YORK STEAKS
WITH RED WINE BUTTER

SERVES: 4 | PREP TIME: 15 MINUTES | STANDING TIME: 1 HOUR | GRILLING TIME: 29 TO 39 MINUTES
SPECIAL EQUIPMENT: CHARCOAL GRILL, 2 LARGE HANDFULS HICKORY WOOD CHIPS, INSTANT-READ THERMOMETER

4 well-marbled New York strip steaks,
    each about 8 ounces and
    1¼ to 1½ inches thick
4 teaspoons extra-virgin olive oil
1½ teaspoons fine sea salt
2 teaspoons ground fennel
1½ cups dry red wine, such as cabernet
½ teaspoon red wine vinegar
1 medium shallot, minced
    Freshly ground black pepper
6 tablespoons (¾ stick) salted butter,
    cut into cubes, cold
1 tablespoon snipped fresh chives

As an alternative to the traditional sear-n-slide method of grilling thick steaks, in which you sear them over direct heat and finish them over indirect heat, the reverse-sear method has recently captured the hopes and dreams of deeply devoted barbecue enthusiasts. Here, the steaks are first slow-roasted over low, indirect heat before they are finished over a ripping hot direct fire. The benefit is that the interior of the meat achieves an even pink color from top to bottom (instead of the gray outer ring of overcooked meat in a sear-n-slide steak), and almost no precious juices are lost.

1 Brush the steaks on both sides with the oil. Combine the salt and fennel, and then rub evenly onto both sides of each steak. Let the steaks stand at room temperature for 1 hour before grilling.

2 Soak the wood chips in water for at least 30 minutes.

3 In a small, heavy saucepan combine the wine, vinegar, and shallot. Bring to a simmer over medium-low heat on the stove and simmer until reduced to about 2 tablespoons. Remove from the heat and let stand at room temperature until 5 minutes before serving. (This may be done up to 2 hours in advance.)

4 Fill a chimney starter one-third full with charcoal (about 30 briquettes), and ignite. When covered with gray ash, dump the coals on one side of the charcoal grate, put the cooking grate in place, and preheat for 10 minutes. The temperature of the grill should be about 300°F. Drain and add one handful of the wood chips to the charcoal. Grill the steaks over **indirect low heat**, with the lid closed, until the interior temperature reaches 110° to 115°F, 25 to 35 minutes.

5 While the steaks are cooking over indirect heat, light a full chimney starter filled with briquettes on a heatproof surface away from the grill. When the coals are very hot, transfer the steaks to a plate, remove the cooking grate, and dump the hot coals over the remaining coals. Replace the cooking grate and lid and preheat the grate for 5 minutes. Drain and add the remaining wood chips to the charcoal. Grill the steaks over **direct high heat**, with the lid closed, until the interior temperature reaches about 130°F, about 4 minutes, turning once. Remove from the grill, season with pepper, and let rest for 5 minutes.

6 Meanwhile, return the saucepan with the wine mixture over medium-low heat on the stove or over direct heat on the cooking grate; cook until steaming. Remove from the heat and whisk in one cube of the cold butter. Whisk the butter constantly until the mixture is emulsified, and then begin to slowly add the remaining cubes of butter until the mixture is pale and smooth. Swirl in the chives. Serve the red wine butter over the warm steaks.

SANTA MARIA–STYLE TRI TIP
WITH GARLIC BREAD

SERVES: 4 TO 6 | **PREP TIME:** 15 MINUTES | **CHILLING TIME:** 30 MINUTES TO 4 HOURS | **GRILLING TIME:** ABOUT 30 MINUTES
SPECIAL EQUIPMENT: CHARCOAL GRILL, 2 LARGE HANDFULS OAK OR PECAN WOOD CHUNKS, INSTANT-READ THERMOMETER

1 tri-tip roast, 2½ to 3 pounds and
  1¼ to 1½ inches thick
1 tablespoon extra-virgin oil
1½ teaspoons kosher salt
1 teaspoon granulated garlic
  Freshly ground black pepper
¼ cup (½ stick) salted butter, melted
2 garlic cloves, minced
12 slices sourdough bread, each about
  ½ inch thick
  Store-bought salsa

Santa Maria BBQ has quietly persevered in a swath of central California since the mid-1800s, when the region was still part of Mexico. To this day cooks from Santa Barbara to San Luis Obispo continue to cook like the vaqueros (cowboys), who grilled tri tip over a hot fire of coastal red oak, turning and flipping the meat occasionally to avoid scorching it. Another approach is to first roast the meat over indirect heat and then char it directly over the fire. Most Santa Maria locals still use tri tips, but I've seen rib eyes and hefty sirloin steaks cooked there in a similar fashion—with just a simple rub and no sauce to speak of. The usual accompaniments are a mixed green salad, pinquito beans (small pink beans similar to kidneys), and fresh salsa. Sometimes there is a cold macaroni salad and always there is excellent garlic bread.

1 Rub the roast all over with the oil. Combine the salt and granulated garlic, and then rub evenly all over the roast, pushing it into the nooks and crannies. Place the roast on a rack set over a rimmed baking sheet and refrigerate for at least 30 minutes or up to 4 hours.

2 Fill a chimney starter one-third full with charcoal (about 30 briquettes), and ignite. When covered with gray ash, dump the coals on one side of the charcoal grate, place half of the wood chunks on the charcoal, put the cooking grate in place, and preheat the grill until the temperature is 200° to 250°F. Grill the roast over **indirect very low heat**, with the lid closed, until the interior temperature of the roast reaches 120° to 125°F, about 20 minutes.

3 Soon after the roast begins cooking, light a full chimney starter filled with briquettes on a heatproof surface away from the grill. When the coals are very hot, transfer the tri tip from the grill to a plate. Remove the cooking grate, dump the hot coals over the remaining coals, and add the remaining wood chunks to the charcoal. Replace the cooking grate, close the lid, and preheat the grill for direct cooking over high heat (450° to 550°F). Grill the tri tip over **direct high heat**, with the lid closed, until the interior temperature reaches 130° to 135°F and the exterior is nicely charred, 10 to 12 minutes, turning every 2 to 3 minutes or as necessary if flare-ups arise. Transfer to a cutting board, season with pepper, and let rest for 5 minutes.

4 Meanwhile, combine the melted butter and garlic, and then brush both sides of each piece of bread with the garlic butter. Grill the bread over **direct high heat** until golden brown, about 1 minute, turning once or twice. Cut the roast across the grain into ¼-inch-thick slices and serve warm with the garlic bread and salsa.

SANTA MARIA STYLE
— Barbecue —

Way out in the ranching country of Central California, there's a little known but proudly named barbecue style that bears as much resemblance to what they serve in Kansas City as a rattlesnake to a possum. It's called Santa Maria style—after the town of the same name—and here's the kicker: there's no sauce involved and, in its truest form, the beef is only cooked over a hardwood fire, specifically red (aka coastal live) oak. Sounds like what others call "grilling." Bite your tongue! "We don't say 'grill,' we say 'barbecue,'" explains Sandy Knotts, current custodian of Jocko's Steak House in nearby Nipomo. And, with all due respect to other styles of barbecue across this great land, without any sauce, you really taste the smoky-delicious meat.

Back in the 1900s, local ranchers and their vaqueros collaborated to create an asado-like method of turning local livestock into an outrageously great dinner. Almost as important as the meat are some classic sides: local pinquito beans (small pink beans indigenous to the area) are served with very mild salsa, and there's always plenty of butter-drenched garlic bread plus a simple green salad (this is California, after all).

In some spots, there's been no tampering with tradition. Santa Maria native Ike Simas, 87, has been cooking Santa Maria–style barbecue for most of his life. He's fed 4,500 people at the Cow Palace in San Francisco and President Reagan at the Western White House. He cooks for the Elks Lodge most weekends, and can feed 900 people for lunch, and then help a friend serve 300 that evening. He manhandles huge pieces of salt- and garlic salt–crusted sirloins with a long hook, and admits to disliking the cut that is—these days, anyway—most often associated with Santa Maria style: tri tip. Little known outside of California until recently, the cut was born back in the fifties, when a local grocer had the idea of barbecuing a funny-shaped piece of bottom sirloin that usually was just ground up into burger blend. But: "We don't like that word," Simas says of tri tip. "That's not the meat that made us famous. In the old days, we always used rib eye, and I liked to poke holes in it and push in some pieces of garlic. But then it got too expensive, and we started using top sirloin."

About an hour's drive north of Santa Barbara, a free-spirited chef and winemaker wearing a safari hat and Groucho Marx moustache is broadening the Santa Maria traditions with his own high-end sensibilities. At his roadside restaurant, Hitching Post II, Frank Ostini grills dry-aged filet mignon, bone-in Angus rib chops, and other pricey proteins (like Texas quail and Gulf shrimp) over red oak. Forget the beans. He serves his steaks with thick, hand-cut French fries cooked twice in rendered beef fat, and somehow he still manages to call all that Santa Maria–style barbecue. Ostini is completely comfortable in his role as a culinary maverick, as long as the food is cooked over a live fire of red oak and tastes top notch. "Tradition is a good excuse not to work at it," he says. "I like to take tradition into the future where it's even better than before."

STEAK SANDWICHES ON TEXAS TOAST
WITH ESPRESSO BARBECUE SAUCE

SERVES: 4 | **PREP TIME:** 20 MINUTES, PLUS ABOUT 50 MINUTES FOR THE SAUCE
GRILLING TIME: 9 TO 11 MINUTES | **SPECIAL EQUIPMENT:** 2 LARGE HANDFULS MESQUITE WOOD CHIPS

SAUCE
- 1 tablespoon extra-virgin olive oil
- 1 small yellow onion, finely chopped
- 1 garlic clove, finely chopped
- 1 tablespoon prepared chili powder
- 1 teaspoon ground cumin
- ½ teaspoon paprika
- ½ cup ketchup-style chili sauce
- ½ cup drip-brewed espresso or dark roast coffee
- 2 tablespoons packed light brown sugar
- 2 tablespoons balsamic vinegar

RUB
- 1½ teaspoons kosher salt
- 1 teaspoon prepared chili powder
- ½ teaspoon ground cumin
- ½ teaspoon freshly ground black pepper

- 1 flank steak, about 1½ pounds and ¾ inch thick
  Extra-virgin olive oil
- ¼ cup (½ stick) salted butter, softened
- 2 garlic cloves, minced
- 4 slices white, French, or Italian bread, each about 1 inch thick
- 2 cups baby arugula

Increasingly, coffee has broken out of its role as a beverage to become a cooking ingredient, too. In fact, it shows up in some old cowboy recipes as a slightly bitter flavor to complement spiciness and sweetness, as in this barbecue sauce. This sauce can be made with drip-brewed espresso or dark roast coffee, so you don't have to run out to your local café. The sauce works beautifully with the full, meaty flavors of flank steak. Texas toast is a specialty of that state, made from extra-thick slices of white bread, spread with butter and grilled until golden brown—a warm bed for the sliced steak and eye-opening sauce.

1 In a heavy, medium saucepan over medium-low heat, warm the oil. Add the onion and cook until super soft and very dark, about 30 minutes, stirring occasionally. Stir in the garlic and cook until fragrant, about 1 minute. Add the chili powder, cumin, and paprika and stir well. Add the remaining sauce ingredients and bring to a boil over medium-high heat. Reduce the heat to low and simmer, uncovered, until the sauce thickens and is reduced to about 1 cup, 15 to 20 minutes, stirring occasionally.

2 Soak the wood chips in water for at least 30 minutes.

3 Mix the rub ingredients. Lightly brush the steak on both sides with oil and season evenly with the rub. Allow the steak to stand at room temperature for 15 to 30 minutes before grilling.

4 Combine the butter and garlic, and then spread on both sides of the bread slices. Stand the slices upright, cut sides together, on a plate until ready to grill.

5 Prepare the grill for direct cooking over medium heat (350° to 450°F).

6 Drain and add the wood chips to the charcoal or to the smoker box of a gas grill, following manufacturer's instructions, and close the lid. When smoke appears, grill the steak over **direct medium heat**, with the lid closed, until cooked to your desired doneness, 8 to 10 minutes for medium rare, turning once. During the last minute of grilling time, brush the steak on both sides with some of the sauce, and turn once or twice to glaze the steak. Remove from the grill and let rest for 3 to 5 minutes.

7 Grill the bread slices over **direct medium heat** until lightly toasted, about 1 minute, turning once.

8 Cut the steak across the grain into thin slices. Build the sandwiches on the toasted bread with arugula, steak, and sauce. Drizzle the sandwiches with the carving juices. Serve warm with additional sauce on the side. Any leftover sauce can be stored in the refrigerator in a covered container for up to 2 weeks.

The grain of a flank steak looks a little like countless pieces of thread running in the same direction. If you make a cut in that same (parallel) direction, you get long stretches of thread that are hard to chew. But if you cut across (perpendicular to) the threads in very thin slices, you get short, little bits of thread that are easy to chew. Because flank steak is so wide, make the slicing more manageable by cutting the steak in half lengthwise before slicing each half across the grain.

HOMEMADE PASTRAMI
WITH CORIANDER-PEPPER RUB

SERVES: 6 TO 8 | PREP TIME: 10 MINUTES | SOAKING TIME: 8 TO 16 HOURS | COOKING TIME: 4½ TO 5½ HOURS
STANDING TIME: 1 HOUR | CHILLING TIME: AT LEAST 8 HOURS | SPECIAL EQUIPMENT: SPICE MILL; WATER SMOKER; 2 LARGE
HANDFULS APPLE WOOD CHUNKS; HEAVY-DUTY ALUMINUM FOIL; SPRAY BOTTLE FILLED WITH WATER; INSTANT-READ THERMOMETER

RUB
1½ tablespoons black peppercorns
1½ tablespoons coriander seed
1½ teaspoons yellow mustard seed
1½ teaspoons paprika
¾ teaspoon granulated garlic
¾ teaspoon granulated onion
¾ teaspoon crushed red pepper flakes

1 corned beef brisket, about
  4 pounds, preferably the flat end
  Vegetable oil

A butcher in a New York deli might take weeks to make cured, spice-crusted, and smoked pastrami from raw brisket, but my streamlined version starts with a store-bought corned beef, greatly reducing the prep time.

1 In a spice mill coarsely grind the peppercorns, coriander seed, and mustard seed (see tip No. 2 below). Put the ground spices in a bowl and add the remaining rub ingredients.

2 Drain the brisket and rinse well under cold running water. If necessary, trim the fat cap so it is about ⅓ inch thick, but no less. Place the brisket in a deep roasting pan or other food-safe container and cover it completely with cold water. Refrigerate for at least 8 hours or up to 16 hours, changing the water every few hours.

3 Drain the brisket and pat dry with paper towels. Very lightly brush the brisket all over with oil and season evenly with the rub, pressing the rub firmly with your hands to make sure it adheres securely to the meat.

4 Prepare the smoker for indirect cooking with low heat (as close to 250°F as possible).

5 Add the wood chunks to the charcoal, and then cook the brisket over *indirect low heat*, with the lid closed, for 2 hours. Remove the brisket from the smoker and place it on a large sheet of heavy-duty

aluminum foil. Spray the brisket on both sides with water, and then tightly wrap in the foil. Return the brisket to the smoker and continue cooking over *indirect low heat*, with the lid closed, until an instant-read thermometer inserted into the thickest part of the meat registers 190°F to 195°F, 2½ to 3½ hours more. Remove from the grill, open the foil, lift the brisket from the juices, and place it on a clean piece of foil. Wrap it well and let stand for 1 hour. Refrigerate until completely chilled, at least 8 hours.

6 Unwrap the pastrami and cut it across the grain into very thin slices. Place a collapsible steamer inside a large saucepan. Add enough water to come up to ¼ inch from the bottom of the steamer and bring the water to a boil over high heat on the stove. Add the sliced pastrami to the steamer and tightly cover the saucepan. Reduce the heat to very low. Steam, occasionally moving the slices from top to bottom, until the pastrami is hot and the fat is translucent, 15 to 20 minutes. Serve warm with bagels and scrambled eggs, if desired.

TIPS} HOMEMADE PASTRAMI

1
Purchase corned beef from the flat end of the brisket, not the thicker, fattier point end. Corned beef of the proper size (about 4 pounds) may not be easy to find outside of its St. Patrick's Day sales window. Look for it at warehouse stores. If you can only find a very large corned beef brisket (about 8 pounds), cut it in half and double the recipe.

2
The peppercorns, coriander seed, and mustard seed vary in size and hardness, so grind each spice separately to get the right coarseness. Use an electric spice mill.

3
Resist the temptation to tear into the pastrami right off the smoker, as it needs to be chilled overnight to facilitate thin slicing. Use a sharp, thin-bladed carving knife for slicing.

4
The classic way to reheat pastrami is over steam. If you prefer, reheat the slices in a microwave: spread the slices in a heatproof dish, sprinkle them with 2 tablespoons of water, cover the dish, and microwave at medium until they are hot, 3 to 5 minutes.

5
Leftovers will keep for about 5 days in the refrigerator. Smoked meats do not freeze well.

RED MEAT

BEEF DEBRIS PO'BOYS

SERVES: 6 | **PREP TIME:** 20 MINUTES | **GRILLING TIME:** 3¼ TO 4¼ HOURS
SPECIAL EQUIPMENT: 3 LARGE HANDFULS PECAN OR OAK WOOD CHIPS, LARGE (6-QUART) GRILL-PROOF DUTCH OVEN

1 chuck roast, about 3 pounds and
  2 inches thick
  Extra-virgin olive oil
  Kosher salt
  Freshly ground black pepper
1 can (14 ounces) low-sodium
  beef broth
½ cup hearty red wine
3 tablespoons tomato paste
2 tablespoons Worcestershire sauce
2 yellow onions, 1½ to 2 pounds total,
  cut into thin half-moons
8 large garlic cloves, coarsely chopped
2 teaspoons finely chopped fresh thyme
2 bay leaves
6 crusty, oblong French rolls or
  French sandwich rolls, split
  Mayonnaise
  Lettuce leaves
  Tomato slices

Let's face it: Debris is not a very appetizing word, even if it does sound French. In New Orleans parlance, it refers to a beef pot roast that is cooked until it is fall-apart tender, making the scrap-like pieces that inspire its name. The added smoke makes a good thing even better. Tuck the succulent meat (and the onions cooked along with it), into a crusty roll, and you have a po'boy sandwich fit for the sandwich gods. The story of po'boy is another colorful, and questionable, bit of culinary lore that supposedly started with sandwiches being handed out to unemployed poor workers during a strike.

1 Soak the wood chips in water for at least 30 minutes.

2 Brush the roast all over with 1 tablespoon oil and season evenly with salt and pepper. Allow the roast to stand at room temperature for 30 minutes before grilling.

3 Prepare the grill for direct cooking over high heat (450° to 550°F).

4 Drain and add two handfuls of the wood chips to the charcoal or to the smoker box of a gas grill, following manufacturer's instructions, and close the lid. When the wood begins to smoke, sear the roast over **direct high heat**, with the lid closed, until lightly browned, 8 to 10 minutes, turning once.

5 Reduce the temperature of the grill and prepare it for indirect cooking over medium heat (350° to 400°F). Slide the roast over **indirect medium heat** and continue cooking, with the lid closed, until it is more deeply browned, 25 to 30 minutes (do not turn).

6 Meanwhile, in a large bowl whisk the broth, wine, tomato paste, Worcestershire sauce, and 1 tablespoon oil until the tomato paste is dissolved. Add the onions, garlic, thyme, 1½ teaspoons salt, and ½ teaspoon pepper and mix well. Transfer half of the onion mixture, including about half of the liquid, to a large grill-proof Dutch oven. When the roast is browned, place it on the onions, and then top with the remaining onion mixture and liquid. Tuck the bay leaves into the liquid. Do not cover the Dutch oven at this point.

7 Drain and add the remaining wood chips to the charcoal or smoker box. Cook the roast in the Dutch oven over **indirect medium heat**, with the lid closed, until the onions begin to soften, 15 to 20 minutes. Tightly cover the Dutch oven with foil. Continue cooking, with the lid closed, until the roast is so tender that there is no resistance at all when a fork is inserted, 2½ to 3¼ hours, turning once.

8 Remove the Dutch oven from the grill, transfer the roast to a cutting board, and let stand for 5 minutes. If you wish, toast the rolls, cut side down, on the grill over direct heat, about 1 minute. Spread the rolls with mayonnaise as desired. Cut the roast across the grain into thick slices. Stir any "debris" that falls off back into the onions. Season the onion mixture and cooking juices with salt and pepper. Pile the beef, onion mixture, lettuce, and tomato on the rolls. Serve warm.

ANCHO BEEF AND BEAN CHILI

SERVES: 6 TO 8 | **PREP TIME:** 40 MINUTES
GRILLING TIME: 2 TO 2½ HOURS | **SPECIAL EQUIPMENT:** LARGE (6-QUART) GRILL-PROOF DUTCH OVEN

3 ancho chile peppers, about 1½ ounces total, stemmed and seeded
3 guajillo chile peppers, about ¾ ounce total, stemmed and seeded
1–1½ quarts low-sodium beef broth
1 chuck roast, about 3 pounds, trimmed and cut into 1-inch pieces
  Kosher salt
  Freshly ground black pepper
  Extra-virgin olive oil
1 white onion, about 12 ounces, finely chopped
4 garlic cloves, minced
2 tablespoons pure chile powder
1 tablespoon ground cumin
1 tablespoon paprika
2 teaspoons dried oregano
½ teaspoon ground allspice
3 tablespoons masa harina
2 cans (each 14 ounces) diced fire-roasted tomatoes in juice
2 cans (each 15 ounces) red kidney beans, rinsed and drained
1 ounce semisweet chocolate, chopped
  Chopped scallions
  Grated cheddar cheese
  Your favorite hot sauce

The origin of chili has long been debated, sometimes to a point of infuriation. Many legends point to the Incan, Aztec, and Mayan people as the first to make it, but even more stories center on cattle drivers and cowboys of the American West who popularized the dish. One thing that is fairly certain is that chili is essentially a stewed mixture of meat, peppers, herbs, spices, and, sometimes, beans. We can argue for days about who makes the best chili, or where it can be found, but the recipe right here is darn good, and you can make it right in your own backyard.

1 Bring a medium saucepan of water to a boil over high heat. Add the chile peppers, remove from the heat, and let stand until softened, about 30 minutes. Drain the chiles, transfer to a blender, and add 1 quart of broth. Puree and set aside.

2 Prepare the grill for direct cooking over medium-low heat (300° to 325°F) and preheat a large grill-proof Dutch oven, without its lid, for 10 minutes.

3 Season the meat with 1 teaspoon salt and ½ teaspoon pepper. Warm 1 tablespoon oil in the Dutch oven and add half of the meat. Cook over **direct medium-low heat**, with the grill lid closed, until lightly browned, about 5 minutes, stirring twice. Transfer the meat to a plate. Repeat with the remaining meat, adding another tablespoon of oil, if necessary.

4 Return all of the meat to the Dutch oven and stir in the onion and garlic. Close the grill lid and cook until the onion is slightly softened, 4 to 5 minutes. Stir in the chile powder, cumin, paprika, oregano, and allspice and cook until fragrant, about 1 minute, stirring to coat the meat evenly with the spices. Add the pureed chile mixture, masa harina, diced tomatoes and their juice, and ½ teaspoon salt. Put the lid on the Dutch oven, leaving it slightly ajar, close the grill lid, and adjust the temperature to **direct low heat** (250° to 300°F). Simmer the chili until the meat is fork tender, 1¾ to 2¼ hours, stirring occasionally with a metal spatula and loosening the chili from the bottom and sides of the Dutch oven as needed. Add more broth if the chili is becoming too thick, checking about every 20 minutes. Stir in the beans during the last 15 minutes of cooking time.

5 Wearing insulated barbecue mitts or gloves, carefully remove the lid of the Dutch oven and add the chocolate, stirring until it is melted, about 1 minute. Remove the chili from the grill and season with salt and pepper. Serve in bowls topped with scallions, cheese, and your favorite hot sauce.

It is no accident that three of the most significant, indigenous ingredients in Mexican food—corn, chiles, and chocolate—are featured in this Mexican-American recipe. Dried corn is the basis for masa harina, the ground mixture we use to thicken chili. Of course, the ancho and guajillo peppers give the chili its deep, spicy character, and the chocolate takes the edge off the spiciness and rounds out the flavors.

HICKORY-SMOKED PRIME RIB
WITH SHALLOT-CABERNET REDUCTION SAUCE

SERVES: 8 TO 10 | **PREP TIME:** 30 MINUTES, PLUS ABOUT 1 HOUR FOR THE SAUCE | **GRILLING TIME:** 2 TO 2½ HOURS
SPECIAL EQUIPMENT: 2 LARGE HANDFULS HICKORY WOOD CHIPS, BUTCHER'S TWINE, INSTANT-READ THERMOMETER

RUB

1½ tablespoons kosher salt
1 tablespoon ancho chile powder
2 teaspoons dried basil
1½ teaspoons paprika
1½ teaspoons ground cumin
1½ teaspoons freshly ground black pepper

1 prime rib roast with 3 bones, about 7 pounds

SAUCE

6 tablespoons (¾ stick) unsalted butter, divided
1½ cups finely chopped shallots (8 to 9 ounces)
6 garlic cloves, minced
1 large carrot, finely chopped
1 large rib celery, finely chopped
2 bay leaves
1 tablespoon fresh thyme leaves
1 bottle (750 ml) cabernet sauvignon or other dry red wine
2¼ cups low-sodium beef broth
1½ tablespoons tomato paste
½ teaspoon kosher salt
½ teaspoon freshly ground black pepper

Bring on the top-dollar barbecue and open your best bottle of wine or Scotch. The hardest part of making this dish is buying the groceries. After that, cut the bones off the meat so you can season more surface areas, make a decedent red wine sauce, and cook the beast with smoke until the internal temperature is just under 120°F. It will continue to cook off the heat, producing utterly luscious, rosy slices and meaty ribs with gorgeously charred crusts.

1. Soak the wood chips in water for at least 30 minutes.

2. Combine the rub ingredients. Using a sharp knife, cut between the rib bones and the meat, keeping the three bones together as one unit, and leaving about 2 inches of the meat attached to the bottom of the bones. Season the meaty side of the rib bones and the roast all over with the rub. Using butcher's twine, tie the rib bones back onto the roast in its original form (see photos below). Allow the roast to stand at room temperature for 1 hour before grilling.

3. In a large saucepan over medium-high heat on the stove, melt 2 tablespoons of the butter. Add the shallots, garlic, carrot, celery, bay leaves, and thyme and cook until slightly softened, 4 to 5 minutes, stirring occasionally. Add the wine, bring to a boil, and cook until the mixture resembles coarse, wet sand, 15 to 17 minutes. Add the broth and tomato paste, return to a boil, reduce the heat to medium, and simmer until reduced to 2½ cups, about 30 minutes. Remove the saucepan from the heat and pour the sauce through a fine-mesh strainer set over a medium bowl. Press on the solids with a spatula or large spoon to release the liquids. Discard the solids. Return the sauce to the saucepan and reserve.

4. Prepare the grill for indirect cooking over medium-low heat (as close to 350°F as possible).

5. Drain and add one handful of the wood chips to the smoker box of a gas grill, following manufacturer's instructions, and close the lid. When smoke appears, grill the roast, bone side down, over **indirect medium-low heat**, with the lid closed, until an instant-read thermometer inserted into the thickest part of the roast (not touching the bone) registers about 118°F for medium rare, 2 to 2½ hours. Drain and add the remaining wood chips to the smoker box after the first hour of grilling. Remove the roast from the grill.

6. Separate the roast from the rib section, cover the ribs and roast with foil, and let rest for 20 minutes (the internal temperature will rise 5 to 10 degrees during this time). Meanwhile, warm the sauce over medium heat on the stove until just hot. Remove the sauce from the heat and whisk in the remaining 4 tablespoons butter until just melted. Season the sauce with the salt and pepper.

7. Cut the roast into thick slices and cut between the bones to make three individual ribs. Serve immediately with the warm sauce.

RACKS OF LAMB
WITH MUSTARD-CAPER BOARD DRESSING

SERVES: 4 | **PREP TIME:** 20 MINUTES | **MARINATING TIME:** 3 TO 4 HOURS (OPTIONAL) | **GRILLING TIME:** 16 TO 20 MINUTES
SPECIAL EQUIPMENT: 2 LARGE HANDFULS MESQUITE WOOD CHIPS, INSTANT-READ THERMOMETER

2 lamb racks, each
    about 1½ pounds, frenched
    Extra-virgin olive oil
    Kosher salt
    Freshly ground black pepper
¾ teaspoon dried thyme, crumbled

BOARD DRESSING
¼ cup capers, drained and
    finely chopped
¼ cup finely chopped fresh Italian
    parsley leaves
2 tablespoons Dijon mustard
2 tablespoons plus 2 teaspoons
    brandy (optional)
2 tablespoons plus 2 teaspoons extra-
    virgin olive oil
1 tablespoon minced garlic
2 teaspoons red wine vinegar
1 teaspoon kosher salt
1 teaspoon freshly ground black pepper

My friend Adam Perry Lang first coined the term "board dressing" for the technique of assembling a handful of flavorful ingredients directly on a cutting board and then carving meat directly on top. The juices from the meat mingle together with the flavorings to create a dressing or sauce, and ingredients are almost infinitely variable. The technique, if not the name, has been surging in popularity among grill aficionados lately, so with this recipe I'll show you how it's done.

1 Soak the wood chips in water for at least 30 minutes.

2 Trim off most of the fat from the meaty side of the lamb racks, exposing the meat in a few places. Lightly coat both sides of the racks with oil and season generously with salt, pepper, and the thyme. If possible, refrigerate the racks, uncovered, for 3 to 4 hours. Allow the racks to stand at room temperature for 15 to 30 minutes before grilling.

3 Prepare the grill for direct cooking over medium-high heat (400° to 450°F).

4 Mound the board dressing ingredients in the center of a large cutting board and place it near the grill (place the cutting board inside a rimmed baking sheet, if desired).

5 Drain and add the wood chips to the charcoal or to the smoker box of a gas grill, following manufacturer's instructions, and close the lid. When smoke appears, grill the racks, meaty side down, over **direct medium-high heat**, with the lid closed, for 8 minutes, moving them around if flare-ups occur. Turn the racks over, bone side down, and then place a rectangle of foil underneath the bones to prevent them from burning. Continue grilling until the internal temperature reaches about 135°F and the meat is springy to the touch, 8 to 12 minutes more. To crisp the "eye" of the meat at either end, use tongs to hold the racks with the ends directly on the cooking grate for a few seconds.

6 Using a fork, blend the board dressing ingredients together and gather into an oval shape. Transfer the racks directly to the cutting board, meaty side down, right on top of the dressing. Let the meat rest for 3 minutes, and then cut into individual chops. Drag both sides of the chops through the board dressing. Serve warm.

When the lamb racks are cooked, immediately transfer them to the cutting board and let them rest for a few minutes so that the meat juices can meld with the board dressing ingredients. Then cut the racks into individual chops and dredge them through the dressing on both sides.

LAMB CHOPS
WITH MOROCCAN RUB AND TOMATO-GARBANZO SALAD

SERVES: 4 | **PREP TIME:** 25 MINUTES
GRILLING TIME: 8 TO 10 MINUTES

RUB
- 2 teaspoons pure chile powder
- 1 teaspoon kosher salt
- ½ teaspoon freshly ground black pepper
- ½ teaspoon ground coriander
- ½ teaspoon ground cumin
- ½ teaspoon caraway seed
- ¼ teaspoon garlic powder

- 2 lamb racks, each 1½ to 2 pounds, chine bones removed, frenched, and trimmed of excess fat and silver skin
  Extra-virgin olive oil

SALAD
- 1½ tablespoons fresh lemon juice
- ½ teaspoon kosher salt
- ¼ teaspoon freshly ground black pepper
- 1 can (14 ounces) garbanzo beans (chickpeas), rinsed and drained
- 8 ounces multicolored cherry tomatoes or grape tomatoes, each cut in half
- ¼ cup roughly chopped fresh basil leaves
  Sea salt
- 2 cups thinly sliced hearts of romaine

  Lemon wedges

Most lamb chops are just too thin and tiny for high heat. In the time it takes to char the outsides, the insides become overcooked. My recommendation is to scale back on the heat, buy whole racks of lamb, and cut them into double chops, each about 1½ inches thick. This method does require some work with a knife to remove the layer of fat covering the meaty side and the bones. You also need to methodically cut away the meat and fat between the bones.

1 Mix the rub ingredients.

2 For each rack of lamb, remove the thick cap of fat covering the chops by slipping a thin-bladed knife into the seam below it and pulling away the fat with your hands. Make one long crosswise cut over the top of the bones about 2 inches above the meaty center of each chop. Slip your knife under the thin layer of meat and fat clinging to the bones and pull off that layer with your hands. Cut out the individual strips of meat between the bones. Scrape the bones clean with the blade of your knife. Then cut each rack into four chops, each about 1½ inches thick and including two rib bones (see photos below).

3 Lightly brush the chops on both sides with oil and season evenly with the rub. Allow the chops to stand at room temperature for 15 to 30 minutes before grilling.

4 Prepare the grill for direct cooking over medium heat (350° to 450°F).

5 In a serving bowl whisk 3 tablespoons oil, the lemon juice, salt, and pepper. Add the garbanzo beans, tomatoes, and basil and mix well.

6 Grill the chops over **direct medium heat**, with the lid closed, until cooked to your desired doneness, 8 to 10 minutes for medium rare, turning four times to grill all sides (if flare-ups occur, move the chops temporarily over indirect heat). Remove the chops from the grill, season with sea salt, and let rest for 3 to 5 minutes.

7 Add the romaine to the salad and mix well. Serve the chops warm with the salad and lemon wedges.

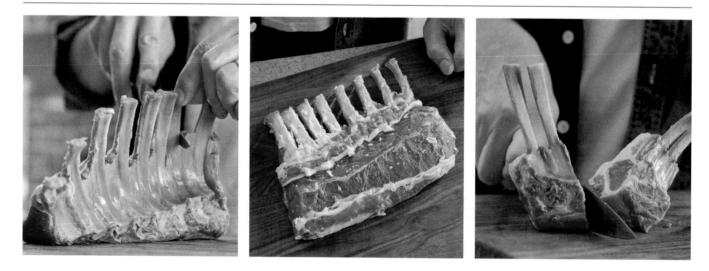

LAMB AND BELL PEPPER KABOBS
WITH PICKLE JAR MARINADE

SERVES: 4 TO 6 | **PREP TIME:** 25 MINUTES | **MARINATING TIME:** 4 TO 8 HOURS
GRILLING TIME: 8 TO 10 MINUTES | **SPECIAL EQUIPMENT:** 12 METAL OR BAMBOO SKEWERS

Don't let that brine in the pickle jar go to waste! It can make a terrific marinade that gives a boost to lamb. The amount of salt in brines tends to vary a lot from brand to brand, so taste the meat after cooking. If it needs a little more oomph, sprinkle some salt over the kabobs. When choosing the meat itself, it is helpful to know that top round lamb is a leaner, tenderer cut of meat than leg of lamb, but the leg meat will be more flavorful.

MARINADE
 1 cup brine from a jar of dill pickles
 1 red onion, 5 to 6 ounces, minced
 1 teaspoon caraway seed
 ½ teaspoon crushed red pepper flakes

 2 pounds top round lamb or
   boneless leg of lamb, cut into
   1- to 1½-inch pieces
 4 medium dill pickle halves, cut into
   1-inch chunks
 1 red bell pepper, cut into 1-inch pieces
   Kosher salt or sea salt

1 Whisk the marinade ingredients. Place the lamb pieces in a large, resealable plastic bag and pour in the marinade. Press the air out of the bag and seal tightly. Turn the bag to distribute the marinade, place the bag in a bowl, and refrigerate for 4 to 8 hours, turning the bag occasionally.

2 If using bamboo skewers, soak them in water for at least 30 minutes.

3 Prepare the grill for direct cooking over medium-high heat (400° to 450°F).

4 Remove the lamb pieces from the bag, leaving any spices on the meat. Discard the marinade. Thread the lamb pieces, pickle chunks, and bell pepper pieces alternately onto skewers, and then grill over **direct medium-high heat**, with the lid closed, until cooked to your desired doneness, 8 to 10 minutes for medium, turning occasionally. Remove from the grill and season with salt, if desired. Serve warm.

MESQUITE-SMOKED BEEF RIBS
WITH BEER MOP

SERVES: 4 TO 5 | **PREP TIME:** 15 MINUTES, PLUS ABOUT 20 MINUTES FOR THE MOP | **COOKING TIME:** 6 TO 7 HOURS
SPECIAL EQUIPMENT: WATER SMOKER, 4 LARGE HANDFULS MESQUITE WOOD CHUNKS

Beef back ribs are the unsung, underrated understudies of American barbecue. Everybody loves the star—beef short ribs (which aren't really short at all)—because they are so irresistibly meaty. Butchers cut beef back ribs off of prime rib roasts, almost always leaving most of the meat on the roasts and making the bones almost bare. If you ever meet an agreeable butcher, ask him to cut a couple racks of back ribs with meat at least one inch thick. Barbecue those Jurassic bones until the meat between the ribs is tender enough that you can slide a fork in and out with very little resistance.

2 racks beef back ribs, each 7 bones and 5 to 6 pounds, preferably meaty bones No. 6 through No. 12
2 tablespoons kosher salt
1 tablespoon freshly ground black pepper

MOP
2 cups tomato sauce
1 bottle (12 ounces) amber beer
¼ cup packed dark brown sugar
¼ cup yellow mustard
¼ cup cider vinegar
1 teaspoon ground cumin
½ teaspoon kosher salt
½ teaspoon ground cloves

1 Prepare the smoker for indirect cooking with very low heat (200° to 250°F), filling the water pan about three-fourths of the way with water.

2 Peel off the thin membrane on the underside of each rack of ribs. Rub the salt and pepper into the meat on both sides of the racks.

3 When the smoker reaches 250°F, add the wood chunks to the charcoal. Set the beef racks on the cooking grate bone side down, and cook over **indirect very low heat**, with the lid closed, for 3 hours.

4 Meanwhile, in a heavy, medium saucepan over medium-high heat on the stove, whisk the mop ingredients until the brown sugar is dissolved. Bring to a boil, reduce the heat to low, and

simmer slowly until reduced to about half the original volume, 15 to 20 minutes, stirring occasionally with a wooden spoon.

5 After 3 hours, mop the ribs all over, and then continue cooking over **indirect very low heat**, with the lid closed, until you can slide a fork in and out of the meat with very little resistance, 3 to 4 hours more, mopping every hour. Maintain a steady, even temperature between 200° and 250°F for the duration of the cooking time.

6 Remove the racks from the smoker, tent with foil, and let rest for 10 to 15 minutes. Cut the racks between the bones so there is plenty of meat on both sides of each rib. Serve warm.

KOREAN SHORT RIB TACOS
WITH KOGI SAUCE AND PICKLED CUCUMBERS

SERVES: 6 | **PREP TIME:** 30 MINUTES | **PICKLING TIME:** 1 HOUR
MARINATING TIME: 24 HOURS | **GRILLING TIME:** 4 TO 6 MINUTES

MARINADE
6 garlic cloves
1 Granny Smith apple, about 8 ounces, cored and cut into quarters
1 yellow onion, about 6 ounces, cut into quarters
1 piece fresh ginger, about 2 inches long, peeled and coarsely chopped
1 cup soy sauce
½ cup packed light brown sugar
¼ cup Asian rice wine or sherry
2 tablespoons toasted sesame oil
1 teaspoon freshly ground black pepper
½ teaspoon ground cayenne pepper

3 pounds flanken-style beef short ribs

PICKLED CUCUMBERS
1 English cucumber, about 12 ounces, very thinly sliced
1 red jalapeño chile pepper, finely chopped
2 tablespoons unseasoned rice vinegar
1 teaspoon kosher salt
½ teaspoon granulated sugar

KOGI SAUCE (see headnote*)
¼ cup *gochujang* (Korean fermented hot pepper paste)
¼ cup soy sauce
3 tablespoons granulated sugar
1 tablespoon toasted sesame oil
2 teaspoons unseasoned rice vinegar

1 large head butter lettuce, leaves separated
12 flour tortillas
½ cup fresh cilantro leaves

Korean-American chefs like Roy Choi (in Los Angeles), David Chang (in New York City), and Edward Lee (in Louisville) have made it cool and modern to reimagine tacos and introduce words like gochujang (ko-chew-jang) into barbecue conversations. A thick paste of red chiles, fermented soy beans, and glutinous rice, gochujang (see photo, facing page, top left) is a key ingredient in kogi sauce, which we might as well call a Korean barbecue sauce because of its spicy-sweet-salty nature and its affinity for charred meat. If you are unable to find gochujang, squeeze a little Sriracha sauce just by itself on these tacos.*

1 In a food processor combine the garlic, apple, onion, and ginger and process until finely chopped. Add the remaining marinade ingredients and process until pureed and well blended. Place the short ribs in a large, resealable plastic bag and pour in the marinade. Press the air out of the bag and seal tightly. Turn the bag to distribute the marinade, place in a bowl, and refrigerate for 24 hours, turning the bag occasionally. Allow the ribs to stand at room temperature for 30 minutes before grilling.

2 In a medium bowl combine the pickled cucumber ingredients and stir to combine. Let stand at room temperature for 1 hour.

3 If you are using *gochujang*, whisk the kogi sauce ingredients.

4 Prepare the grill for direct cooking over high heat (450° to 550°F).

5 Remove the ribs from the bag and discard the marinade. Grill the ribs over **direct high heat**, with the lid closed, until charred, caramelized, and cooked to medium rare, 4 to 6 minutes (depending on the thickness of the ribs), turning once. Remove from the grill and let rest for 3 to 5 minutes. Remove the bones and cut the meat crosswise into thin slices.

6 Arrange a lettuce leaf on a tortilla. Top with meat, pickled cucumbers, kogi sauce (or Sriracha), and cilantro. Roll up and eat.

NEW MEXICO SHORT RIBS

SERVES: 6 | **PREP TIME:** 30 MINUTES
GRILLING TIME: 3½ TO 4 HOURS | **SPECIAL EQUIPMENT:** LARGE (6-QUART) GRILL-PROOF DUTCH OVEN

4 pounds bone-in beef short ribs, cut into 3- to 4-inch pieces

3 tablespoons extra-virgin olive oil

BRAISING SAUCE

5 slices thick-cut bacon, chopped

2 cups packed chopped red onion

2 green bell peppers, about 1 pound total, chopped

1 tablespoon chopped canned chipotle chile peppers in adobo sauce

1 tablespoon adobo sauce (from the can)

2 teaspoons minced garlic

2 tablespoons pure chile powder, preferably New Mexico

1 tablespoon smoked paprika

2 teaspoons dried oregano

2 teaspoons ground cumin

1¼ teaspoons kosher salt

½ teaspoon freshly ground black pepper

1 can (28 ounces) crushed tomatoes in juice

1 bottle (12 ounces) amber beer

⅔ cup fresh orange juice

2 tablespoons packed finely grated orange zest

In Texas they barbecue whole racks of beef plate ribs with a peppery bark. In New Mexico you are more likely to see those racks cut into blocks that are slowly braised in moist heat. By browning the short ribs right over direct heat and then braising them in a pot to the side of the hot coals, you create a smoky supper full of the flavors of the American Southwest. Tortillas would be a nice, natural accompaniment. Rice and beans would also go well with this meat. Or you might want to set the ribs on a soft bed of mashed potatoes and let the braising juices trickle onto the plate.

1 Prepare the grill for direct and indirect cooking over medium heat (350° to 400°F).

2 Generously brush the short ribs all over with the oil, and then grill over **direct medium heat**, with the lid closed, until browned, about 10 minutes, turning occasionally. Move the short ribs over indirect heat and prepare the braising sauce.

3 Place a large grill-proof Dutch oven over **direct medium heat**. Add the bacon to the Dutch oven, close the grill lid, and fry until browned, 6 to 7 minutes, stirring occasionally. Add the onion and bell peppers and cook until softened, 8 to 9 minutes, stirring often (don't allow the temperature of the grill to go over 400°F). Stir in the chipotle chile pepper, adobo sauce, and garlic and cook for 1 minute. Add the chile powder, paprika, oregano, cumin, salt, and pepper, stirring until aromatic, about 20 seconds. Pour in the tomatoes, beer, and orange juice. Scrape up any browned bits on the bottom of the Dutch oven.

4 Transfer the short ribs to the Dutch oven, stir well, and bring to a full boil over **direct medium heat**, raising the heat, if necessary, to bring the liquid to a boil. Cover the Dutch oven and slide it over indirect heat. Reduce the temperature of the grill to low heat (about 300°F), and cook over **indirect low heat**, with the lid closed, until the meat is very tender, 3 to 3½ hours (if the ingredients seem to be getting dry, stir in ½ cup water every hour). Remove the Dutch oven from the grill and stir in the orange zest. Let rest for 10 minutes, and then skim off the fat from the top of the sauce. Serve warm with rice and beans, wrapped in tortillas, or over mashed potatoes.

CENTRAL TEXAS BEEF SHORT RIBS

SERVES: 6 TO 8 | PREP TIME: 15 MINUTES | COOKING TIME: 6 TO 7 HOURS | RESTING TIME: 1 TO 2 HOURS
SPECIAL EQUIPMENT: WATER SMOKER; 4 LARGE HANDFULS MESQUITE OR OAK WOOD CHUNKS; SPRAY BOTTLE FILLED WITH WATER; INSTANT-READ THERMOMETER; DRY, INSULATED COOLER

RUB
1 tablespoon plus 2 teaspoons coarsely ground black pepper
1 tablespoon kosher salt
2 teaspoons granulated garlic

2 racks beef short (plate) ribs, 4 bones per rack, each 4 to 4½ pounds and meat about 2 inches thick, trimmed of excess fat

This recipe comes straight out of an epic day I spent with third-generation pit master Wayne Mueller at Louie Mueller Barbecue in Taylor, Texas. He makes the greatest beef ribs I've ever tasted. Period.

1 Mix the rub ingredients, and then season the racks with the rub, putting almost all of it on the meaty side.

2 Prepare the smoker for indirect cooking with low heat (275° to 300°F). Fill the water pan about halfway with water. When the temperature reaches 275°F, add the wood chunks to the charcoal.

3 Cook the racks, bone side down, using the upper and lower cooking grates of the smoker, if needed, over **indirect low heat**, with the lid closed, for 6 to 7 hours. After the first 3 hours, spray each rack a few times with water and swap their positions, if using both grates, putting the rack that was on the top grate on the bottom grate and vice versa. Continue cooking over **indirect low heat**, with the lid closed, until the racks are so tender that the probe of a thermometer slides through the meat between the bones with very little resistance. When you press the meat with your fingertips, it should feel as soft as a marshmallow. The internal temperature in the thickest part of the meat should be about 200°F, but the tenderness of the meat is much more important than the temperature. Spray each rack one more time with water. Wrap each rack individually in three layers of plastic wrap, and transfer to a dry, insulated cooler for 1 to 2 hours.

4 Unwrap the racks and cut between the bones into individual ribs. Serve warm. (Texans serve them without sauce.)

LOUIE MUELLER BARBECUE ▼

The keys to Mueller's jaw-dropping results are not so much in a recipe as they are in understanding fire and thermal dynamics. He doesn't teach his restaurant cooks how many tablespoons of this or that to use; he teaches them how to stoke a proper fire and how to retain temperatures and humidity for consistency day after day. He teaches them how green wood burns differently than seasoned or cured wood. As he said to me, "The hardest thing I do is to train people to be human thermostats. Apparently small, innocuous changes in the pits with things like wind speed, wind direction, barometric pressure, and humidity will affect the way meat cooks—and so will what a cook did last night for fun. Barbecue is a matter of controlling all those variables with an intuition that you can only acquire with experience." Mueller did, nevertheless, share some words of wisdom that all of us can use right away:

1 *In the beef short rib world, we have two distinct choices: There's the chuck rib, which is close to the shoulder of a steer. Then there's the plate rib, a rack a little lower on the steer and about 50% larger than the chuck rib. Its meat-to-bone ratio is much higher than that of chuck ribs. That's why Mueller cooks plate ribs.*

2 *He seasons the plate ribs with salt and pepper only, but more coarse ground pepper than you would think. He uses a ratio of 9:1 (pepper:salt).*

3 *He leaves the membrane on the racks and cooks them bone side down for the entire time (6 to 7 hours). At his restaurant, a wood fire of post oak burns at one end of a long, horizontal pit made of bricks and metal. The hot smoke flows horizontally over the top of the meat, right where he wants it. Occasionally he turns a rack 90 degrees to face it into the stream of heat, giving a particular side a bit more of a thermal blast, although the overall temperature in his pit never gets above 300°F.*

STAGING A COMEBACK WITH
LAMB AND BISON

Colorado

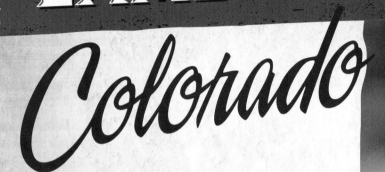

Colorado newspapers from the late 1800s and early 1900s regaled their readers with tales of "monster"—their way of saying "awesome"—barbecues where up to 30,000 people gorged on an eclectic buffet of domesticated livestock and wild game. Of this bounty, the locals held a special place in their hearts and mouths for American bison (mistakenly called "buffalo") and Colorado-raised lamb. Later pushed off barbecue restaurant menus by beef, pork, and poultry, bison and lamb are now poised to recapture their glory.

"We feature bison because my tribe is a Plains tribe (the Osage Nation), and bison was our main protein," explains Ben Jacobs, co-owner of Tocabe, an American Indian eatery in Denver. The ribs are seasoned with a dry rub, refrigerated for 24 hours, and then seared on a hot grill, six to seven minutes per side. Next, the meat is slotted upright in a rib rack, placed in a pan half-filled with a bison stock or stout beer, covered with foil, roasted for two hours in a 425°F oven, and quickly seared again on a smoky grill for a couple of minutes before serving. As a nod to the traditional condiment used by Jacobs' ancestors, Tocabe pairs its bison ribs with a seasonal berry barbecue sauce of blackberries, blueberries, or huckleberries.

Colorado's wildest barbecued bison ambassador was the late Sam'l P. Arnold (1926–2006), who meticulously researched historical sources before opening up The Fort Restaurant in Morrison, Colorado; this iconic restaurant, opened in 1963, served up traditional American West cuisine. Executive chef Randy Savala now tends The Fort's smoker and notes that the restaurant has served bison ribs consistently for the last 10 years. "We use hickory for the wood and also a hickory-based liquid smoke to finish off the process," says Savala. "We smoke our ribs for 10 hours at 205°F, and then finish them off when ordered in a 425°F oven for eight minutes to get them hot. We also put our [whiskey] barbecue sauce on them during the finishing process. It seals in the flavor and doesn't dry them out." Savala advises home cooks to treat bison like beef and start by finding the right rub. In this case "right" means black and white. "We only use salt and pepper before the smoking process because bison is sweeter than beef. We want to stand behind the product and not overpower it with a rub."

Chef Coy Webb had "something different" in mind in 2014 when he opened Roaming Buffalo Bar-B-Que in Denver. "I grew up raising sheep on a Texas farm, and I was introduced to Colorado lamb while cooking in New Mexico. When I moved to Denver and decided to open up a barbecue joint, I wanted a place that would reflect my rustic cowboy heritage and show a unique part of Colorado history." Along with beef, pork, and poultry, Webb settled on a barbecue menu that showcases bison short ribs, lamb shanks, and lamb shoulder. Depending on the size of the cut of meat and how much meat is on the bone, Webb cooks the bison short ribs for 5 to 7 hours, the lamb shoulder for 14 to 16 hours, and the lamb shanks for 4½ hours at a temperature between 215°F to 240°F. Webb uses a pecan wood blend, and recommends the same (or some other mellow wood) to cooks who want to try bison and lamb at home.

BRISKET

Aaron Franklin is the brightest star in the barbecue galaxy right now. Cooking at a joint that he opened in a trailer by Interstate 35 in Austin, Texas, he recently won the James Beard Award for Best Chef: Southwest (2015). Almost every day barbecue fanatics from all over the country (and the world) line up along a concrete sidewalk, through a parking lot, and up a residential street for several hours before the joint opens its doors. They eat with frenzied delight, sending selfies with Franklin's food all over the Internet and blogosphere, fueling even more Franklin Barbecue mania.

When I sat down with Franklin, I asked him straight up: What is barbecue, anyway? His response was a little surprising: "By definition, barbecue is anything cooked on live fire. Real simple. It could be grilling. It could be a hot dog. Hot dogs are cool. They take a few minutes. But to me barbecue is a soulful investment of time and love. It means something. On a personal level, I think of long-cooked meats and logs of wood. Here in Central Texas we have a pretty hard-core German-Czech scene going on, so I have tunnel vision about our style of barbecue .... If other people want to think of barbecue as something else, that's cool .... People should make barbecue however they like."

A brisket is two muscles held together in one big hunk of meat that happens to be from the chest of the cow, so those muscles grow mighty tough while bearing a lot of weight and moving around the feedlot. The first muscle is the "point" (sometimes called "deckle"), which is a relative fatty section shown here between my hands.

Then there is the flat, a lean rectangular slab of beef that sits under the point and extends all the way to the opposite side of a brisket. A fundamental challenge in cooking brisket is getting two different cuts of meat to cook well in the same length of time. It's a little like getting the dark meat and light meat of a turkey to cook just right—only much more difficult.

One way of helping yourself is to buy brisket with a flat section that is nice and thick all the way to the skinny end. If the brisket tapers down to thinner than an inch, forget it. That thin meat will dry out long before the rest of the brisket is done. Another consideration is the overall size and weight. If you cook anything less than about 10 pounds, you are asking for trouble. You want something big enough that it can stay on the smoker long enough to melt a brisket's impressive amount of collagen to gelatin. Ideally, you will find a "whole packer" in the range of 12 to 16 pounds.

TRIMMING

Franklin advises that as you trim your brisket you should try to imagine how smoke and heat will flow over it on your smoker. The meat should be aerodynamic, without any odd sections protruding into the airflow and potentially drying out or burning. For this reason, he cuts away more meat than most people. He cuts off long strips of meat, an inch or so wide, along the two longest sides of the brisket. At the end of the flat, he rounds off the corners like the bumpers of a sports car.

A thick layer of fat covers one entire side of a brisket. You need to trim that fat to an even thickness about ¼ inch, but no less. Otherwise the smoke can't penetrate very well.

Make sure you trim down any hard fat along the side of the brisket, and if you see any grayish meat in that area (a sign that area was sitting too long in its own juices), cut it off, too.

On the underside of the brisket, slip a thin-bladed knife under any thin sections of fat and silver skin clinging to the meat, and remove them.

With this side facing up, you should also see a big chunk of fat where the point and flat meet on one side. Cut that chunk off—it's too big and thick to render (melt).

SEASONINGS

A brisket will spend anywhere from 10 to 16 hours in a smoker, during which time ½ teaspoon of cumin or mustard powder or whatever spice you like would be overwhelmed (and essentially wasted) by all the smoke, so stick with two or three basic seasonings. In true Central Texas style, Franklin uses equal parts kosher salt and coarsely ground black pepper sprinkled lightly over all sides of the meat.

BEGINNER BRISKET

SERVES: 10 | **PREP TIME:** 30 MINUTES
COOKING TIME: 6 TO 7 HOURS | **RESTING TIME:** 2 TO 3 HOURS
SPECIAL EQUIPMENT: WATER SMOKER; SPRAY BOTTLE FILLED WITH WATER; 6 TO 8 LARGE
HANDFULS MESQUITE, OAK, OR APPLE WOOD CHUNKS; INSTANT-READ THERMOMETER;
HEAVY-DUTY ALUMINUM FOIL; DRY, INSULATED COOLER

To cook a brisket of 14 pounds or so, you are looking at about 16 hours from start to finish. Understanding that you may not always have that kind of time available, I wanted to give you a relatively easy recipe that you can start in the morning and enjoy by dinnertime. So here it is. It calls for a fairly small brisket (10 to 12 pounds) that is on the smoker for 6 to 7 hours and then in an insulated cooler for 2 to 3 hours. It may not produce the ultimate brisket, but it should be very satisfying. If you find that your slices in the flat are a little dry, that's not uncommon. Even the barbecue pros get dry slices occasionally. You can still enjoy the flat by chopping it up with some of the moist meat from the point and serving it on buns, maybe with some barbecue sauce for extra flavor and moisture.

After about 4 hours of cooking, the brisket should have a nice dark crust on the surface. This is when you should remove it from the smoker, spritz it with water on all sides, and wrap it tightly in heavy-duty aluminum foil. Put it back on the smoker until it is as tender as a marshmallow. This usually happens when the internal temperature reaches 195° to 205°F, but not always. When the meat is soft, move your brisket to a dry, insulated cooler to rest for 2 to 3 hours. Do not skip this last step. It is crucial for helping the muscles relax.

1 whole, untrimmed beef brisket, including both the flat and point sections, 10 to 12 pounds
⅓ cup kosher salt
¼ cup freshly ground black pepper
2 cups your favorite barbecue sauce
10 hamburger buns, split

1   Using a very sharp knife, trim the fat on the fatty side of the brisket so that it is about ¼ inch, but no less. On the meatier side, remove the web-like membrane so that the coarsely grained meat underneath is visible. Be sure to remove any hard clumps of fat on either side of the brisket.

2 Mix the salt and pepper, and then rub the brisket evenly on all sides with the seasoning. Refrigerate the brisket until ready to cook.

3 Prepare a smoker for indirect cooking with very low heat (about 225°F).

4 Spray the brisket on both sides with water to make the surface wet. Add half of the wood chunks to the charcoal. When smoke appears, place the brisket, fat side down, on the top cooking grate, close the lid, and cook over *indirect very low heat* until it has a nice dark crust on the surface, usually about 4 hours. After the first hour, add the remaining wood chunks to the charcoal. The surface color of the meat is your indication that you have created a good "bark" and the brisket will no longer absorb much smoke, so it is time to wrap it. Color is the primary indication of this, but you should also check the internal temperature

of the meat now. It should be somewhere between 150° and 160°F in the thickest part of the meat.

5 Remove the brisket from the smoker, spray it on both sides with water, and double or triple wrap it tightly with heavy-duty aluminum foil.

6 Place the wrapped brisket, fat side down, on the top grate of the smoker and continue cooking over *indirect very low heat*, with the lid closed, until the meat is so tender that when you press it with your fingers through the foil it feels like a giant marshmallow and the internal temperature is 195° to 205°F, 2 to 3 hours more (tenderness is a more important indicator of doneness than temperature). The amount of time required will depend on the particular breed of cattle and other characteristics of the meat.

7 Transfer the brisket, still wrapped in foil, to a dry, insulated cooler. Close the cooler and let the meat rest for 2 to 3 hours.

8 Unwrap the brisket and set it on a cutting board, being careful to keep the precious meat juices in the foil.

9 Warm the barbecue sauce over medium heat on the stove for about 5 minutes. Cut the brisket across the grain into thin slices and serve with as much or as little sauce as you like. If desired, add the meat juices to the sauce. If the meat from the flat is a little dry, coarsely chop it and mix with as much sauce as you like. Serve warm on buns.

BARBECUED BRISKET
WITH DALMATIAN RUB

SERVES: 10 TO 12 | **PREP TIME:** 30 MINUTES | **COOKING TIME:** 8 TO 10 HOURS | **RESTING TIME:** 2 TO 3 HOURS
SPECIAL EQUIPMENT: 3 LARGE HANDFULS MESQUITE AND 3 APPLE/CHERRY WOOD CHUNKS; WATER SMOKER; SPRAY BOTTLE FILLED WITH WATER; INSTANT-READ THERMOMETER; EXTRA-LARGE, HEAVY-DUTY ALUMINUM FOIL ROASTING PAN; DRY, INSULATED COOLER

If you aspire to make a really good brisket, seek out a piece of meat you can trust and season it simply with salt and pepper (aka Dalmatian rub). Rather than taking your chances with a small brisket of questionable quality, look for a larger one from a reputable brand like Certified Angus Beef, raised to meet higher standards of taste and tenderness. You may need to go to a specialty meat market or ask your butcher to special order the brisket for you, but a top-quality cut will improve your chances of success more than any other single step.

RUB
- ¼ cup kosher salt
- 3 tablespoons freshly ground black pepper
- 3 tablespoons turbinado sugar (optional)

- 1 whole, untrimmed beef packer cut brisket, including both the flat and point sections, 12 to 14 pounds
- ½ cup beef broth

After spending 12+ hours preparing your brisket, it's important to cut it properly, that is, against the grain (as much as possible) so that it is tender. I follow the method that I learned at Franklin Barbecue. Set the brisket on your board with the point facing up. Start making slices crosswise about ¼ inch thick on the flat end (see photo, top left). When you reach the part of the flat where it meets the point, stop and set the slices aside, held firmly together so they do not dry out. Now, rotate the remaining brisket 90 degrees so that the side you were just slicing is facing away from you. Cut this piece in half (see photo, top right). You will know that you have done a good job of cooking the brisket if the band of fat and collagen running between the flat and point is nicely softened and the meat looks juicy (see photo, bottom left). Now you can start slicing each half a little thicker than the slices from the flat (see photo, bottom right). Remember not to cut the meat until you are ready to serve it. It stays warmer and juicier when it is uncut.

1 Combine the rub ingredients.

2 Using a very sharp knife, trim the fat on the fatty side of the brisket so that it is aboutabout ¼ inch, but no less. On the meatier side, remove the web-like membrane so that the coarsely grained meat underneath is visible. Be sure to remove any hard clumps of fat on either side of the brisket. Try to round off the corners of the brisket and make them as aerodynamic as possible. Also, if you notice any grayish corners or areas, trim those off.

3 Season the brisket evenly on all sides, even the narrow sides, with the rub. Cover and refrigerate the brisket until ready to cook, up to one day ahead.

4 Prepare the smoker for indirect cooking with very low heat (about 225°F and no higher).

5 Add the wood chunks to the charcoal. When smoke appears, spray the brisket on the top and bottom with water to make the surface damp (not wet). Place the brisket, fat side down, on the top cooking grate and close the lid. Cook over **indirect very low heat**, with the lid closed, until

the surface looks like the photo below, usually 4 to 5 hours. The surface color of the meat is your indication that you have created a good "bark" and the brisket will no longer absorb much smoke, so it is time to cover it. Color is the primary indication of this, but you should also check the internal temperature in the thickest part of the meat now. It should be somewhere between 150° and 160°F.

6 Remove the brisket from the smoker and place it fat side down in an extra-large, heavy-duty aluminum foil roasting pan. Pour the broth over the brisket. Cover the pan tightly with foil and return the brisket in the covered pan to the smoker. Try to adjust the temperature of the smoker a bit lower, somewhere between 210° and 220°F, and continue cooking until the meat is so tender that when you press it with your fingers through the foil it feels like a giant marshmallow. This will probably take 4 to 5 hours more. Brisket is done when it is done, so it's a good rule of thumb to check the brisket hourly for both tenderness and temperature. The internal temperature should reach 195° to 205°F, although tenderness is a more important indicator of doneness than the temperature. The amount of time required will depend on the particular breed of cattle and other characteristics of the meat.

7 Transfer the brisket, still covered with foil in the roasting pan, to a dry, insulated cooler. Close the cooler and let the meat rest for 2 to 3 hours. Don't skip this step; it will really help loosen the muscles.

8 Uncover the brisket and transfer to a cutting board, being careful to keep the precious meat juices in the pan. Then very carefully transfer the meat juices to a small bowl. If you notice that the color of the brisket is not very dark, give it a couple of minutes out of the foil. The oxygen will help turn the outer color nice and dark. Cut the brisket across the grain into thin slices. Dip each slice into the meat juices. Serve the brisket warm, with any extra juices drizzled on top.

AMERICAN KOBE BRISKET
WITH BURNT ENDS

SERVES: 10 TO 12 | PREP TIME: 30 MINUTES | COOKING TIME: 10 TO 12 HOURS | RESTING TIME: 2 TO 3 HOURS
SPECIAL EQUIPMENT: EXTRA-LARGE, HEAVY-DUTY ALUMINUM FOIL ROASTING PAN; WATER SMOKER;
6 LARGE HANDFULS CHERRY WOOD CHUNKS; INSTANT-READ THERMOMETER; HEAVY-DUTY ALUMINUM FOIL;
DRY, INSULATED COOLER; LARGE DISPOSABLE FOIL PAN

The sport of barbecue has grown so intense and lucrative lately that some competitive barbecue teams are willing to shell out big bucks for super-premium meats like American-style Kobe. The name Kobe refers to a certain strain of Wagyu cattle raised in the Kobe region of Japan. In America some ranchers are crossbreeding Japanese Wagyu cattle with Angus cattle to produce an American-style Kobe beef with intensely marbled flesh and complex flavors. This quality of brisket (see photo below) is what competitors are buying from companies like Snake River Farms in the Pacific Northwest.

1 whole, untrimmed Wagyu beef
packer cut brisket, including both
the flat and point sections,
12 to 14 pounds
¼ cup Worcestershire sauce

RUB
¼ cup kosher salt
2 tablespoons paprika
1 tablespoon granulated onion
1 tablespoon ground cayenne pepper
1 tablespoon freshly ground
black pepper

SAUCE (optional)
1 cup your favorite barbecue sauce
1 cup low-sodium beef broth

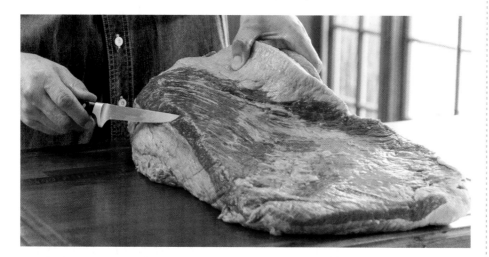

Years ago burnt ends were the crispy, fatty odds and ends of a brisket that pit masters in Kansas City would set aside on the cutting board because they weren't worthy to sell. Nowadays customers pay more for mouthwatering burnt ends and competitors often try to impress judges with meticulously chosen cubes of meat dressed with sauce. The finest part of the brisket for burnt ends is the fatty point. Separate that first from the flat by cutting diagonally under the point and over the flat (see photo, left). Cut the point into long strips about 1 inch thick, and then cut the strips into 1-inch cubes (see photo, right). Toss those in a small pan with a little sauce and barbecue them for an hour or so longer, until the sauce caramelizes on the surface and the burnt ends look good enough to win a trophy.

1   Using a very sharp knife, trim the fat on the fatty side of the brisket so that it is about ¼ inch, but no less On the meatier side, remove the web-like membrane so that the coarsely grained meat underneath is visible. If the thin end (tip) of the flat section is thinner than 1 inch, trim that off so that the thin end is now at least 1 inch thick. Be sure to remove any hard clumps of fat on either side of the brisket. Try to round off the corners of the brisket and make them as aerodynamic as possible. Also, if you notice any grayish corners or areas, trim those off.

2   Place the brisket in an extra-large, heavy-duty aluminum foil roasting pan. Spread the Worcestershire sauce all over the brisket. Mix the rub ingredients, and then season the brisket evenly on all sides with the rub. Cover and refrigerate the brisket until ready to cook, up to one day before.

3 Prepare the smoker for indirect cooking with very low heat (about 250°F).

4 Add half of the wood chunks to the charcoal. When smoke appears, take the brisket out of the foil roasting pan, place it, fat side down, on the top grate, and close the lid. Set aside the foil roasting pan. Cook the brisket over **indirect very low heat**, with the lid closed, until the surface is very dark brown, usually about 6 hours. After the first hour, add the remaining wood chunks to the charcoal. The surface color of the meat is your indication that you have created a good "bark" and the brisket will no longer absorb much smoke.

5 Place the brisket, fat side down, back in the foil roasting pan. Cover the pan tightly with foil and continue cooking until the meat is so tender that when you

press it with your fingers through the foil it feels like a giant marshmallow. This will probably take 4 to 6 hours more. Brisket is done when it is done, so it's a good rule of thumb to check the brisket hourly for both tenderness and temperature. Be patient! The internal temperature should reach 195° to 205°F, although tenderness is a more important indicator of doneness than the temperature.

6 Transfer the brisket, still covered with foil in the roasting pan, to a dry, insulated cooler. Close the cooler and let the meat rest for 2 to 3 hours. Don't skip this step; it will really help loosen the muscles.

7 If you want to serve the brisket with a sauce, mix the barbecue sauce and broth in a saucepan and bring to a simmer over medium heat on the stove, stirring often.

8 Transfer the brisket to a cutting board, being careful to keep the precious meat juices in the pan (if desired, you can add the meat juices to the sauce, if using). Remove the brisket flat from the point (see photo, facing page, bottom left). Return the flat to the roasting pan, cover the pan with foil, and place it back in the cooler to keep warm. Cut the point into 1- or 2-inch cubes. Arrange them in a single layer in a large disposable foil pan. If desired, pour enough of the sauce over them to coat them lightly. Set the pan, uncovered, back on the smoker and cook for about 1 hour more.

9 When ready to serve, unwrap the flat and cut it across the grain into slices about as thick as a No. 2 pencil. Serve the brisket slices and burnt ends warm with the sauce (if using) or with the meat juices.

SAN ANTONIO BRISKET ENCHILADAS

SERVES: 4 TO 8 | **PREP TIME:** 1 HOUR | **GRILLING TIME:** ABOUT 40 MINUTES
SPECIAL EQUIPMENT: 13-BY-9-INCH GRILL-PROOF BAKING PAN; NONSTICK ALUMINUM FOIL

SAUCE

- 7 dried New Mexican chile peppers, stemmed and seeded
- 4 dried mulato chile peppers, stemmed and seeded (see caption and photo below)
- 5 tomatoes, about 1½ pounds total, each cut in half
- 1 large yellow or white onion, cut crosswise into ½-inch slices
- 2 tablespoons extra-virgin olive oil
- 1 medium garlic clove
- 1 teaspoon Mexican dried leaf oregano
- 1 teaspoon ground cumin
- ½ teaspoon ground cinnamon
- ½ teaspoon kosher salt
- ½ teaspoon freshly ground black pepper

- 1¼ pounds shredded smoked beef brisket
- 4 ounces grated pepper jack cheese
- 8 flour tortillas (8 inch)
- 6 ounces grated mild cheddar cheese
- 4–8 large eggs
  Sour cream (optional)
- 2 scallions, thinly sliced

What are you going to do with leftover brisket? Do like they do in San Antonio, Texas, and make enchiladas, a combination of Tex-Mex cuisine and Southwestern barbecue that is a local point of pride. The key is that the brisket must be quite tender—in fact, shreddable with a fork. If you are using leftover brisket that's more suitable for slicing than shredding, spray the whole chunk with water, wrap it in aluminum foil, and set the packet on the grate over indirect medium heat until the meat shreds easily with a fork (1 hour or so).

1 Break up the dried chile peppers and put them in a large bowl. Cover with boiling water and set aside to soak for 20 minutes. Drain in a colander set over a bowl, catching and reserving the soaking liquid.

2 Prepare the grill for direct and indirect cooking over medium heat (350° to 450°F).

3 Brush the tomato halves and onion slices with the oil, and then grill over **direct medium heat**, with the lid closed, until charred and softened, 10 to 12 minutes, turning once or twice.

4 Place the tomatoes, half of the onion slices, the drained chile peppers, garlic, oregano, cumin, cinnamon, salt, and pepper in a blender. Cover and blend until smooth, adding just enough of the reserved soaking liquid to make a thick sauce. Strain the sauce through a medium-mesh strainer into a medium bowl.

5 Roughly chop the remaining onion slices and put in a large bowl. Add the shredded brisket and pepper jack cheese and toss to combine.

6 Spread ½ cup of the sauce on the bottom of a 13-by-9-inch grill-proof baking pan. Lay out all the tortillas on a work surface and brush each with 2 tablespoons of the sauce. Then place ½ cup of the brisket mixture in a line down the center of each tortilla. Roll up the tortillas fairly tight and place them close together, seam side down, in the prepared baking pan so they are parallel to the short end of the pan. Pour the remaining sauce over the enchiladas and then distribute the cheddar cheese evenly on top. Cover with a large sheet of nonstick aluminum foil and seal the edges tightly all around the pan.

7 Cook the enchiladas over **indirect medium heat**, with the lid closed, for 20 minutes. Remove the aluminum foil from the pan and continue cooking over **indirect medium heat**, with the lid closed, until the enchiladas are bubbling and the cheese is melted, 8 to 10 minutes more. Remove the pan from the grill and let rest for 5 minutes. While the enchiladas rest, fry the eggs over easy. Serve the enchiladas warm with a fried egg on top and a dollop of sour cream on the side, if desired. Garnish with scallions.

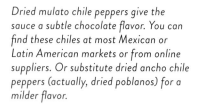

Dried mulato chile peppers give the sauce a subtle chocolate flavor. You can find these chiles at most Mexican or Latin American markets or from online suppliers. Or substitute dried ancho chile peppers (actually, dried poblanos) for a milder flavor.

4

POULTRY

LEMON CHICKEN
WITH CHARRED CORN, TOMATOES, AND FARRO

SERVES: 4 | **PREP TIME:** 45 MINUTES
MARINATING TIME: 1 TO 4 HOURS | **GRILLING TIME:** 16 TO 22 MINUTES

MARINADE

- 2 teaspoons finely grated lemon zest
- ¼ cup fresh lemon juice
- 1 tablespoon Dijon mustard
- ½ teaspoon dried oregano
- 2 garlic cloves, minced

  Extra-virgin olive oil
  Freshly ground black pepper
  Kosher salt
- 4 boneless, skinless chicken breast halves, each 6 to 8 ounces
- 1½ cups pearled farro (about 9 ounces)
- 3 cups low-sodium chicken broth or water

CILANTRO PUREE

- 1 cup loosely packed fresh cilantro leaves
- 1 cup loosely packed fresh Italian parsley leaves
- 1 tablespoon fresh lemon juice
- 1 tablespoon red wine vinegar
- 2 garlic cloves, chopped
- ¼ teaspoon crushed red pepper flakes

SALAD

- 2 ears fresh corn, husked
- 12 ounces grape or cherry tomatoes, each cut in half
- 2 scallions (white and light green parts only), thinly sliced
- ¼ cup chopped fresh Italian parsley leaves
- 1 tablespoon fresh lemon juice

If you have a charcoal grill, fire it up for this dish, because the sweet smell of burning embers will imbue the chicken and corn with greater depth. Don't overcook either one. The breast meat should be moist and the corn kernels should be crisp-tender in the salad. Farro is an ancient grain that has attracted a lot of attention lately from chefs for its earthy nuttiness and pleasantly chewy texture. Be sure to buy the pearled variety, which has had the bran removed, so you don't have to soak the grain overnight. Feel free to substitute cooked rice or couscous, if you like.

1 Whisk the marinade ingredients, including 2 tablespoons oil, 1½ teaspoons pepper, and 1 teaspoon salt. Place the chicken breasts in a large, resealable plastic bag and pour in the marinade. Press the air out of the bag and seal tightly. Turn the bag to distribute the marinade, place in a bowl, and refrigerate for 1 to 4 hours, turning the bag occasionally.

2 In a medium saucepan combine the farro, broth, and 1½ teaspoons salt. Bring to a boil on the stove, reduce the heat to medium-low, cover, and simmer until the farro is tender, 15 to 20 minutes. Drain off any remaining liquid and set aside off the heat.

3 In a food processor combine the cilantro puree ingredients, including ⅓ cup oil, ½ teaspoon pepper, and ½ teaspoon salt. Process until blended and almost smooth. Transfer to a bowl.

4 Prepare the grill for direct cooking over medium heat (350° to 450°F).

5 Lightly brush the corn with oil, and then grill over **direct medium heat**, with the lid closed, until lightly charred and crisp-tender, 8 to 10 minutes, turning as needed. Remove from the grill and, when cool enough to handle, cut the kernels from the cobs and transfer to a bowl. Add the remaining salad ingredients, including 2 tablespoons oil, 1 teaspoon salt, and ½ teaspoon pepper, and stir to combine. Fold in the farro and cilantro puree.

6 Grill the chicken, smooth (skin) side down first, over **direct medium heat**, with the lid closed, until firm to the touch and opaque all the way to the center, 8 to 12 minutes, turning once. Remove from the grill and let rest for 3 to 5 minutes. Serve the chicken warm with the salad.

SMOKED CHICKEN BANH MI
WITH PICKLED JALAPEÑOS

SERVES: 4 | **MARINATING TIME:** 1 HOUR | **PREP TIME:** 40 MINUTES | **GRILLING TIME:** ABOUT 20 MINUTES
SPECIAL EQUIPMENT: 2 LARGE HANDFULS APPLE OR CHERRY WOOD CHIPS

MARINADE

¼ cup Vietnamese or Thai fish sauce
¼ cup fresh lime juice
2 tablespoons minced shallot
2 tablespoons vegetable oil
1 tablespoon toasted sesame oil
2 garlic cloves, minced

4 boneless, skinless chicken breast
  halves, each about 6 ounces
⅓ cup plus 1 tablespoon unseasoned
  rice vinegar
1 tablespoon granulated sugar
2 teaspoons kosher salt
2 medium jalapeño chile peppers, cut
  crosswise into ⅛-inch rings
½ cup mayonnaise
  Finely grated zest of 1 lime
1 tablespoon fresh lime juice
¼ teaspoon hot chili-garlic sauce, such
  as Sriracha
4 crusty, oblong sandwich rolls, split
5 ounces store-bought smooth
  chicken liver mousse or pâté, duck
  liver mousse, or liverwurst, at
  room temperature
½ cup thinly sliced, thin-skinned
  seedless cucumbers
½ small red onion, cut into thin rings
½ cup tightly packed fresh
  cilantro leaves

For decades the banh mi sandwich lingered in obscurity as an unlikely love child of French and Vietnamese cooking. Recently, though, its unique layering of flavors, colors, and textures has mainstream America taking notice. You can even find versions of it in barbecue restaurants (see story, page 107). The fresh herbs and pickled vegetables represent authentic Vietnamese touches that now seem entirely natural mingled with the French elements of crusty bread and chicken liver mousse.

1   Soak the wood chips in water for at least 30 minutes.

2   Whisk the marinade ingredients. Place the chicken breasts in a large, resealable plastic bag and pour in the marinade. Press the air out of the bag and seal tightly. Turn the bag to distribute the marinade, place in a bowl, and set aside at room temperature to marinate for 1 hour, turning the bag occasionally.

3   Meanwhile, combine the vinegar, sugar, and salt and whisk to completely dissolve the sugar. Add the jalapeños, cover, and refrigerate for 1 hour.

4   Mix the mayonnaise, lime zest and juice, and hot chili-garlic sauce. Cover and refrigerate until ready to serve.

5   Prepare the grill for indirect cooking over medium-low heat (as close to 350°F as possible).

6   Remove the chicken from the bag and blot the excess marinade off the chicken with paper towels. Discard the marinade. Drain and add the wood chips to the charcoal or to the smoker box of a gas grill, following manufacturer's instructions, and close the lid. When smoke appears, grill the chicken, smooth (skin) side up, over ***indirect medium-low heat***, with the lid closed, until the meat is firm to the touch and opaque all the way to the center, about 20 minutes (the color of the chicken will still be pale). Remove the chicken from the grill and let rest for 3 minutes. Cut the chicken diagonally and across the grain into ½-inch slices.

7   Spread one side of each roll with the mayonnaise mixture. Spread the other half of each roll with chicken liver mousse. Divide the chicken, jalapeños, cucumbers, onion, and cilantro evenly among the rolls. Serve immediately.

DUCK BREASTS
WITH SMOKY PEACH AND GINGER CHUTNEY

SERVES: 4 | **PREP TIME:** 20 MINUTES | **GRILLING TIME:** ABOUT 35 MINUTES
SPECIAL EQUIPMENT: 2 LARGE HANDFULS CHERRY WOOD CHIPS, GRILL-PROOF SKILLET

CHUTNEY

4 firm but ripe peaches (freestone, if available)
2 tablespoons unsalted butter, melted
½ cup packed dark brown sugar
¼ cup finely chopped shallots
¼ cup cider vinegar
2 tablespoons peeled, minced fresh ginger
½ teaspoon ground cinnamon

4 duck breast halves, each 6 to 8 ounces
1 teaspoon kosher salt
¼ teaspoon freshly ground black pepper

No doubt, grilling duck breasts presents some challenges. There's so much fat in the skin that if the fire is too hot, the fat rushes out quickly and ignites in a blaze. If the fire is too low, the meat turns rubbery before the skin is barely as tan as khakis. Recall the Goldilocks principle: the one in the middle (medium heat) is "just right." But don't get too comfortable. Even with medium heat, flare-ups occasionally happen, so you may need to move the duck over indirect heat temporarily. Forget it, you say? Please don't. Your diligence and responsiveness will be rewarded with one of my favorite recipes in the whole book.

1 Soak the wood chips in water for at least 30 minutes.

2 Prepare the grill for direct and indirect cooking over medium heat (350° to 450°F).

3 Cut each peach in half and save any juices. Brush the peach halves all over with the melted butter. Set aside any remaining butter.

4 Drain and add one handful of the wood chips to the charcoal or to the smoker box of a gas grill, following manufacturer's instructions, and close the lid. When smoke appears, grill the peach halves, cut side up, over **direct medium heat**, with the lid closed, until charred and beginning to soften, 7 to 10 minutes. Remove from the grill, pull off and discard the skin, and cut the peach halves into thin slices.

5 In a grill-proof skillet combine the peach slices, brown sugar, shallots, vinegar, ginger, cinnamon, and any reserved peach juices and remaining melted butter. Place the skillet over **direct medium heat**, close the lid, and bring the mixture to a simmer, 7 to 9 minutes. Cook, stirring occasionally, until the chutney has thickened, about 10 minutes more. Remove from the heat and let cool.

6 While the chutney is cooking, use a very sharp knife to score the skin of each duck breast on the diagonal in a crisscross pattern (do not cut through to the meat). Season the duck evenly on both sides with the salt and pepper.

7 Drain and add the remaining wood chips to the charcoal or smoker box and close the lid. When smoke appears, grill the duck breasts, skin side down first, over **direct medium heat**, with the lid closed, until the skin is browned and the meat is cooked to your desired doneness, 8 to 10 minutes for medium rare, turning once (as flare-ups occur, move the duck temporarily over indirect heat). Remove the duck from the grill, tent with foil, and let rest for 3 to 5 minutes. Cut the duck crosswise into slices and serve warm with the chutney.

One of the keys to rendering (melting) fat from duck breasts skillfully over medium heat is first crosshatching the skin without cutting into the meat. Using a very sharp knife, score the skin on the diagonal in lines spaced about one-half inch apart. Then score crisscrossing lines, also about one-half inch apart, to create an even pattern.

DRUNKEN NOODLES
WITH CHICKEN AND BASIL

SERVES: 2 TO 4 | **PREP TIME:** 25 MINUTES | **GRILLING TIME:** 6 TO 8 MINUTES
SPECIAL EQUIPMENT: GRILL-PROOF WOK OR VERY LARGE SKILLET

8 ounces dried wide rice noodles

SAUCE

3 tablespoons oyster sauce
2 tablespoons Thai or Vietnamese
  fish sauce
2 tablespoons water
1 tablespoon soy sauce
1 tablespoon packed light brown sugar

2 tablespoons vegetable oil
4 boneless, skinless chicken thighs, each
  about 4 ounces, cut into 1-inch pieces
1 medium red bell pepper, cut into
  ½-inch strips
6 ounces fresh shiitake mushrooms,
  stemmed, caps cut into ½-inch strips
4 scallions, cut diagonally into thin
  slices, divided
12 canned baby corn, rinsed, drained,
  and cut diagonally into ¾-inch pieces
3 garlic cloves, minced
1 small red chile pepper, such as Thai,
  minced, including seeds
¼ cup water
1 cup very coarsely chopped fresh
  Thai or holy basil leaves
1 lime, cut into wedges
  Hot chili-garlic sauce, such as Sriracha

Drunken noodles do not actually contain a drop of liquor; the name is derived from their alleged power to cure a hangover. While this Thai stir-fry is not particularly smoky, the high heat from the grill gives the chicken a quick, deep sear that the average American stove top cannot achieve. Experiment by adding other vegetables, such as thin asparagus or broccoli florets, or try peeled and deveined shrimp instead of chicken. Standard basil will work well in this recipe, but Thai basil is worth looking for in Asian markets because even when the serrated leaves are cooked, they retain distinct licorice and anise flavors.

1 In a large bowl completely cover the noodles with very hot tap water. Let stand until the noodles are softened but not fully tender, 12 to 15 minutes, stirring occasionally (they will cook and soften a bit more during cooking, so do not over soak). Drain the noodles, rinse under cold water, and drain again.

2 Prepare the grill for direct cooking over high heat (450° to 550°F) and preheat a grill-proof wok for 5 to 10 minutes.

3 Whisk the sauce ingredients until the sugar is dissolved.

4 Have all the ingredients prepped and ready to go before you begin cooking. Bring the noodles, sauce, oil, chicken thighs, bell pepper, mushrooms, half of the scallions, baby corn, garlic, chile pepper, water, and basil to the grill and keep close by.

5 When the wok is smoking hot, pour the oil into the wok, letting it run down the sides. Add the chicken and cook over **direct high heat**, with the lid open, until seared on both sides, about 1 minute, stirring occasionally. Add the bell pepper, mushrooms, scallions, and baby corn and cook, with the lid open, until the vegetables soften, 2 to 4 minutes, stirring often. Stir in the garlic and chile pepper and cook until fragrant, about 30 seconds.

6 Add the noodles and water and cook until the water evaporates and the noodles are warm, about 1 minute, stirring and tossing constantly. Pour the sauce over the noodles and stir until the noodles are hot and coated with the sauce, about 1 minute more. Stir in the basil and cook until just wilted, about 30 seconds. Remove the wok from the grill. Transfer the noodles to plates or bowls and garnish with the remaining scallions. Serve hot with lime wedges and hot chili-garlic sauce.

For thousands of years, the focal point of a typical Chinese kitchen was a round hole over a firebox of burning wood and embers, with a wok fit snugly inside the hole, making efficient use of a small amount of an expensive fuel. You can replicate the ancient art of stir-frying over a live fire by resting a wok in the hole of a special grate made for a backyard grill.

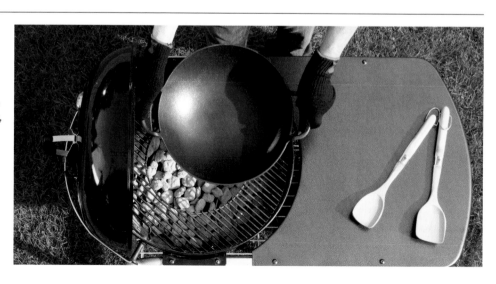

CHICAGO:

THERE'S A NEW 'CUE IN TOWN

Chicago loves a good reinvention story. Whether it's the brutal, bone-stinging winters giving way to glorious summers, the habitually losing athletic teams emerging as champions, or even the reversing current of its eponymous river, Chi-towners are accustomed to turning things around. With barbecue, it's no different.

"I think Chicago was a barbecue town waiting to happen," said Barry Sorkin, a former IT executive and now owner of Smoque BBQ, an excellent upper-scale 'cue joint in the Irving Park neighborhood. "There were all these pent-up barbecue fanatics and there was no outlet for it, at least not for the generation of eaters weaned on cooking shows and food as a hobby." And, if the line of people usually extending out the door at Smoque BBQ is any indication, he's right. Young Chicagoans craved the quality of 'cue proudly hailed in places like Kansas City and Austin. Chicago had its styles, true, but the people were ready for the next phase.

And boy, did that next phase come with a bang.

"We've seen a surge in fine-dining barbecue," says Chicago-based food writer Kevin Pang of the flurry of restaurant openings since 2010. "Barbecue has been elevated with sophisticated presentations and cooking techniques." He is referring to places like Chicago q, in the ritzy Gold Coast neighborhood, one of several places now barbecuing with fully automated, digitally controlled smokers that run on gas. Barbecue purists can argue about the authenticity of this approach, but with the benefit of wood logs, these smokers produce consistently great barbecue month after month.

Walking into Chicago q, you immediately feel a hip, urban vibe. This posh place pulses with energy, especially at night when crowds of young diners and drinkers pack the place for competition-worthy ribs, American-style Kobe brisket, and more than a few surprises, such as blackened alligator with Creole mustard aioli. The chef there is Lee Ann Whippen, a top-tier barbecue competitor who was approached by an investor to marry her cooking skills with country club class. The barbecue techniques are beyond reproach. The number of wines, craft beers, and whiskeys is staggering. And the prices? Well, customers come prepared to pay.

"You ask people how they feel at the end of the meal, after they have shelled out a lot of money," Whippen reflected. "In most cases they say, 'I feel wonderful, and I'll be back, and I'll bring more people.'"

This is a starkly different scene from what Chicago barbecue was—and still is, but might not be much longer. Rarely ranked in the pantheon of originators, the Windy City's contribution to this cuisine reflects its gritty history of intermingling traditions. Essentially, up until very recently, it had been a tale of two 'cues, with north and south sides finding themselves divided. To the north,

Eastern Europeans seeking opportunity flooded the city from its inception, accompanied by sausages and rib racks boiled to the point of falling off the bone, and, as the style evolved, finished on a grill and drenched in sweet sauce. Restaurants such as Twin Anchors Restaurant & Tavern and Gale Street Inn Chicago built local empires on the practice. To the south, at stalwarts such as Lem's Bar-B-Q and Leon's BBQ, you will find techniques drawn from the migration of African Americans during the early 20th century. Popular rib tips and hot links are cooked in aquarium smokers—the fire-code-compliant cousins to open pits, which look exactly like you think they should—topped in house-made sauce, stuffed in a white plastic clamshell with a slice of white bread, and often delivered through a bullet-proof turnstile.

South-side barbecue is in crisis now. Diners are now awash in nicer-looking options, and pit masters are aging without apprentices training to take over. "It's this history that is slowly dying off," Pang said. "I think the most shameful thing is that [this style of] barbecue is not a young person's game."

But Chicago's next wave of barbecue is. While the city is not unique in offering gourmet 'cue, Chicago's stature as arguably America's foremost food city pits (ahem) it as a bit of a vanguard. Restaurateurs don't have to pledge allegiance to one style. Instead, history and creativity overlap. Old traditions and new technologies meet in the middle. Texas brisket and Carolina pulled pork coexist with a white tablecloth treatment. And so begins yet another chapter in Chicago's riveting food story—one where all barbecue finds a hospitable home, where IT execs and traveling competitors become restaurant stars, and where reinvention reigns.

LESSONS FROM THE LEGENDS
CHICKEN THIGHS

In 2015, while serving as a judge at the Memphis in May World Championship Barbecue Contest, I spent several hours with the Danish National BBQ team (pictured above), watching how they cook chicken and other meats. These intense Vikings had beaten out many wannabe contenders to make it on their country's elite team, and then they had trained for months to compete at this international spectacle on the banks of the Mississippi River. Considered one of the world's most prestigious competitions, with more than 250 teams working hard to qualify, it is a one-of-a-kind experience that includes two days of raucous parties with men dressed in drag and rubber pig masks followed by two days of serious business, that is, finessing luscious pieces of barbecue, including chicken, so they glisten like jewels for the judges.

BRINE TIME

If brining sounds like a chore to you, I understand. Sometimes I skip this step, too, but barbecue competitors will tell you that if you can drop some chicken thighs in a saltwater bath in the morning, here is what will happen by dinnertime:

1

Salt, being the good chemical that it is, will dissolve muscle proteins in the meat, loosening up the fibers in the chicken and making them more absorbent.

2

In will rush the flavors of the brine. I usually combine ½ cup of kosher salt and ½ cup of sugar with a quart of water in a large saucepan. I bring that to a boil to dissolve the salt and sugar, and then I add about 2 quarts of ice cubes to chill the mixture before adding the raw chicken.

3

After 6 to 8 hours, when the chicken is on the grill, much of that flavor and moisture will stay inside the meat. The relaxed muscle fibers will not constrict and drive out juices as much as they would without a brine. Your reward will be moist, succulent thighs.

PREPARING THIGHS FOR THE GRILL

To achieve crispy brown skins, you must start with dry chicken thighs. The skins naturally have a lot of water, fat, and protein in them. They can be especially watery if you have brined them (as you should), so be sure to pat dry all surfaces with paper towels, and then season them on both sides. A little bit (not a lot) of oil will help the thighs to brown without sticking to the cooking grate.

BROWNING BEFORE SAUCING

To achieve golden brown colors and crisp textures on the skins, direct heat helps a lot, as it quickly cooks out a lot of the remaining water and fat in the skins. After the step of browning over direct heat, you can move the thighs over indirect heat and brush them with the sauce of your choice. Sweet barbecue sauces could burn, so wait until the final 10 to 15 minutes of cooking time to apply those.

CHICKEN THIGHS
WITH SWEET APRICOT-HOISIN GLAZE

SERVES: 4 | PREP TIME: 20 MINUTES | GRILLING TIME: 31 TO 36 MINUTES
SPECIAL EQUIPMENT: 2 LARGE HANDFULS CHERRY OR APPLE WOOD CHIPS,
LARGE DISPOSABLE FOIL PAN

It used to be that I ate hoisin sauce only when I ordered Peking duck, moo shu pork, or pho in Chinese and Vietnamese restaurants. But if you think about it, hoisin sauce's sweet, pungent flavors (sugar, vinegar, soybeans, spices, etc.) have all the elements of a worthy alternative to tomato-based barbecue sauces. When you simmer it with apricot preserves, fresh lemon juice, and ginger, you have a contemporary, Asian-style glaze for barbecued chicken.

For this recipe I have developed a sauce that would seem out of place in Memphis because it is so tropical in character, but I love the blend of pineapple and hoisin flavors. Feel free to use your own style of sauce, adding yet another twist to this ongoing story of American barbecue.

RUB
1½ teaspoons kosher salt
1½ teaspoons garlic powder
1 teaspoon ground cumin
¾ teaspoon freshly ground black pepper
½ teaspoon prepared chili powder
½ teaspoon ground ginger
⅛ teaspoon ground cinnamon

8 chicken thighs (with bone and skin), each 5 to 6 ounces, trimmed of excess skin and fat, patted dry

GLAZE
½ cup apricot preserves
¼ cup hoisin sauce
1 tablespoon fresh lemon juice
2 teaspoons peeled, minced fresh ginger

1–2 tablespoons chopped fresh cilantro leaves

1 Soak the wood chips in water for at least 30 minutes.

2 Prepare the grill for direct and indirect cooking over medium-low heat (350° to 400°F).

3 Combine the rub ingredients, and then season the chicken thighs all over with the rub.

4 In a small saucepan over medium heat on the stove, bring the glaze ingredients to a simmer. Cook until slightly thickened, about 3 minutes, stirring occasionally. Remove from the heat.

5 Drain and add the wood chips to the charcoal or to the smoker box of a gas grill, following manufacturer's instructions, and close the lid. When smoke appears, grill the thighs, skin side down first, over **direct medium-low heat**, with the lid closed, until lightly browned, about 16 minutes, turning once. Place the thighs in a large disposable foil pan, place the pan over **indirect medium-low heat**, and brush the thighs with some of the glaze. Close the lid, and cook until the juices run clear and the meat is no longer pink at the bone, 15 to 20 minutes more, brushing occasionally with the glaze. If the glaze becomes too thick as it cools, warm it briefly over medium heat. Brush with any remaining glaze just before removing the thighs from the grill. Serve the thighs warm, garnished with the cilantro.

BRINED CHICKEN THIGHS
WITH BLACK CHERRY BARBECUE SAUCE

SERVES: 6 | **PREP TIME:** 20 MINUTES | **BRINING TIME:** 6 TO 8 HOURS OR OVERNIGHT | **GRILLING TIME:** ABOUT 2 HOURS
SPECIAL EQUIPMENT: 2 LARGE HANDFULS CHERRY WOOD CHIPS, 2 LARGE DISPOSABLE FOIL PANS

One of the surest ways to barbecue chicken so it's juicy is to brine it. Incorporating some black cherry juice into the brine will help with the overall flavor. If you use this kind of juice in the sauce, the brine and sauce will echo the same black cherry flavors.

BRINE

- 1 quart water
- 2 cups tart black cherry juice
- ½ cup kosher salt
- ½ cup packed brown sugar
- 2 quarts ice cubes

- 12 large chicken thighs (with bone and skin), each about 7 ounces, trimmed of excess skin and fat, patted dry

RUB

- 2 teaspoons paprika
- 1½ teaspoons kosher salt
- 1½ teaspoons prepared chili powder
- 1½ teaspoons dried thyme
- ¾ teaspoon freshly ground black pepper

SAUCE

- 1 cup tart black cherry juice
- ½ cup ketchup
- ¼ cup prepared yellow mustard
- 2 tablespoons honey
- 1 teaspoon Worcestershire sauce

In the barbecue competition world, one of the techniques that teams use to gain an edge is scraping the skin of each thigh so that when judges bite into it, their teeth cut easily through the skin. Scraping requires removing each skin from the meat, scoring the underside, and then, using a very sharp blade, scraping away most of the fat. The skins are then reattached, sometimes with toothpicks. It's a lot of tedious work, but "bite-through skin" is now considered a must-have for earning top scores.

1   In a large pot combine all the brine ingredients except the ice cubes. Bring to a boil on the stove, mixing well to dissolve the salt and sugar. Remove from the heat and add the ice cubes to cool down the brine. When the brine is cool, submerge the thighs in the brine and refrigerate for 6 to 8 hours or overnight.

2   Soak the wood chips in water for at least 30 minutes.

3   Mix the rub ingredients. Reserve ½ teaspoon of the rub to use in the sauce.

4   Prepare the grill for indirect cooking over low heat (about 300°F).

5   Remove the thighs from the pot and discard the brine. Season the thighs evenly with the rub, and then arrange them snugly, skin side down, in a single layer in two large disposable foil pans (six thighs in each pan).

6   Drain and add the wood chips to the charcoal or to the smoker box of a gas grill, following manufacturer's instructions, and close the lid. When smoke appears, place the pans over **indirect low heat**, close the lid, and cook for 1½ hours, turning the thighs once after 45 minutes.

7   In a medium saucepan combine the sauce ingredients, including the ½ teaspoon reserved rub, and bring to a simmer over medium heat on the stove. Cook for 3 to 5 minutes, stirring occasionally.

8   Take the thighs out of the pan and brush them all over with sauce. Grill the thighs on the cooking grates over **indirect low heat**, with the lid closed, until the sauce is set, 20 to 30 minutes. Remove from the grill and brush the thighs one more time with the sauce. Serve warm.

CHICKEN AND SAUSAGE GUMBO

SERVES: 8 | **PREP TIME:** 1 HOUR | **GRILLING TIME:** ABOUT 3½ HOURS | **SPECIAL EQUIPMENT:** 3 LARGE HANDFULS PECAN OR HICKORY WOOD CHIPS, GAS GRILL, LARGE (6-QUART) GRILL-PROOF DUTCH OVEN

6 chicken thighs (with bone and skin), each 5 to 6 ounces, trim of excess skin and fat, patted dry
Vegetable oil
Kosher salt
Freshly ground black pepper
1 pound smoked sausages, such as andouille or spicy kielbasa
6 slices bacon, cut crosswise into 1-inch pieces
1 cup unbleached all-purpose flour
2½ cups finely chopped yellow onions
1½ cups finely chopped celery
1¼ cups ½-inch-diced green bell pepper
4 garlic cloves, minced
2 quarts low-sodium chicken broth
4 teaspoons Worcestershire sauce
Hot pepper sauce
1½ teaspoons dried thyme leaves
2 bay leaves
8 ounces okra, ends trimmed, cut crosswise into ½-inch slices
¼ cup roughly chopped fresh Italian parsley leaves
4 cups cooked long-grain rice

Gumbo is an epic Southern dish famous for the range of interpretations it permits. Each cook tends to make it the way he or she learned as a child, but every Southern family comes at gumbo from a different path of ethnic and idiosyncratic distinctions. Consequently, the "right" mix of meats and vegetables is debatable. Even the essential element of the roux has inspired fierce debate, with people arguing over the correct shade of browning in the roux before adding the vegetables. Gumbo comes from West African dialect for okra, so you would think this vegetable is mandatory—but if you aren't an okra fan, you can leave it out or substitute one-half pound of green beans cut into bite-sized pieces. (Keep in mind, though, that the relatively long simmering time eliminates okra's gluey texture.)

Note: This recipe requires a lot of fluctuating temperatures on the grill, so it is best to use a gas grill.

1 Soak the wood chips in water for at least 30 minutes.

2 Brush the chicken thighs on both sides with oil and season evenly with 1 teaspoon salt and ½ teaspoon pepper. Set aside at room temperature while you prepare the grill.

3 Prepare the gas grill for indirect cooking over medium-low heat (about 350°F).

4 Drain and add half of the wood chips to the smoker box, following manufacturer's instructions, and close the lid. When smoke appears, grill the chicken thighs, skin side up, over **indirect medium-low heat**, with the lid closed, until the meat is firm to the touch and the juices run clear, about 50 minutes. After 20 minutes, drain and add the remaining wood chips to the smoker box. Transfer the chicken to a bowl and set aside. Increase the temperature of the grill and the cooking method to direct medium heat (350° to 450°F).

5 Grill the sausages over **direct medium heat**, with the lid closed, until browned on all sides, about 8 minutes, turning occasionally. Remove from the grill, let rest for 5 minutes, and then cut crosswise into ¼-inch-thick slices.

6 In a large grill-proof Dutch oven over **direct medium heat**, fry the bacon, with the grill lid closed, until browned and crisp, 8 to 10 minutes, stirring occasionally. Using a slotted spoon, transfer the bacon to paper towels to drain, and keep the bacon fat in the Dutch oven.

7 Add ¾ cup oil to the bacon fat in the Dutch oven. Whisk in the flour to make a thin roux. Cook over **direct medium heat** until the roux is about the color of a skinned peanut, 8 to 10 minutes, whisking almost constantly. You may stop cooking the roux at this point, but longer cooking gives the best flavor. Reduce the temperature of the grill to **direct medium-low heat** (about 350°F) and continue cooking and whisking constantly until the roux smells toasted, smokes lightly, and is just a shade lighter than milk chocolate, watching closely to prevent over browning, 10 to 15 minutes more.

8 Add the onions, celery, and bell pepper to the Dutch oven. Cook over **direct medium heat**, with the lid closed, until the onion is slightly softened and the mixture is quite sticky, 8 to 10 minutes, stirring often. Stir in the garlic and cook for 1 minute. Gradually whisk in the broth. Stir in the Worcestershire sauce, 2 teaspoons hot sauce, the thyme, bay leaves, ¾ teaspoon salt, and ½ teaspoon pepper. Increase the temperature of the grill to high heat (450° to 550°F) and bring the mixture to a boil. Then reduce the temperature of the grill to low heat (250° to 350°F) and simmer the gumbo over **direct low heat**, with the lid closed, for 1 hour, stirring occasionally.

9 Add the chicken (and any accumulated juices) and sausage pieces to the gumbo and cook over **direct low heat**, with the lid closed, for 30 minutes. Add the okra and parsley and cook until the okra is very tender, 20 to 30 minutes more. Remove from the heat. Discard the bay leaves. Transfer the chicken to a cutting board to cool slightly. Cover the Dutch oven to keep the gumbo hot.

10 Cut the chicken into bite-sized pieces, discarding the bones and skin, and chop the bacon. Add the chicken and bacon to the gumbo. Adjust the seasoning with more salt, pepper, and hot sauce, if desired.

11 Heap about ½ cup of rice into each serving bowl and ladle gumbo over the rice. Serve hot, with hot sauce on the side.

JERK CHICKEN

SERVES: 4 | **PREP TIME:** 30 MINUTES | **MARINATING TIME:** 4 TO 18 HOURS | **GRILLING TIME:** 1¼ TO 1¾ HOURS
SPECIAL EQUIPMENT: RUBBER GLOVES, 2 LARGE HANDFULS APPLE OR PIMENTO WOOD CHIPS

MARINADE

- 1 Scotch bonnet or habanero chile pepper, seeded and coarsely chopped (see caption and photo below)
- 6 large scallions (white and light green parts only), coarsely chopped
- ¼ cup vegetable oil
- 2 tablespoons soy sauce
- 2 tablespoons fresh lime juice
- 2 tablespoons ground allspice, preferably freshly ground Jamaican allspice berries
- 2 tablespoons packed light brown sugar
- 1 tablespoon peeled, minced fresh ginger
- 1 tablespoon coarsely chopped fresh thyme leaves
- 1 teaspoon kosher salt
- ½ teaspoon freshly grated nutmeg
- ½ teaspoon ground cinnamon
- 2 garlic cloves, coarsely chopped

- 1 whole chicken, 4½ to 5 pounds
- 1 lime, cut into wedges

Somewhere out in the sun-soaked West Indies lies American barbecue's point of origin (see page 5 for the real history), so I think it's fitting to feature a contemporary recipe in this cookbook from that part of the world, specifically Jamaica. With an intriguing blend of ingredients that includes chiles, spices, herbs, and soy sauce, the thick marinade for this recipe uses the minimum amount of chiles; try to use the traditional Scotch bonnet type, and add a second chile if you dare. The local trick from jerk aficionados is to let the chicken cook "low and slow" to smoky tenderness over pimento wood. If the fire is too hot, the meat tends to scorch. If you would rather not shell out big bucks for pimento wood, which you'll need to buy online, use a more common fruitwood instead.

1 To avoid burning your skin, wear rubber gloves when you handle the chile. In a blender combine the marinade ingredients. Puree the marinade, stopping to scrape down the inside of the jar as needed, and add a little water if it is too thick. (A blender works best because it is easy to clean, and a plastic food processor bowl could pick up the marinade's strong flavor.)

2 Cut the chicken into six pieces: two breast halves, two leg quarters, and two wings (cut off and discard the wing tips), and then place in a 13-by-9-inch glass or ceramic baking dish. Pour the marinade over the chicken and use tongs to turn and coat the chicken. Cover with plastic wrap and refrigerate for at least 4 hours or up to 18 hours, turning the chicken occasionally.

3 Soak the wood chips in water for at least 30 minutes.

4 Prepare the grill for direct and indirect cooking over medium-low heat (350° to 400°F).

5 Remove the chicken from the dish, letting any excess marinade drip back into the dish. Transfer the marinade and juices in the dish to a small bowl, cover, and refrigerate.

6 Drain and add half of the wood chips to the charcoal or to the smoker box of a gas grill, following manufacturer's instructions, and close the lid. When smoke appears, grill the chicken, skin side up, over *indirect medium-low heat*, with the lid closed, for 45 minutes. Drain and add the remaining wood chips to the charcoal or smoker box before the old chips burn out. Turn the chicken over and baste with some of the reserved marinade. Continue grilling, with the lid closed, until the juices run clear and the meat is no longer pink at the bone, 30 to 55 minutes more, occasionally basting with the reserved marinade up until the last 20 minutes of grilling time. Discard any remaining marinade. If desired, to crisp and brown the skin, during the last 2 to 4 minutes, grill the chicken, skin side down, over *direct medium-low heat*, turning once. Remove from the grill and let rest for 3 to 5 minutes.

7 Using a heavy knife, cut the leg pieces in half at the joint and cut the breast pieces crosswise in half. Serve warm with a squeeze of lime on top.

Scotch bonnet chiles (pictured here), and their look-alike cousin, habaneros, are two of the hottest chiles on the consumer market. Caribbean cooks have been cooking with these chiles for centuries and know to handle them with care. Learn from their experience! If you have sensitive skin, wear rubber gloves. Take care not to inhale the very strong fumes, especially when pureeing in a blender, and make the marinade in a well-ventilated kitchen.

SPATCHCOCKED BBQ CHICKEN
WITH ALABAMA WHITE SAUCE

SERVES: 2 TO 4 | **PREP TIME:** 15 MINUTES | **GRILLING TIME:** 25 TO 30 MINUTES
SPECIAL EQUIPMENT: 1 LARGE HANDFUL HICKORY OR PECAN WOOD CHIPS, POULTRY SHEARS, INSTANT-READ THERMOMETER

PASTE

1 tablespoon extra-virgin olive oil
1 tablespoon fresh lime juice
1 tablespoon packed dark brown sugar
1 teaspoon ground cumin
1 teaspoon dried oregano
1 teaspoon dried thyme
1 teaspoon paprika
1 teaspoon kosher salt
1 teaspoon freshly ground black pepper
½ teaspoon garlic powder

1 whole chicken, 4 to 4½ pounds, spatchcocked (see how-to below)

SAUCE

1 cup mayonnaise
¼ cup white wine vinegar
2 teaspoons freshly ground black pepper
¾ teaspoon granulated sugar
¼ teaspoon kosher salt

In Alabama, white barbecue sauce is a special point of state pride. It is a vinegary, creamy sauce laced with lots of ground black pepper, and it has almost nothing in common with classic red barbecue sauce. A white color is mandatory, but beyond that there are hundreds of variations. Some people make it sweeter. Some make it spicier by using cracked black peppercorns rather than ground pepper. The restaurant most famous for this kind of sauce is Big Bob Gibson's Bar-B-Q in Decatur. There, my friend Chris Lilly mixes his version in a big vat so he can dunk whole barbecued chickens into it. For this recipe I suggest spatchcocking (or butterflying) a chicken so you can get the most surface area right on the grate—and get the most flavor imaginable into the meat. Have a stack of napkins on hand! You'll want lots of sauce with every bite.

1 Soak the wood chips in water for at least 30 minutes.

2 Combine the paste ingredients. Massage the paste evenly all over the chicken. Set aside at room temperature while preparing the grill.

3 Prepare the grill for direct cooking over medium heat (350° to 450°F).

4 Drain and add the wood chips to the charcoal or to the smoker box of a gas grill, following manufacturer's instructions, and close the lid. When smoke appears, grill the chicken, bone side down first, over **direct medium heat**, with the lid closed, for 10 minutes. Turn the chicken over and continue grilling until the juices run clear and an instant-read thermometer inserted into the thickest part of the thigh (not touching the bone) registers 160° to 165°F, 15 to 20 minutes more. Remove from the grill and let rest for 10 minutes (the internal temperature will rise 5 to 10 degrees during this time).

5 Meanwhile, in a medium bowl whisk the sauce ingredients until smooth. Cut the chicken lengthwise in half or into pieces, and serve warm with the sauce for dipping.

1 *To spatchcock, place the chicken, breast side down, on a cutting board. Using poultry shears, cut from the neck to the tail end along either side of the backbone.*

2 *Once the backbone is out, you'll be able to see the interior of the chicken. Make a small slit in the cartilage at the bottom end of the breastbone. This will help the chicken to lie flat. Then, placing both your hands on the rib cage, crack the chicken open like a book.*

3 *Remove the breastbone by running your fingers along either side of the cartilage that lies between the breast halves to loosen it from the flesh. Grab the bone and pull up to remove it with the attached cartilage.*

4 *Turn the chicken over and press on the skin side to finish flattening the chicken. Cut off the wing tips because they would likely burn.*

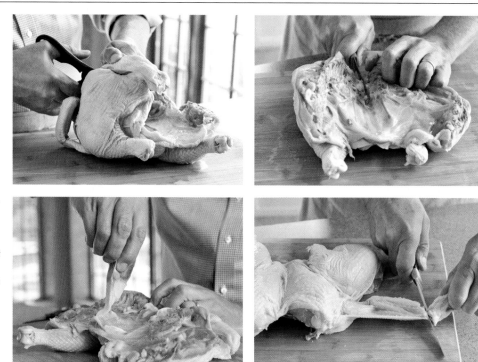

ROSEMARY-LEMON BRICK CHICKEN
WITH BREAD SALAD

SERVES: 4 TO 6 | PREP TIME: 30 MINUTES | MARINATING TIME: 4 TO 24 HOURS | GRILLING TIME: ABOUT 1 HOUR
SPECIAL EQUIPMENT: POULTRY SHEARS, 3 LARGE HANDFULS PECAN WOOD CHIPS, CHARCOAL GRILL,
2 FOIL-WRAPPED BRICKS OR LARGE CAST-IRON SKILLET, INSTANT-READ THERMOMETER

MARINADE

Freshly grated zest and juice of
2 lemons
2 tablespoons finely chopped fresh
rosemary leaves
4 garlic cloves, minced
1 teaspoon smoked paprika

Extra-virgin olive oil
Kosher salt
Freshly ground black pepper
1 whole chicken, about
5 pounds, spatchcocked
(see how-to, page 196)
1 French baguette, trimmed to a length
of 8 inches, cut lengthwise in half

DRESSING

1 tablespoon fresh lemon juice
1 tablespoon red wine vinegar
1 garlic clove, minced

12 ounces cherry or grape tomatoes,
each cut in half
⅓ cup roughly chopped fresh Italian
parsley leaves

Spatchcocking a chicken and barbecuing it under foil-wrapped bricks will score you points for style and a higher degree of difficulty than roasting it uncut; beyond style, however, this technique makes good culinary sense. The dark meat of the legs almost always takes longer to cook than the breasts, but not in this case because here the legs are more exposed to the fire. Try as best you can to balance the bricks over the breasts so they will protect the lean meat from too much heat. If you want a browner, crisper skin (and who doesn't?), toward the end of cooking, slide the whole bird carefully over direct heat.

1   Whisk the marinade ingredients, including ¼ cup oil, 2 teaspoons salt, and 1 teaspoon pepper. Lay the chicken flat in a baking dish. Pour the marinade over the chicken and massage it into both sides. Cover with plastic wrap and refrigerate for 4 to 24 hours.

2   Soak the wood chips in water for at least 30 minutes.

3   Prepare the charcoal grill for direct and indirect cooking over medium-high heat (about 400°F) creating a crescent moon fire, with the charcoal arranged around one-half of the perimeter of the charcoal grate.

4   Lightly brush the cut side of the baguette with oil, and then grill, cut side down, over **direct medium-high heat**, with the lid closed, until toasted, about 2 minutes, turning once. Remove from the grill and cut into bite-sized pieces.

5   In a large bowl whisk the dressing ingredients, including ¼ cup oil, ½ teaspoon salt, and ¼ teaspoon pepper. Add the bread and tomatoes and stir to coat. Let the salad stand at room temperature while you grill the chicken.

6   Drain and add the wood chips to the charcoal. Lay the chicken, bone side down and with the legs facing the fire, over **indirect medium heat**, and put two foil-wrapped bricks on top of the chicken. Close the lid and grill for 25 minutes. Remove the bricks. Using a large spatula, carefully turn the chicken over (keep the legs facing the fire), being careful not to tear the pieces apart. Replace the bricks and continue grilling over **indirect medium-high heat**, with the lid closed, for 25 minutes more. Remove the bricks. If the skin needs more browning, carefully slide the chicken over **direct medium-high heat** and grill, with the lid off, for 5 to 10 minutes. The chicken is fully cooked when the juices run clear and an instant-read thermometer inserted into the thickest part of the thigh (not touching the bone) registers 160° to 165°F. Carefully remove the chicken from the grill and let rest for 10 minutes (the internal temperature will rise 5 to 10 degrees during this time). Cut the chicken into serving pieces.

7   Stir the parsley into the salad, and then spoon the salad onto a serving platter. Place the chicken pieces over the salad. Serve immediately.

BEER CAN CHICKEN
WITH CHIPOTLE SPICE RUB

SERVES: 4 | **PREP TIME:** 20 MINUTES | **GRILLING TIME:** 45 MINUTES TO 1 HOUR | **SPECIAL EQUIPMENT:** 3 LARGE HANDFULS MESQUITE WOOD CHIPS, WEBER STYLE™ POULTRY INFUSION ROASTER, INSTANT-READ THERMOMETER, FAT SEPARATOR

RUB

- 1 tablespoon extra-virgin olive oil
- 2 teaspoons kosher salt
- 1 teaspoon packed brown sugar
- 1 teaspoon chipotle chile powder
- 1 teaspoon ground cumin
- 1 teaspoon smoked paprika
- ½ teaspoon freshly ground black pepper
- ¼ teaspoon ground cayenne pepper

- 1 whole chicken, 4 to 5 pounds, neck, giblets, and any excess fat removed
- 1 cup beer, at room temperature

For all the fun and folklore surrounding a chicken standing tall with a beer can crammed inside it (oh, how undignified!), it's not the beer that really matters. Almost any liquid will do, because what really matters is steam. The key is that you use no more than a few ounces of beer, wine, juice, water, or whatever. Otherwise, the liquid will take ages to reach a simmer, and simmering is what pays off for you. The evaporating liquid makes a moist and juicy bird, restoring almost all of its dignity. If you want to skip the whole act of a chicken teetering on a can, get yourself a poultry roaster—it will sit flat and sturdy on the cooking grate of your grill and hold a few ounces of whatever liquid floats your boat.

1 Soak the wood chips in water for at least 30 minutes.

2 Using a fork, mix the rub ingredients into a smooth paste.

3 Using your fingers, gently separate the chicken skin from the meat, starting at the neck cavity and moving along the breast, being careful not to tear the skin. Turn the chicken and, starting at the tail cavity, separate the skin from the thighs and legs. Carefully and gently spread half of the rub under the skin, massaging it directly onto the meat. Massage the remaining rub all over the skin on both the front and back sides of the chicken. Fold the wing tips behind the chicken's back. Allow the chicken to stand at room temperature while you prepare the grill.

4 Prepare the grill for indirect cooking over medium heat (350° to 450°F).

5 Fill the cup of a Weber Style™ poultry roaster with beer. Lower the larger cavity of the chicken over the cup.

6 Drain and add two handfuls of the wood chips to the charcoal or to the smoker box of a gas grill, following manufacturer's instructions, and close the lid. When smoke appears, place the poultry roaster with the chicken over **indirect medium heat**, close the lid, and cook until the juices run clear and an instant-read thermometer inserted into the thickest part of the thigh (not touching the bone) registers 160° to 165°F, 45 minutes to 1 hour. After the first 15 minutes of cooking time, drain and add the remaining wood chips to the charcoal or smoker box. After 30 minutes of cooking time, wearing insulated barbecue mitts or gloves, swivel the poultry roaster with the chicken 180 degrees to ensure even cooking. If the neck and wings begin to brown too quickly, cover them with aluminum foil. If using a charcoal grill, replenish the charcoal as needed to maintain a steady temperature.

7 Remove the poultry roaster with the chicken from the grill and place on a heatproof surface. Use a large spoon to collect and transfer the majority of the cooking juices from the roaster to a fat separator; set aside for the fat and juices to separate. Let the chicken rest for 10 minutes (the internal temperature will rise 5 to 10 degrees during this time). Lift the chicken from the roaster and cut the chicken into serving pieces. Drizzle with the reserved, degreased cooking juices. Serve warm.

TIPS
BEER CAN CHICKEN

1

Use any beer you like. The truth is, the flavor of the beer is almost impossible to taste in the chicken, but it does help keep the chicken moist. Any 12-ounce can works well for chickens in the range of 3½ to 5 pounds. A bigger chicken requires a 16-ounce can. Let the beer come to room temperature before cooking so it will get hot faster on the grill.

2

Tent the top. In this preparation the chicken's neck and wings tends to brown first. If they get dark too soon, loosely tent that area of the bird with aluminum foil. Nonstick aluminum foil works well here.

3

There is a safer way. Precariously balancing a chicken on a can may not be for everyone. If you have visions of your chicken falling over and beer spilling into your grill, you may want to invest in a dedicated poultry roaster than can achieve the same results more safely. It allows a chicken to stand upright over a small container you fill with beer that is attached to a sturdy pan, so the chicken and beer remain steady from start to finish.

ROTISSERIE CHICKEN
BRINED IN HERBS AND BUTTERMILK

SERVES: 4 | **PREP TIME:** 25 MINUTES | **BRINING TIME:** 8 TO 24 HOURS | **GRILLING TIME:** ABOUT 1¼ HOURS
SPECIAL EQUIPMENT: ROTISSERIE, BUTCHER'S TWINE, LARGE DISPOSABLE FOIL PAN, INSTANT-READ THERMOMETER

BRINE

- 1½ quarts buttermilk
- ⅓ cup hot pepper sauce
- ¼ cup kosher salt
- ¼ cup granulated sugar
- 12 garlic cloves, minced
- 2 tablespoons chopped fresh oregano leaves
- 1 tablespoon fresh thyme leaves

- 3 tablespoons chopped fresh rosemary leaves, divided
- 1 whole chicken, about 5 pounds, neck, giblets, wing tips, and excess fat removed
- 2 tablespoons extra-virgin olive oil

Have you noticed lately that we are living in the United States of Rotisserie Chicken? It's ubiquitous. You see it in warehouse stores, in supermarkets, and in fast-casual restaurants. We the People love it, especially when the flesh is moist and the skin is crispy. For top-notch results, start with an organic, air-chilled chicken, which you can buy at many specialty food stores. They are more expensive, but well worth it for their savory depths of taste. An easy, herby brine with buttermilk will add a nice bit of tangy richness to the natural flavor. Cook your chicken as close to 400°F as possible, and after it is done, let it rest for about 10 minutes before you cut into it.

1. Combine the brine ingredients, including 2 tablespoons of the rosemary, and stir until the salt and sugar are dissolved. Place the chicken, legs up, into a 1-gallon, resealable plastic bag and pour in the brine, making sure to fill the chicken's cavity so all the brine will fit in the bag. Squeeze the air out of the bag and seal tightly. Place the bag in a large bowl to prevent any leakage. Refrigerate for 8 to 24 hours.

2. Place a large disposable foil pan underneath the cooking grate to catch the drippings. You may have to smash the foil pan a bit, but that's okay. Or, if you are using a charcoal grill, place the foil pan on the charcoal grate between the two piles of charcoal. Then prepare the grill for rotisserie cooking over indirect medium heat (as close to 400°F as possible).

3. Remove the chicken from the bag and discard the brine. Pat the chicken dry, inside and outside, with paper towels. Truss the chicken with butcher's twine, securing the legs and wings.

4. Combine the remaining 1 tablespoon rosemary with the oil and brush it all over the chicken. Slide one pronged fork onto the spit, with the tines facing inward, about 10 inches from the end of the spit. Secure the fork, but don't tighten it thoroughly yet. Slide the spit through the center of the chicken and gently push it onto the fork tines so that they are deep inside the chicken. Add the other pronged fork to the spit, with the tines facing inward, and slide it down until they are firmly in the chicken. Secure the fork, but don't tighten it yet. Wearing insulated barbecue mitts or gloves, place the pointed end of the spit into the rotisserie motor. If necessary, adjust the chicken so that it is centered on the spit. Tighten both forks into place and turn on the motor.

5. Grill the chicken over **indirect medium heat**, with the lid closed, until an instant-read thermometer inserted into the thickest part of the thigh (not touching the bone) registers 160° to 165°F, about 1¼ hours. Before checking the temperature, turn off the rotisserie motor. If the skin is not nicely browned at the end of the cooking time, turn on the infrared burner for medium heat (if your grill has one). With the rotisserie still rotating, cook the chicken for a few minutes longer, watching *very* carefully so the chicken doesn't burn.

6. Turn off the rotisserie motor. Wearing insulated barbecue mitts or gloves, carefully remove the spit from the grill. Gently loosen the forks and slide the chicken off the spit. Transfer to a cutting board and let rest for 10 minutes (the internal temperature will rise 5 to 10 degrees during this time). Cut the chicken into serving pieces. Serve warm.

HONEY-GLAZED GAME HENS

SERVES: 2 TO 4 | **PREP TIME:** 20 MINUTES | **GRILLING TIME:** 30 TO 40 MINUTES
SPECIAL EQUIPMENT: 1 LARGE HANDFUL HICKORY WOOD CHIPS, POULTRY SHEARS

½ cup honey
¼ cup unseasoned rice vinegar
2 tablespoons soy sauce
1 canned chipotle chile pepper in adobo sauce, seeded and minced
2 game hens, each 1½ to 1¾ pounds, neck, giblets, and wing tips removed
Sea salt

This little recipe for shiny glazed game hens highlights a few classic elements of American barbecue: simple but bold flavors, a strategic use of smoke, and vigilance about the use of fire. Moving the game hens off the flame after a brief period of browning and basting gives you succulent meat with a glistening sheen. The final touch of a little salt sprinkled over the top brightens all the tastes involved.

1 Soak the wood chips in water for at least 30 minutes.

2 Prepare the grill for direct and indirect cooking over medium heat (350° to 450°F).

3 Combine the honey, vinegar, soy sauce, and chipotle chile and stir until the honey dissolves. Reserve ⅓ cup to use as a dipping sauce.

4 Set the game hens, with the breast side facing down, on a work surface. Using poultry shears, cut along both sides of the backbone and discard. Spread the hens open like a book and use a large, sturdy knife to cut through the middle of the breast. The breastbone will stay attached to one of the halves.

5 Drain and add the wood chips to the charcoal or to the smoker box of a gas grill, following manufacturer's instructions, and close the lid. When smoke appears, grill the hens, skin side down, over ***direct medium heat***, with the lid closed, until well browned, about 5 minutes. Baste with the honey mixture, turn, and continue cooking, skin side up, for 5 minutes more. (Resist the urge to move the hens unless you see big flare-ups underneath. This will allow the sweet glaze to caramelize as the skin browns.)

6 Baste the hens again, move them over ***indirect medium heat***, close the lid, and continue cooking until the meat is firm to the touch and opaque all the way to the center, 20 to 30 minutes more, brushing often with the honey mixture. Remove from the grill, season generously with sea salt, and let rest for 5 minutes. Serve the hens warm with the reserved honey mixture for dipping.

SMOKED TURKEY PASTRAMI ON RYE

SERVES: 6 TO 8 | **PREP TIME:** 15 MINUTES | **REFRIGERATION TIME:** 24 TO 48 HOURS | **COOKING TIME:** ABOUT 2 HOURS
SPECIAL EQUIPMENT: SPICE MILL, WATER SMOKER, 3 LARGE HANDFULS CHERRY WOOD CHUNKS, INSTANT-READ THERMOMETER

RUB

1 tablespoon black peppercorns
1 tablespoon coriander seed
2 teaspoons yellow mustard seed
2 tablespoons packed light brown sugar
1 tablespoon kosher salt
2 teaspoons paprika
1 teaspoon ground cumin

1 boneless turkey breast half (with skin), 2½ to 3 pounds
1 tablespoon extra-virgin olive oil
Sliced rye bread
Lettuce leaves
Tomato slices
Mayonnaise
New York–style deli mustard

Classic pastrami, like the ragged, fatty slices you get piled high on rye in a Jewish deli, comes from the brisket (chest area) of a cow. Because that thick, muscular slab of beef is smoked with low heat to break down its connective tissues, my friend Meathead Goldwyn of Amazingribs.com has declared that America's oldest, continually operated barbecue restaurant is Katz Deli, which opened in New York City in 1888. Traditionally the beef is cured in a brine, seasoned with spices such as coriander, black pepper, mustard seed, and paprika, and then put into a smoker to transform before it is steamed and sliced. In this recipe I have applied similar techniques and seasonings to a turkey breast because, let's face it, that normally bland cut really benefits from an earthy, peppery burst of flavor and the quintessential dark bark of old-world pastrami.

1   In a small skillet over medium heat on the stove, stir and shake the peppercorns, coriander seed, and mustard seed until lightly toasted and fragrant, 3 to 4 minutes. Transfer to a small bowl and cool for 5 minutes. Pour into a spice mill and pulse 15 to 20 times until coarsely ground. Transfer back to the small bowl, add the remaining rub ingredients, and mix well.

2   Brush the turkey breast with the oil and season evenly with the rub. Wrap tightly in a double layer of plastic wrap, place on a plate, and refrigerate for 24 to 48 hours.

3   Prepare the smoker for indirect cooking with very low heat (225° to 275°F). When the temperature reaches 225°F, add the wood chunks to the charcoal.

4   Cook the turkey breast, skin side up, over **indirect very low heat**, with the lid closed, until an instant-read thermometer inserted into the thickest part of the breast registers 160°F, about 2 hours. Remove the turkey from the smoker and let rest for 20 minutes, uncovered (the internal temperature will rise 5 to 10 degrees during this time). Cut the turkey into slices and make sandwiches with rye bread, lettuce, tomato, mayonnaise, and mustard.

STATE FAIR TURKEY LEGS

SERVES: 6 | **PREP TIME:** 15 MINUTES | **BRINING TIME:** 12 HOURS | **COOKING TIME:** 1¾ TO 2 HOURS
SPECIAL EQUIPMENT: WATER SMOKER, 2 LARGE HANDFULS CHERRY OR APPLE WOOD CHUNKS, INSTANT-READ THERMOMETER

BRINE

- 1 quart water
- 3 cups turbinado sugar
- 1½ cups kosher salt
- 1 tablespoon celery seed
- 1 tablespoon coriander seed
- 1 tablespoon cumin seed
- 1 tablespoon yellow mustard seed
- 1 quart ice cubes

- 6 turkey drumsticks, each ¾ to 1 pound
- 2 tablespoons canola oil

SAUCE

- ⅔ cup ketchup
- 2 teaspoons unsulfured molasses (not blackstrap)
- 2 teaspoons cider vinegar
- 2 teaspoons Worcestershire sauce
- 1 teaspoon prepared chili powder
- 1 teaspoon granulated garlic
- ½ teaspoon freshly ground black pepper
- ½ teaspoon ground cumin

Every August, Des Moines, Iowa, is overrun with turkeys! Well, actually, with turkey legs. Brined and barbecued, they're a signature dish of the state fair, an 11-day event that highlights the best produce, livestock, and home crafts from this agriculturally rich state. Don't skip the 12-hour brine. That and the gentle heat of a smoker are crucial for breaking down the tight turkey tendons and yielding tender meat dripping with juices. Have a crunchy, summery salad with a creamy dressing and some grilled ears of corn to accompany this American classic.

1 In a large pot combine all the brine ingredients except the ice cubes. Cook over high heat on the stove until the salt and sugar are dissolved, about 5 minutes, whisking constantly. Add the ice and stir until it melts. Submerge the turkey drumsticks in the cool brine. Cover and refrigerate for 12 hours. If any parts of the drumsticks are not completely submerged, reposition them occasionally to make sure they all get enough time in the brine.

2 Prepare the smoker for indirect cooking with very low heat (250° to 300°F).

3 Remove the drumsticks from the brine, pat dry with paper towels, and brush them all over with the oil. Discard the brine.

4 Add the wood chunks to the charcoal and, when smoke appears, cook the drumsticks over ***indirect very low heat***, with the lid closed, until well browned and an instant-read thermometer inserted into the thickest part of the meat (not touching the bone) registers 165°F, 1¼ to 1½ hours. Meanwhile, make the sauce.

5 In a small saucepan combine the sauce ingredients. Bring to a simmer over medium heat on the stove, and then lower the heat and simmer for about 2 minutes, stirring occasionally.

6 After the internal temperature of the drumsticks has reached 165°F, brush them all over with the sauce. Continue cooking over ***indirect very low heat***, with the lid closed, until the internal temperature reaches 175° to 180°F, 20 to 30 minutes more. Remove the drumsticks from the smoker and let rest for 15 minutes (the internal temperature will rise 5 to 10 degrees during this time). Serve warm.

SMOKED TURKEY
WITH HERB GRAVY

SERVES: 8 TO 10 | **PREP TIME:** 20 MINUTES, PLUS ABOUT 4 HOURS FOR THE STOCK | **CHILLING TIME:** 12 TO 16 HOURS
COOKING TIME: 4½ TO 5½ HOURS | **SPECIAL EQUIPMENT:** WOODEN SKEWER; BUTCHER'S TWINE; 1 PIECE DOUBLE-THICK CHEESECLOTH, ABOUT 2½ FEET LONG; WATER SMOKER; 3 LARGE HANDFULS PECAN, APPLE, OR HICKORY WOOD CHUNKS; INSTANT-READ THERMOMETER

1 whole turkey, about 13 pounds, thawed if frozen

STOCK

3 pounds turkey wings or backs, preferably chopped with a cleaver into 2- to 3-inch chunks, plus reserved tail, fat, giblets, and neck from the turkey
1 tablespoon vegetable oil
1 small yellow onion, chopped
1 small carrot, chopped
1 small celery rib with leaves, chopped
1 cup dry white wine
4 sprigs fresh Italian parsley
1½ teaspoons kosher salt
½ teaspoon dried thyme
½ teaspoon black peppercorns
1 bay leaf

RUB

2 tablespoons kosher salt
2 teaspoons dried sage
1 teaspoon dried marjoram
1 teaspoon dried rosemary
1 teaspoon dried thyme
1 teaspoon freshly ground black pepper

Vegetable oil
1 yellow onion, 3 to 4 ounces, very coarsely chopped
½ small orange, very coarsely chopped
4 sprigs fresh Italian parsley
2 bay leaves, coarsely crumbled

GRAVY

Melted unsalted butter, as needed (up to 4 tablespoons)
½ cup unbleached all-purpose flour
1 teaspoon finely chopped fresh thyme leaves
1 teaspoon finely chopped fresh rosemary leaves
Kosher salt
Freshly ground black pepper

Because the drippings from a barbecued turkey can sometimes be too smoky to make gravy, here I make the gravy separately with a homemade stock prepared earlier with oven-roasted turkey wings and giblets. The charcoal also gives off smoke and flavor, so resist the temptation to add extra wood chunks.

1 Pat the turkey dry, inside and outside, with paper towels. Cut off the turkey tail, if necessary. Pull any fat from inside the body cavity near the tail. Remove the giblets and neck (discard the liver). Using a heavy knife or poultry shears cut the neck into 2-inch chunks. Remove and discard the pop-up thermometer and any plastic or metal pieces. Save the tail, fat, giblets, and neck. Preheat the oven to 400°F. Place the turkey wings or backs, the tail, fat, giblets, and neck in a large roasting pan, and then roast until well browned, about 1 hour, turning the pieces once.

2 In a large stockpot over medium-high heat on the stove, warm the oil. Add the onion, carrot, and celery. Cook until softened and lightly browned, about 3 minutes, stirring occasionally. Add the turkey pieces to the stockpot and set the roasting pan aside. Pour enough cold water into the stockpot to just barely cover the ingredients. Bring to a boil over high heat, skimming off any foam that rises to the surface. Add the remaining stock ingredients. Reduce the heat to low and simmer until the stock is full flavored, about 2 hours, skimming occasionally. Strain the stock through a fine-mesh strainer into a large bowl. Let stand 5 minutes to allow the fat to separate. Skim and discard the fat. Return the stock to the stockpot and boil over high heat until reduced to 1 quart, 15 to 20 minutes.

3 Meanwhile, heat the roasting pan over high heat on the stove until the fat is sizzling. Pour the fat from the pan into a small bowl. Return the pan to the heat. Add 1 cup water and bring to a boil, scraping up all the browned bits in the pan. Cook until reduced to ½ cup, about 1 minute. Transfer these deglazed drippings to a separate, small bowl. Cool, cover, and refrigerate the stock, fat, and ½ cup of deglazed drippings for up to 2 days.

4 While the stock is cooking, combine the rub ingredients. Brush the turkey with 2 tablespoons oil and season evenly, inside and outside, with the rub. Tuck the wing tips behind the turkey's back. Carefully coat the turkey all over with a little oil to keep the herbs moist. Place the turkey on a wire rack set over a rimmed sheet pan and refrigerate, uncovered, for 12 to 16 hours.

5 Stuff the onion, orange, parsley, and bay leaves into the turkey body and neck cavities. Using a wooden skewer, pin the neck skin to the back skin to enclose the seasoning mixture. Tie the ends of the drumsticks together with butcher's twine. Let the turkey stand at room temperature for 1 hour before cooking. Meanwhile, rinse the cheesecloth under cold running water. Wring it out, put it in a medium bowl, and saturate it with 2 tablespoons oil.

6 Prepare the smoker for indirect cooking with very low heat (225° to 250°F). When the temperature reaches 225°F, add the wood chunks to the charcoal.

7 Brush the bottom of the turkey again with oil. Wrap the moistened cheesecloth around the turkey. Smoke the turkey over *indirect very low heat*, with the lid closed, for 3½ hours. Discard the cheesecloth and tent the breast area loosely with aluminum foil. Continue smoking, with the lid closed, until the turkey is deep golden brown and an instant-read thermometer inserted in the thickest part of the thigh (not touching the bone) reaches 170° to 175°F, 1 to 2 hours more, checking the temperature every 30 minutes.

8 Remove the turkey from the smoker. Tilt the body cavity over a 1-quart measuring cup to catch any juices that have accumulated. Add enough stock to measure 1 quart. Let the turkey rest for 30 minutes (the internal temperature will rise 5 to 10 degrees during this time).

9 In a medium saucepan over medium heat, warm the turkey fat. Measure it and add enough melted butter to make ½ cup. Return the fat mixture to the saucepan. Whisk in the flour and let bubble over medium heat until the flour smells cooked and turns light golden brown, 2 to 3 minutes. Whisk in the stock mixture, deglazed drippings, thyme, and rosemary. Bring to a simmer, and then reduce the heat to medium-low and cook until slightly thickened, 5 to 8 minutes, stirring often. Season with salt and pepper.

10 Carve the turkey, discarding the ingredients in the body cavity, and serve warm with the gravy.

5

SEAFOOD

CEDAR-PLANKED SALMON
WITH PICKLED FENNEL SALAD AND HORSERADISH CREAM

SERVES: 4 | **PREP TIME:** 30 MINUTES | **GRILLING TIME:** 15 TO 20 MINUTES
SPECIAL EQUIPMENT: 1 UNTREATED CEDAR PLANK, ABOUT 12 INCHES LONG AND 7 INCHES WIDE

PICKLING LIQUID
1 cup dry white wine or vermouth
¾ cup white wine vinegar
2 tablespoons granulated sugar
2 teaspoons fennel seed
8 juniper berries
2 small garlic cloves, crushed

Kosher salt
½ large fennel bulb, cored and cut into 1-inch strips
½ small head radicchio, cored and cut into 2-inch strips
2 tablespoons prepared horseradish
1½ teaspoons finely chopped fresh dill
½ cup crème fraîche or sour cream
Freshly ground black pepper
1 center-cut salmon fillet (with skin), about 2 pounds and 1 inch thick, pin bones removed
Extra-virgin olive oil
1 small bunch watercress, torn into small sprigs

One chef who inspires me is Edward Lee, a Korean American who grew up in Brooklyn, trained in chichi French kitchens, and now runs his own restaurants in the South. He has a special way of weaving together the threads of his eclectic background and exploring the boundaries of barbecue. "Nothing cuts the intensity of smokiness like a sharp pickle," he writes in his first cookbook. "Together they are harmonious, the perfect yin and yang." That's why pickles show up so often with barbecue, including this recipe that skips the traditional dill pickles for a vegetable salad with pickled fennel and radicchio. After all, this is new American barbecue.

1 Soak the cedar plank in water for at least 1 hour.

2 In a small, nonreactive saucepan combine the pickling liquid ingredients, including 2½ tablespoons salt. Bring to a boil over medium heat on the stove, add the fennel strips, and simmer until tender but not mushy, 3 to 4 minutes. Using a slotted spoon, transfer the fennel strips to paper towels to dry. Add the radicchio to the simmering pickling liquid and cook for 1½ minutes only, just until wilted. Using a slotted spoon, transfer the radicchio to paper towels to dry.

3 Whisk the horseradish, dill, and crème fraîche, and season lightly with salt and generously with pepper.

4 Prepare the grill for direct cooking over medium heat (350° to 450°F).

5 Cut the salmon fillet into four equal portions, cutting down to, but not all the way through the skin. Brush the salmon with oil and season evenly with salt and pepper.

6 Drain the cedar plank. Place it over **direct medium heat** and close the lid. When the plank begins to smoke and char, turn it over. Place the salmon, skin side down, on the plank. Grill over **direct medium heat**, with the lid closed, until cooked to your desired doneness, 15 to 20 minutes for medium rare. Carefully transfer the fillet on the plank to a heatproof surface. Slide a spatula between the skin and flesh and transfer individual portions of the salmon to serving plates.

7 In a bowl combine the pickled vegetables, watercress, and 1½ tablespoons oil and toss gently until evenly coated. Serve the salmon warm with the salad and horseradish cream.

Before cooking fish on a cedar plank, start the plank smoking. Submerge it in water for at least one hour, drain it, and set it over the fire until you smell smoke. Then turn it over and lay the fish on top. If the plank ever catches fire, put out the flames with a spray bottle filled with water. Cedar is the classic pairing with salmon, but if you can find fruitwood or mesquite planks, try one of those for an interesting variation.

SALMON
IN TOMATO-ANDOUILLE BROTH

SERVES: 4 | **PREP TIME:** 25 MINUTES
GRILLING TIME: 16 TO 18 MINUTES

BROTH

- 2 cups low-sodium chicken broth
- ⅔ cup dry white wine or vermouth
- 2 teaspoons white wine vinegar
- 3 sprigs fresh thyme
- 3 garlic cloves, smashed and peeled
- ½ teaspoon ground cumin
- ½ teaspoon hot chili-garlic sauce, such as Sriracha
- ¼ teaspoon kosher salt
- ¼ teaspoon smoked paprika

- 3 medium, vine-ripened tomatoes, about 12 ounces total, cored, each cut crosswise in half, seeds scraped away
- 3 fully cooked andouille sausages, each 3 to 4 ounces
  Extra-virgin olive oil
  Kosher salt
  Freshly ground black pepper
- 1¼ pounds salmon fillet (with skin), about ¾ inch thick, pin bones removed
- ¼ teaspoon smoked paprika
- 4 large slices rustic bread, each about ½ inch thick
- ⅓ cup loosely packed fresh cilantro leaves

One reason that salmon is such a popular fish for grilling is because you can taste the flavors of fire in the fish after just a few minutes on the hot grate. This recipe echoes those flavors in a warm, savory broth made quickly with grilled smoky sausages and charred tomatoes. I like how the broth keeps the fish moist and tender in the bowl.

1 In a small saucepan combine the broth ingredients. Bring to a simmer over medium heat on the stove, and then reduce the heat to low. Cover and simmer gently for 15 minutes to infuse the broth with flavor. Remove from the heat and keep covered.

2 Prepare the grill for direct cooking over medium-high heat (425° to 450°F).

3 Brush the tomato halves and sausages with oil and season the tomato halves with ¼ teaspoon salt and ¼ teaspoon pepper. Grill the tomatoes and sausages over **direct medium-high heat**, with the lid closed, until the tomatoes are slightly charred and the sausages are deep brown in spots, about 5 minutes for the tomatoes and about 8 minutes for the sausages, turning occasionally. Remove from the grill to cool slightly.

4 Lightly brush the salmon with oil and season with ¼ teaspoon salt, ¼ teaspoon pepper, and ¼ teaspoon paprika. Lightly brush the bread slices with oil. Grill the salmon, skin side down, over **direct medium-high heat**, with the lid closed, until opaque in the center, 8 to 10 minutes (do not turn). During the last minute of grilling time, toast the bread over direct heat, turning once.

5 Reheat the broth, if necessary, and discard the thyme and large chunks of garlic. Dice the tomatoes and cut the sausages crosswise into ¼-inch-thick slices. Divide the tomatoes, sausages, and salmon among four shallow bowls. Ladle the broth on top and garnish with cilantro. Serve warm with the grilled bread slices on the side.

GRILLED SALMON BLT SANDWICHES

SERVES: 2 | **PREP TIME:** 15 MINUTES
GRILLING TIME: 5 TO 6 MINUTES

Here I have taken a classic American sandwich on a road trip up the West Coast, picking up luscious avocado and fresh salmon along the way. Grilling skinless fish can be a little tricky because the skin usually helps to hold the flesh together, so be sure the cooking grates are really hot and really clean, and don't fiddle too much with the fish. Turn the fillets just once. Also, brushing the fish generously with oil before you start helps prevent sticking.

4 slices thick-cut bacon
2 skinless salmon fillets, each
   5 to 6 ounces and about ½ inch
   thick, pin bones removed
   Extra-virgin olive oil
⅛ teaspoon kosher salt
⅛ teaspoon freshly ground black pepper
4 slices sourdough bread from a
   crusty loaf
1 small Hass avocado, smashed
   Mayonnaise
2 leaves romaine lettuce
1 medium beefsteak tomato, cut
   crosswise into 4 thin slices

1 Prepare the grill for direct cooking over high heat (450° to 550°F).

2 In a large skillet over medium heat on the stove, fry the bacon until crisp, 10 to 12 minutes, turning occasionally. Transfer the bacon to a plate lined with paper towels.

3 Brush the salmon fillets on both sides with oil and season evenly with the salt and pepper. Brush one side of each slice of bread with oil.

4 Grill the fillets over **direct high heat**, with the lid closed, until you can lift them off the cooking grates without sticking, about 3 minutes. Turn the fillets over and continue grilling to your desired doneness, 2 to 3 minutes more for medium rare. During the last 30 seconds of grilling time, toast the bread over direct heat on the oiled side only. Remove from the grill and let the salmon rest for 2 to 3 minutes.

5 To build the sandwiches, generously spread the non-grilled side of two bread slices with avocado and the other two slices with mayonnaise. Then add tomato slices, lettuce, bacon, and salmon. Serve immediately.

SMOKED TUNA PROVENÇAL SLIDERS

SERVES: 4 TO 6 (MAKES 12 SLIDERS) | **PREP TIME:** 35 MINUTES | **GRILLING TIME:** 15 TO 20 MINUTES
SPECIAL EQUIPMENT: 3 LARGE HANDFULS APPLE, CHERRY, OR OAK WOOD CHIPS

This recipe elevates regular ole tuna salad to the nth degree by combining aromatic wood-smoked fish with Provençal favorites such as olives, capers, and garlic. The sliders can be wrapped individually in plastic wrap and refrigerated for a few hours before serving; in fact, you may prefer them that way, giving the flavors a chance to mingle. If, instead, you're serving them right away, insert a toothpick into the center of each sandwich to keep all the ingredients neatly stacked inside the rolls.

⅔ cup mayonnaise
1 large garlic clove, minced
1 pound tuna steaks, about 1 inch
　thick, patted dry
　Extra-virgin olive oil
　Kosher salt
　Freshly ground black pepper
2 tablespoons fresh lemon juice
1 teaspoon Dijon mustard
1 teaspoon anchovy paste
3 tablespoons finely chopped
　Kalamata olives
2 tablespoons capers, rinsed
12 slider buns or dinner rolls, split,
　some of the interior bread pulled out
　from each side
3 ripe plum tomatoes, thinly sliced
3 large hard-boiled eggs, thinly sliced
1 cup packed baby arugula

1　Soak the wood chips in water for at least 30 minutes.

2　Prepare the grill for indirect cooking over medium-low heat (about 350°F).

3　To make aioli, mix the mayonnaise and garlic. Cover and set aside while smoking the tuna.

4　Lightly brush the tuna on all sides with oil and season evenly with ¼ teaspoon salt and ¼ teaspoon pepper. Drain and add the wood chips to the charcoal or to the smoker box of a gas grill, following manufacturer's instructions, and close the lid. When smoke appears, grill the tuna over **indirect medium-low heat**, with the lid closed, until it has a light golden patina and is just turning opaque throughout, 15 to 20 minutes. Remove from the grill and break the tuna into ½-inch pieces.

5　In a large bowl whisk the lemon juice, mustard, anchovy paste, ¼ teaspoon salt, and ¼ teaspoon pepper. Gradually whisk in 3 tablespoons oil. Add the tuna, olives, and capers and mix well.

6　Spread the cut side of each roll lightly with aioli. Top with tomatoes, tuna salad, eggs, and arugula. Serve immediately, or wrap individually and refrigerate for a few hours.

SEARED TUNA
WITH OLIVE-CAPER VINAIGRETTE

SERVES: 4 | **PREP TIME:** 15 MINUTES
GRILLING TIME: 3 TO 4 MINUTES

1½ teaspoons finely grated lemon zest
3 tablespoons fresh lemon juice
½ teaspoon anchovy paste
¼ teaspoon mustard powder
Kosher salt
1 garlic clove, minced
⅛ teaspoon crushed red pepper flakes
Freshly ground black pepper
Extra-virgin olive oil
⅓ cup Kalamata olives,
finely chopped
2 tablespoons capers, drained
1 teaspoon finely chopped fresh
thyme leaves
4 tuna steaks, preferably sushi grade,
each about 6 ounces and 1 inch thick
6 ounces baby arugula
4 large hard-boiled eggs, each cut
into quarters

With its meaty texture, tuna takes especially well to a searing-hot grate and the marks add a nicely charred flavor. You can serve the tuna warm, but when the weather is warm, serve it chilled for a light meal that you can make ahead.

1 Prepare the grill for direct cooking over high heat (450° to 550°F).

2 In a medium bowl whisk the lemon zest and juice, anchovy paste, mustard powder, ¼ teaspoon salt, garlic, red pepper flakes, and ⅛ teaspoon pepper. Gradually whisk in ¼ cup oil. Add the olives, capers, and thyme and mix to create the vinaigrette.

3 Lightly brush the tuna steaks on both sides with oil, season evenly with 1 teaspoon salt and ½ teaspoon pepper, and then grill over **direct high heat**, with the lid open, until cooked to your desired doneness, 3 to 4 minutes for rare, turning once. Remove from the grill and let rest for about 3 minutes. Cut each tuna steak across the grain into ½-inch thick slices, and then cut into bite-sized pieces.

4 Divide the arugula among four serving plates and top with tuna, eggs, and vinaigrette. Serve while the tuna is still warm.

Most of the tuna in supermarkets today is sold in fairly thin slices, and the quality is such that you need to cook it all the way through for safe eating. Occasionally it's worth seeking out sushi-grade tuna for something special. It is particularly wonderful if the tuna "steaks" are cut thick enough that you can sear the outside for flavor and appearance while leaving the centers raw. The color contrast is gorgeous and the taste of the seared surfaces with the raw flesh is dynamite.

SWORDFISH STEAKS
WITH QUICK TOMATO-ANCHOVY SAUCE

SERVES: 4 | **PREP TIME:** 15 MINUTES, PLUS ABOUT 20 MINUTES FOR THE SAUCE | **GRILLING TIME:** 6 TO 7 MINUTES
SPECIAL EQUIPMENT: CHARCOAL GRILL, ALL-NATURAL LUMP CHARCOAL , 4 TO 6 LARGE HANDFULS HICKORY WOOD CHUNKS

SAUCE
 1 tablespoon extra-virgin olive oil
 ½ cup finely chopped yellow onion
 4 garlic cloves, minced
 3 anchovy fillets packed in olive oil,
   finely chopped
 ½ teaspoon crushed red pepper flakes,
   or to taste
 12 ounces grape tomatoes or small
   cherry tomatoes
 ½ cup Kalamata olives,
   coarsely chopped
 ½ cup dry white wine
 1 tablespoon capers, rinsed

 4 swordfish steaks (with skin), each
   6 to 8 ounces and about 1 inch thick
 1 tablespoon extra-virgin olive oil
 ¾ teaspoon kosher salt
 ½ teaspoon freshly ground black pepper

The sharp, pungent flavors of this sauce balance really well with charred fish and shellfish. The anchovies melt into the sauce, adding to the umami-rich flavors, while the chile flakes give a nice kick of heat. Swordfish is dry when overcooked, so don't walk away from the steaks, and be sure to adjust your cooking time according to their thickness.

1 In a large, heavy skillet over medium heat on the stove, warm 1 tablespoon oil. Add the onion and sauté until it begins to soften, about 2 minutes, stirring occasionally. Add the garlic, anchovies, and red pepper flakes. Sauté until fragrant, about 1 minute, stirring often. Add the tomatoes, olives, wine, and capers. Bring to a boil, and then reduce the heat to medium-low. Partially cover the skillet and simmer until the tomatoes begin to break down, 8 to 10 minutes, breaking up some of the tomatoes with the back of a spoon and stirring occasionally. Uncover the skillet and continue to cook until the sauce thickens, 5 to 7 minutes more, stirring occasionally. Remove from the heat and cover to keep warm.

2 Prepare the charcoal grill with all-natural lump charcoal for direct cooking over high heat (450° to 550°F) and add the wood chunks.

3 Lightly brush the swordfish steaks on both sides with 1 tablespoon oil and season evenly with the salt and pepper. When the wood chunks have burned down to embers, grill the swordfish over **direct high heat**, with the lid closed, until just opaque in the center and still juicy, 6 to 7 minutes, turning once. Remove from the grill and serve warm with the sauce.

BLACKENED RED SNAPPER TACOS
WITH GRILLED PINEAPPLE SALSA

SERVES: 4 | **PREP TIME:** 20 MINUTES | **GRILLING TIME:** ABOUT 15 MINUTES
SPECIAL EQUIPMENT: 12-INCH CAST-IRON SKILLET

SALSA
- 1 medium pineapple, peel removed
- 1 tablespoon canola oil
- ¼ cup finely chopped red onion
- 2 tablespoons fresh lime juice
- 2 tablespoons finely chopped fresh cilantro leaves
- ½ teaspoon kosher salt
- ¼ teaspoon ground cumin

RUB
- 1 tablespoon paprika
- 1 teaspoon garlic powder
- 1 teaspoon dried oregano, crumbled
- 1 teaspoon kosher salt
- ½ teaspoon ground cumin
- ¼ teaspoon freshly ground black pepper
- ⅛ teaspoon ground cayenne pepper

- 1½ pounds skinless red snapper fillets, about ½ inch thick
- 2 tablespoons unsalted butter
- 8 flour or corn tortillas (6 inches)
- 2 limes, each cut into 4 wedges

One of the titans of American cooking, Paul Prudhomme of New Orleans, revolutionized regional cooking in the 1980s by highlighting Cajun food as a distinct style worthy to stand beside any other cuisine. Blackened redfish was the dish that launched his revolution. Here's a variation of that dish you can do on the grill, with the blackened snapper wrapped inside tortillas and topped with a salsa.

1   Prepare the grill for direct cooking over medium-high heat (400° to 450°F).

2   Cut the pineapple crosswise into six ½-inch-thick slices (don't cut out the core). You may not need all of the pineapple. Brush the pineapple slices on both sides with the oil.

3   Grill the pineapple slices over **direct medium-high heat**, with the lid closed, until lightly charred and softened, 5 to 8 minutes, turning once. Remove from the grill, cut out the core, and discard. Coarsely chop the pineapple and place in a medium bowl. Add the remaining salsa ingredients to the pineapple and stir until evenly combined.

4   Mix the rub ingredients. Season the fillets evenly on both sides with the rub.

5   In a 12-inch cast-iron skillet over **direct medium-high heat**, melt the butter. Before the butter begins to brown, add the fillets to the skillet (see caption and photo below) and cook over **direct medium-high heat**, with the lid closed, for 5 minutes. Using a metal spatula, turn the fillets over and continue cooking until the flesh barely begins to flake when poked with the tip of a knife, 2 to 3 minutes more. Remove the skillet from the grill. Break the fillets into large chunks.

6   Warm the tortillas over direct heat for about 10 seconds on each side. Fill the tortillas with equal amounts of the fish and top with the salsa. Serve right away with the lime wedges.

When chef Paul Prudhomme introduced America to blackened redfish (also called red drum), it grew so popular that it had to be protected from overfishing. Red snapper works well with this technique, as do grouper and mahimahi. Turn the fish away from you so that any splattering butter does not burn you.

ZITI AND SMOKED TROUT
WITH PEAS AND CREAM

SERVES: 4 | PREP TIME: 20 MINUTES | GRILLING TIME: ABOUT 10 MINUTES
SPECIAL EQUIPMENT: 1 LARGE HANDFUL PECAN OR APPLE WOOD CHIPS, WIDE FISH TURNER

2 whole trout, each about
   8 ounces, butterflied
1 tablespoon extra-virgin olive oil
   Kosher salt
   Freshly ground black pepper
12 ounces dried ziti or penne pasta
¼ cup (½ stick) unsalted butter, cut
   into small chunks
⅓ cup minced shallots
1 cup dry white wine, such
   as Chardonnay
1 cup heavy whipping cream
1 cup hulled fresh peas or frozen peas
   (do not thaw)
2 ounces Parmigiano-Reggiano®
   cheese, finely grated
1 teaspoon finely grated lemon zest
2 tablespoons finely chopped fresh dill

This warm pasta supper gets a burst of flavor from home-smoked trout, which is milder and tenderer than what you usually find in supermarkets. It is very nice served on a summer evening with a glass of cold beer or a crisp wine.

1 Soak the wood chips in water for at least 30 minutes.

2 Prepare the grill for indirect cooking over medium heat (350° to 450°F).

3 Rub the skin of the trout with the oil and season the flesh with ¼ teaspoon salt and ¼ teaspoon pepper. Drain and add the wood chips to the charcoal or to the smoker box of a gas grill, following manufacturer's instructions, and close the lid. When smoke appears, grill the trout over **indirect medium heat**, with the lid closed, until the flesh is opaque and flakes easily, about 10 minutes (do not turn). Remove from the grill and cool for a few minutes. Remove the flesh from the trout, discarding the head, tail, skin, and bones. Break the flesh into large, bite-sized pieces.

4 Bring a large pot of salted water to a boil on the stove for the pasta, and cook according to package directions. Drain.

5 Preheat a large skillet over high heat on the stove for 3 to 4 minutes. Add the butter to the skillet to melt. Add the shallots and cook until softened but not browned, about 3 minutes, stirring often. Add the wine and cream. Bring the sauce to a full boil, stirring occasionally, and then boil for 2 minutes to thicken slightly. The sauce should still be a bit soupy. Add the peas and cook for 1 minute, stirring occasionally. Add the pasta. Toss well until heated through and coated with the sauce, about 1 minute. Stir in the cheese, lemon zest, 1 teaspoon salt and ¼ teaspoon pepper and cook until hot and bubbling, about 1 minute. At the last moment, add the trout pieces to the skillet and mix everything very gently to combine the ingredients. Garnish with dill. Serve immediately.

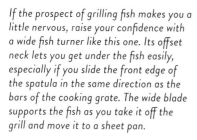

If the prospect of grilling fish makes you a little nervous, raise your confidence with a wide fish turner like this one. Its offset neck lets you get under the fish easily, especially if you slide the front edge of the spatula in the same direction as the bars of the cooking grate. The wide blade supports the fish as you take it off the grill and move it to a sheet pan.

NEW ORLEANS'
SEAFOOD BARBECUE

When fire meets meat, barbecue happens. What also often happens is a lively debate about the correct sauce and the best choice of wood or charcoal. Then there is the question of whether the meat should be beef or pork, or both. At Pêche Seafood Grill, the answer is neither. With a multi-functional, wood-fired grill, chef Ryan Prewitt and his team are fashioning a new, idiosyncratic style of barbecue that is more than surf than turf, and miles from what you might expect of seafood in New Orleans.

"We wanted to open a seafood restaurant that put the focus on the quality of the Gulf seafood," Prewitt told me just before lunch service at the restaurant. Whole pompano straight from the Gulf and grilled over oak and pecan coals was the daily special. It wasn't fried, doused in butter, or topped with crab and crawfish like you'd find elsewhere in town, but covered in a relish of red onions, Italian parsley, and fresh cucumbers. There is a smoky essence in the tender, mild white fish, and a brightness in the garnish that you don't often get with barbecue. Heck, it might even be considered healthy.

Prewitt seems a natural with seafood as he discusses the finer points of Champagne Bay versus Caminada Bay oysters (both from the Louisiana shore), and the James Beard Foundation agreed. They named him Best Chef: South (May 2014), but seafood wasn't his first love. Being a Memphis boy, he was all about pork barbecue growing up.

Prewitt moved to New Orleans four weeks before Katrina hit, having landed a position with chef Donald Link at a white-linen restaurant called Herbsaint, where Link was getting international acclaim for the way he put a Southern spin on French and Italian dishes. It all fell into place when Prewitt's wife got into graduate school at Tulane. "Our fate was sealed," he revealed. Hurricane or not, New Orleans was his new home, and opening a new restaurant with Donald Link was always his goal. They just didn't know what kind of restaurant. "The idea developed concurrently with a period where we were traveling with a lot of barbecue

guys," Prewitt recalls. He and Link were part of the Fatback Collective—a sort of barbecue dream team made up of chefs, writers, and farmers—and they competed in his hometown at the biggest whole hog competition on the planet, Memphis in May. Prewitt was hooked, and knew he wanted to keep cooking with fire.

The idea and passion coalesced on a trip to Uruguay. "Seeing the way they cooked and how they used fire was a completely different view of it than I had previously had," said Prewitt. "There were no smokers or other contraptions to harness the fire. They would just build bonfires and cook over it. They'd build walls of fire so hot you could put a pot next to it and it would boil," he told me while sweating beside the mini-inferno blazing within his kitchen's grill. It might not be a wall of fire, but it's no joke. Soon after the restaurant opened, a cook fainted from dehydration while manning the grill. Now they work the grill in pairs.

In addition to the house specialty of whole fish, there's a seasonal menu and a more fluid daily menu. Wood-grilled sardines (one of the few items not from the Gulf) were fresh enough to bring in as a daily special. They showed their deep grill marks under a garnish of bacon jam and celery hearts. The fire made for some sweet and smoky fish with a nice char.

At the raw bar, they whip up an order of smoked tuna dip from Gulf-caught tuna smoked in a designated chamber within the wood grill. Chunks of smoked drum are tossed with pickled sweet potatoes and sesame seeds. The flavors of smoke with pickled vegetables are familiar, but the combination is exhilarating. The same can be said for what sounds like a simple side dish of corn, but the wood grill makes it anything but simple. The whole ears are grilled with their shucks still on until the kernels are cooked. The shucks and kernels are then removed from the cobs, and a rich, smoky stock is made with the charred shucks and the cobs. That all gets mixed back into the corn along with chile oil and Grana Padano cheese. The depth of the stock and umami from the corn and cheese make this dish taste more like barbecue than any vegetable I can remember.

Lovers of more traditional barbecue are also taken care of at Pêche Seafood Grill. Chicken with Alabama white sauce is on the regular menu, but, of course, it is reimagined into something more fitting for rustic elegance of the restaurant. Rather than the usual half chicken, they grill boneless thighs on wood skewers, and then coat them with the tangy white sauce. It's like a barbecue hors d'oeuvre that you can't stop eating.

The twist on the barbecue paradigm is refreshing, but, as with all great barbecue, it's best when it isn't overcomplicated. "The idea is that we have the wonderful cooking medium and this thoughtfully sourced product. Put them together and give them just a nudge in the right direction," Chef Prewitt says modestly, but he and his staff provide a lot more than a nudge, and the direction they are going is both familiar and uncharted.

SHRIMP COBB SALAD
WITH SMOKED TOMATO–BUTTERMILK DRESSING

SERVES: 4 TO 6 | **PREP TIME:** 25 MINUTES | **CHILLING TIME:** 1 HOUR | **MARINATING TIME:** 1 HOUR | **GRILLING TIME:** 28 TO 50 MINUTES
SPECIAL EQUIPMENT: 2 LARGE HANDFULS APPLE, CHERRY, OR PECAN WOOD CHIPS; 8 METAL OR BAMBOO SKEWERS; 2 SMALL DISPOSABLE FOIL PANS; PERFORATED GRILL PAN

2 scallions
2 tomatoes, each about 6 ounces, cut crosswise in half
Extra-virgin olive oil
10 ounces grape tomatoes
Kosher salt
Freshly ground black pepper
1 garlic clove, coarsely chopped
½ cup buttermilk
⅓ cup mayonnaise
2 tablespoons coarsely chopped fresh dill
1 tablespoon cider vinegar
¼ teaspoon smoked paprika
1½ pounds large shrimp (21/30 count), peeled and deveined, tails left on or removed
1 tablespoon fresh lemon juice
2 romaine lettuce hearts, each about 7 ounces, cut into bite-sized pieces
2 large Hass avocados, diced
5 bacon slices, fried and crumbled
4 ounces crumbled feta cheese
4 large hard-boiled eggs, each cut into 4 wedges (optional)

According to American culinary folklore, the Cobb salad came together for the first time one night in 1937 at the hands of Bob Cobb, the hungry owner of a Hollywood restaurant. He gathered this and that from the restaurant's walk-in refrigerator and snatched some crispy bacon from the chef. Since then cooks have swapped various ingredients in and out. My own variation features grilled shrimp in place of the typical chicken or turkey, and a creamy dressing based on smoked tomatoes.

1 Soak the wood chips and skewers (separately) in water for at least 30 minutes.

2 Prepare the grill for indirect cooking over medium heat (350° to 450°F).

3 Coarsely chop the white and light green parts of the scallions (you will use them in the dressing), and thinly slice and reserve the dark green tops for garnish.

4 Place the tomato halves, cut side up, in a small disposable foil pan and drizzle with oil. Place the grape tomatoes in another small disposable foil pan, drizzle with oil, and season with salt and pepper. Drain and add two handfuls of the wood chips to the charcoal or to the smoker box of a gas grill, following manufacturer's instructions, and close the lid. When smoke appears, place the two foil pans with the tomatoes over **indirect medium heat** and close the lid. Cook the tomato halves until very tender and beginning to brown around the edges, 25 to 45 minutes, and cook the grape tomatoes until the skins begin to split, 12 to 25 minutes. Remove from the grill as they are done, and let cool completely.

5 Using a small spoon, scoop the seeds from the tomato halves and discard them. Cut out and discard the stem ends. In a blender puree the tomato halves with the white and light green scallions and garlic. Add the buttermilk, mayonnaise, dill, vinegar, paprika, ¾ teaspoon salt, and ¼ teaspoon pepper and process until smooth. Transfer the dressing to a bowl.

6 Place the shrimp in a large, resealable plastic bag and add the lemon juice, 1 tablespoon oil, and 2 tablespoons of the dressing. Press the air out of the bag and seal tightly. Turn the bag to distribute the marinade and refrigerate for 1 hour. Also cover and refigerate the remaining dressing for 1 hour.

7 Prepare the grill for direct cooking over medium-high heat (400° to 450°F).

8 Remove the shrimp from the bag, leaving any marinade still clinging to the shrimp, and discard the remaining marinade. Thread the shrimp onto skewers, and then grill over **direct medium-high heat**, with the lid closed, until firm to the touch and just turning opaque in the center, 3 to 5 minutes, turning once.

9 Whisk the dressing until smooth and pourable. In a large bowl toss the lettuce with about half of the dressing and transfer to a large platter. Top with rows of grape tomatoes, shrimp, avocados, bacon, feta, and eggs (if using), and garnish with the reserved dark green scallion tops. Serve immediately with the remaining dressing.

SHRIMP AND GRITS

SERVES: 4 | **PREP TIME:** 15 MINUTES, PLUS ABOUT 20 MINUTES FOR THE GRITS | **GRILLING TIME:** 6 TO 8 MINUTES
SPECIAL EQUIPMENT: 1 LARGE HANDFUL APPLE WOOD CHIPS

½ cup (1 stick) unsalted butter
4 cups water
  Kosher salt
1 cup grits
3 ounces white cheddar cheese,
  finely grated
1 garlic clove, minced
1 teaspoon hot pepper sauce
¼ teaspoon freshly ground black pepper
1½ pounds large shrimp (21/30 count),
  peeled and deveined, tails removed
3 scallions (white and light green parts
  only), minced

This Low Country classic is not typically cooked on a grill, but the sweet apple wood smoke does enhance the shrimp. In another departure from tradition, brown butter gives the grits a warm, nutty flavor, and also serves as a simple sauce.

1 Soak the wood chips in water for at least 30 minutes.

2 Prepare the grill for direct cooking over medium heat (350° to 450°F).

3 In a medium saucepan over medium-low heat on the stove, melt the butter. Cook until brown bits form on the bottom of the pan, swirling the pan occasionally, 3 to 4 minutes (see caption and photo below). Remove from the heat and transfer the browned butter to a small glass or other microwave-safe bowl.

4 In the same saucepan used for the butter, combine the water and 1½ teaspoons salt and bring to a boil over medium-high heat on the stove; use a whisk to scrape up the brown bits from the bottom of the pan. Gradually whisk in the grits. Reduce the heat to low and continue cooking until the mixture thickens and the grits are very tender, 15 to 20 minutes, stirring occasionally. Remove the grits from the heat and stir in the cheese and 3 tablespoons of the browned butter. Keep warm over low heat.

5 In a large bowl whisk 1 tablespoon of the browned butter, the garlic, hot sauce, ½ teaspoon salt, and the pepper. Add the shrimp and toss to coat.

6 Drain and add the wood chips to the charcoal or to the smoker box of a gas grill, following manufacturer's instructions, and close the lid. When smoke appears, grill the shrimp over **direct medium heat**, with the lid closed, until firm to the touch and just turning opaque in the center, 6 to 8 minutes, turning once.

7 If the browned butter has solidified, melt it, covered, in a microwave oven.

8 Divide the grits among four warm plates. Top the grits with the shrimp and the remaining brown butter, and garnish with the scallions. Serve immediately.

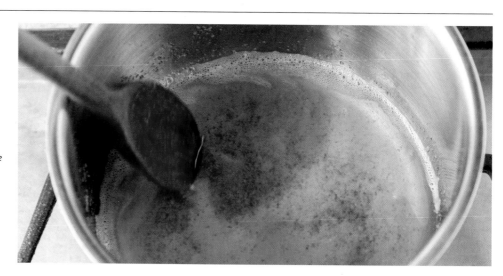

After the butter melts, it will foam up a bit. When the foam subsides, brown specks will appear on the bottom of the pan. These specks are the milk solids in the butter browning and developing nutty aromas. When the butter looks like this, remove the pan from the heat and transfer the butter to a small bowl to prevent the milk solids from burning.

GRILLED SCALLOPS
WITH CAULIFLOWER PUREE AND CRISPY KALE

SERVES: 4 | **PREP TIME:** 30 MINUTES
GRILLING TIME: 5 TO 8 MINUTES

6 large leaves Tuscan (lacinato) kale
  Extra-virgin olive oil
  Kosher salt
1 head cauliflower, about 2 pounds, cored, florets coarsely chopped
1½ cups chicken stock or low-sodium chicken broth
1 small garlic clove
1 ounce Pecorino Romano® cheese, finely grated
3 tablespoons unsalted butter
  Freshly ground black pepper
16 sea scallops, each about 2 ounces, patted dry
2 teaspoons finely grated lemon zest

When cooking scallops be sure to pat them completely dry before oiling them. They hold a lot of water, and sometimes they are soaked in a phosphate solution that makes them look whiter and absorb even more water. To avoid that phosphate solution, look for dry-packed scallops. Get the biggest scallops you can for this recipe.

1 Prepare the grill for direct cooking over medium heat (350° to 450°F).

2 Brush the kale leaves with oil and season with ¼ teaspoon salt. Grill over **direct medium heat**, with the lid closed, until lightly charred and crisp, 2 to 3 minutes, turning once and watching closely to prevent burning. Remove from the grill and, when cool enough to handle, remove and discard the tough ribs and tear the leaves into shards.

3 Place the cauliflower and stock in a large saucepan on the stove. Bring the stock to a boil, and then reduce the heat to medium-low. Cover the pot and simmer until the cauliflower is very tender when pierced with a knife, 18 to 20 minutes. Using a slotted spoon, transfer the cauliflower to the bowl of a food processor. Add ¼ cup of the hot stock and the garlic. Process until the cauliflower is smooth. Add the cheese, butter, 1 teaspoon salt, and ½ teaspoon pepper and pulse to blend. The puree should be smooth and hold its shape when lifted with a spoon. Cover and keep warm.

4 Increase the temperature of the grill to high heat (450° to 550°F).

5 Remove and discard the small, tough side muscle that might be left on each scallop. Lightly brush the scallops on both sides with oil and season evenly with ¾ teaspoon salt and ½ teaspoon pepper. Grill the scallops over **direct high heat**, with the lid closed, until lightly browned and just opaque in the center, 3 to 5 minutes, turning once.

6 Divide the cauliflower puree among serving plates. Using the back of a spoon, spread the puree slightly. Arrange scallops atop the puree and distribute the kale shards around the scallops. Garnish with the lemon zest and serve immediately.

SMOKED MUSSELS
WITH BEER, SHALLOTS, AND GARLIC

SERVES: 4 | **PREP TIME:** 20 MINUTES | **GRILLING TIME:** 18 TO 32 MINUTES | **SPECIAL EQUIPMENT:** 2 LARGE HANDFULS OAK, APPLE, OR CHERRY WOOD CHIPS; LARGE GRILL-PROOF ROASTING PAN OR DISPOSABLE FOIL ROASTING PAN

⅔ cup mayonnaise

2 tablespoons whole-grain Dijon mustard

¼ cup (½ stick) unsalted butter, cut into tablespoons

½ cup chopped shallots

4 garlic cloves, minced

2 bottles (each 12 ounces) wheat beer, amber beer, or pale ale

6 large sprigs fresh thyme

4 pounds live mussels, scrubbed and debearded

1 teaspoon kosher salt

½ teaspoon freshly ground black pepper

3 tablespoons roughly chopped fresh Italian parsley leaves

Meat-loving barbecue purists may scoff at this idea, but early American barbecue actually included a fair amount of shellfish, especially in New England. Mussels were sometimes steamed in wine over a wood fire, but here's a modern take. Try this recipe with a mild-flavored wheat beer. An amber lager or pale ale also works well. To avoid the chore of debearding the mussels, look for the cultivated varieties from Prince Edward Island (PEI). Don't forget to serve lots of crusty bread for wiping the bowl clean of the savory broth.

1 Soak the wood chips in water for at least 30 minutes.

2 Prepare the grill for direct and indirect cooking over medium-low heat (about 350°F).

3 Mix the mayonnaise and mustard, and then divide evenly among four small ramekins. Cover and set aside while cooking the mussels.

4 Put the butter, shallots, and garlic into a large grill-proof roasting pan. Drain and add one handful of the wood chips to the charcoal or to the smoker box of a gas grill, following manufacturer's instructions, and close the lid. When smoke appears, place the pan with the butter, shallots, and garlic over **indirect medium-low heat**, close the lid, and cook until the butter is melted and the shallots are tender, 8 to 10 minutes, stirring occasionally. Add the beer and thyme and cook until the mixture is steaming, 5 to 7 minutes.

5 Drain and add the remaining wood chips to the charcoal or smoker box. Move the pan over direct heat, and then add the mussels to the pan. Cook the mussels, uncovered, over **direct medium-low heat**, with the grill lid closed, until the mussels open, 5 to 15 minutes, stirring occasionally. As each mussel opens, use tongs to transfer it to a large bowl; cover and keep them warm as you wait for the remaining mussels to open. Discard any unopened mussels and the thyme sprigs.

6 Season the cooking liquid with the salt and pepper. Divide the mussels among four deep soup bowls and ladle in the cooking liquid. Garnish with the parsley. Serve hot with the mayonnaise-mustard dip.

COAL-ROASTED CLAMS
WITH BLISTERED CHILES AND LINGUINE

SERVES: 4 | PREP TIME: 25 MINUTES | GRILLING TIME: 7 TO 10 MINUTES
SPECIAL EQUIPMENT: CHARCOAL GRILL, ALL-NATURAL LUMP CHARCOAL, PERFORATED GRILL PAN

4 small red cherry chile peppers
  (pimiento chile peppers)
2 tablespoons extra-virgin olive oil
3 large garlic cloves, chopped
¼ teaspoon crushed red pepper flakes
1 cup dry white wine
¼ cup fresh lemon juice
1 teaspoon kosher salt
2 pounds live littleneck or manila
  clams, scrubbed
1 pound dried linguine or
  spaghetti pasta
4 tablespoons chopped fresh Italian
  parsley leaves, divided
¼ cup (½ stick) unsalted butter, softened
2 teaspoons finely grated lemon zest
  Freshly ground black pepper

How's this for a new way to cook clams? Roast them right over lump charcoal. This technique is a contemporary version of an old Native American tradition called a clambake, which involves digging a pit in the sand and cooking shellfish buried among wood embers, hot stones, and steaming blankets of seaweed. In this recipe I've added the charred flavors and fairly mild spiciness of blistered (not blackened) red cherry peppers. If you prefer your food hotter, use jalapeño chile peppers instead, or add a little more crushed red pepper flakes to the dish.

1 Prepare the charcoal grill with all-natural lump charcoal for direct cooking over medium heat (350° to 450°F).

2 Grill the red cherry peppers over **direct medium heat**, with the lid closed, until blistered, not blackened, all over, 3 to 5 minutes, turning as needed. Remove from the grill and, when cool enough to handle, cut the peppers lengthwise in half, discard the stems and seeds, and cut crosswise into thin slices. Set aside.

3 In a large, deep skillet over medium heat on the stove, warm the oil. Add the garlic and red pepper flakes and sauté until fragrant, about 1 minute. Add the wine, lemon juice, and salt. Bring to a boil, and then reduce the heat to medium-low and simmer for 5 minutes. Remove from the heat and cover.

4 Arrange the clams in single layer on a perforated grill pan. Wearing insulated barbecue mitts or gloves, remove the cooking grate from the grill, and then place the pan with the clams directly on the coals (the coals should be covered with ash, glowing red, with no black remaining). Close the lid and grill the clams until they open, 4 to 5 minutes. Carefully transfer the pan from the grill to a heatproof surface. Discard any unopened clams. Transfer the clams with any of the juices in the shells to the skillet with the wine mixture.

5 Bring a large pot of salted water to a rolling boil. Add the linguine and cook until it's about 1 minute short of al dente. Drain the linguine, reserving ½ cup of the pasta water. Add the linguine, red cherry peppers, 2 tablespoons of the parsley, the butter, and lemon zest to the skillet (add some of the reserved pasta water if desired). Place the skillet over medium-high heat on the stove and toss the pasta until coated with the sauce and heated through. Season with pepper. Serve warm, garnished with the remaining parsley.

This is a case where it's best to cook entirely with all-natural lump charcoal. The chemicals and processed coal sometimes added to briquettes could get into the clams, so use lump charcoal that is nothing more than pieces of hardwood that have been burned down to charcoal in a low-oxygen environment.

The smaller and tenderer varieties of clams taste better here. Littleneck clams from the Atlantic coast are usually the most expensive because of their brilliantly briny sweetness. Manila clams from the Pacific Coast work well, too. Try to get the tender ones that are about an inch wide or less.

6

SIDES

HASSELBACK POTATOES
WITH GARLIC BUTTER AND PARMESAN

SERVES: 6 | **PREP TIME:** 45 MINUTES
GRILLING TIME: 1 HOUR 5 MINUTES TO 1 HOUR 10 MINUTES

6 russet potatoes, each about 12 ounces,
  scrubbed and dried
6 tablespoons (¾ stick) unsalted butter
6 garlic cloves, smashed and peeled
1½ teaspoons kosher salt
¾ teaspoon freshly ground black pepper
2 ounces Parmigiano-Reggiano®
  cheese, finely grated
2 tablespoons finely chopped fresh
  Italian parsley leaves

Hasselback potatoes have been dazzling guests at American barbecues during the last few years, although we cannot claim them as our own. The brilliant idea for these accordion-looking potatoes came from the chefs at Restaurant Hasselbacken in Stockholm, Sweden.

1. Prepare the grill for indirect cooking over medium-high heat (400° to 450°F).

2. So that each potato will lay flat on the cooking grate, cut off a very small piece (¼ inch or less) on the widest side of each potato, which will now be the bottom side. Then, using a very sharp knife, starting 1 inch from the end, cut slits crosswise into each potato, ⅛ to ¼ inch apart, stopping just before you cut through so that the slices stay connected at the bottom.

3. In a small skillet over medium heat on the stove, melt the butter. Add the garlic and cook until lightly browned, 1½ to 2 minutes, stirring occasionally. Remove the skillet from the heat and add the salt and pepper. Fan out the layers of each potato enough that you can get some butter and seasonings inside the layers. Brush the potatoes, including the bottoms, with half of the butter mixture.

4. Grill the potatoes over ***indirect medium-high heat***, with the lid closed, for 30 minutes. Brush the potatoes with the remaining butter mixture, making sure some of the butter drips down inside the slices. Continue grilling, with the lid closed, until the potatoes are almost cooked through, 30 minutes more. Top the potatoes evenly with the cheese and cook until the cheese is melted and slightly browned and the potatoes are crisp on the outside and tender on the inside, 5 to 10 minutes more. Garnish with the parsley and serve hot.

Making all those slices takes work, but creamy potato centers and crispy edges are so worth the time and effort. A helpful trick to keep you from slicing all the way through the potato is to put two chopsticks on either side of each spud to act as a guide and stop your knife from going too far, but as you get near the tapered ends, ignore the chopsticks and just be careful not to cut all the way through the potatoes.

STUFFED POTATOES
WITH CHEDDAR, HORSERADISH, AND CRISPY BACON

SERVES: 4 | **PREP TIME:** 20 MINUTES
GRILLING TIME: 1¼ TO 1½ HOURS | **SPECIAL EQUIPMENT:** PERFORATED GRILL PAN

4 russet potatoes, each about 12 ounces, scrubbed and dried

FILLING
2 slices thick-cut bacon
3 ounces sharp cheddar cheese, finely grated
½ cup sour cream
3 scallions, trimmed, thinly sliced, divided
3 tablespoons tightly packed peeled, finely grated fresh horseradish or 2 teaspoons drained prepared horseradish
2 tablespoons unsalted butter, softened
1½ teaspoons kosher salt
¾ teaspoon freshly ground black pepper

2 tablespoons unsalted butter, melted
1 ounce Parmigiano-Reggiano® cheese, finely grated

What's not to love about stuffed potatoes—especially when they are loaded with cheese and bacon? The extra kick from fresh horseradish adds a peppery bite to the rich filling. Alternatively you could go with a Tex-Mex stuffing with chorizo, sour cream, and roasted chile pepper, or maybe a vegetarian version with blue cheese and fresh thyme.

1 Prepare the grill for indirect cooking over medium heat (350° to 400°F).

2 Pierce the potatoes in several places with a fork, and then grill over **indirect medium heat**, with the lid closed, until tender, 1 to 1¼ hours. Remove from the grill and let stand until cool enough to handle.

3 Meanwhile, in a medium skillet over medium-high heat on the stove, fry the bacon until browned and crisp. Transfer to a plate lined with a paper towel to drain. When cool enough to handle, crumble the bacon into small pieces. Mash together all the filling ingredients, setting aside about 2 tablespoons of the sliced scallions for garnish.

4 Increase the temperature of the grill to high heat (as close to 450°F as possible).

5 Cut off a ½-inch slice, lengthwise, from the top of each potato and discard. Being careful not to tear the skin and leaving a thin layer of flesh intact, gently scoop out the potato flesh. Add the flesh to the filling mixture and, using a fork, stir and mash to blend (the filling will be a little lumpy).

6 Carefully spoon the filling back into the potato skins, dividing equally. Brush a thin film of butter on the (inside) bottom of a perforated grill pan, place the potatoes on the pan, and brush the skins with the remaining melted butter (see top photo, facing page). Distribute the Parmigiano-Reggiano® cheese over the filling.

7 Cook the potatoes on the grill pan over **indirect high heat**, with the lid closed, until the cheese is melted and the tip of a knife inserted deep into the center of each potato comes out piping hot, 8 to 10 minutes. Garnish with the reserved sliced scallions.

VARIATIONS

Tex-Mex (left photo): Mix the potato flesh with 1 cup (6 ounces) cooked and crumbled Mexican chorizo; 4 ounces Mexican cheese blend; ¼ cup sour cream; 1 roasted, chopped poblano chile pepper; 2 tablespoons chopped fresh cilantro; and 1 tablespoon thinly sliced scallion.

Vegetarian (right photo): Mix the potato flesh with 2 ounces crumbled blue cheese, ½ cup sour cream, 2 tablespoons each finely chopped fresh thyme and Italian parsley leaves, and ¼ teaspoon each salt and pepper.

ROASTED FINGERLING POTATOES
WITH MINT GREMOLATA

SERVES: 4 TO 6 | **PREP TIME:** 20 MINUTES
GRILLING TIME: 40 TO 45 MINUTES | **SPECIAL EQUIPMENT:** LARGE CAST-IRON GRIDDLE

A cast-iron griddle opens up a world of new recipe possibilities on the grill. Here is one way to use the griddle—cooking halved fingerling potatoes slowly, encouraging them to turn crisp and brown evenly without burning. Check them once or twice during cooking and move them around on the griddle as needed.

GREMOLATA
1 cup loosely packed fresh Italian parsley leaves
½ cup loosely packed fresh mint leaves
2 tablespoons extra-virgin olive oil
2 teaspoons finely grated lemon zest
1 garlic clove, chopped
¼ teaspoon kosher salt

2 pounds fingerling potatoes, each cut lengthwise in half
2 tablespoons extra-virgin olive oil
1½ teaspoons kosher salt
½ teaspoon freshly ground black pepper
1 garlic clove, minced

1 In the bowl of a food processor pulse the parsley and mint until coarsely chopped. Add the remaining gremolata ingredients and pulse until finely chopped. Transfer the gremolata to a large bowl.

2 Prepare the grill for indirect cooking over medium heat (as close to 400°F as possible) and preheat a large cast-iron griddle.

3 Combine the potatoes, oil, salt, pepper, and garlic and turn to coat. Arrange the potatoes, cut side down, on the griddle and cook over **indirect medium heat**, with the lid closed, until tender, crisp, and golden brown, 40 to 45 minutes, checking occasionally and moving the potatoes around on the griddle to prevent over browning. Transfer the potatoes to the large bowl with the gremolata and toss to combine. Serve immediately.

BABY RED POTATO SALAD
WITH BASIL VINAIGRETTE

SERVES: 4 TO 6 | **PREP TIME:** 20 MINUTES | **GRILLING TIME:** ABOUT 40 MINUTES
SPECIAL EQUIPMENT: 2 LARGE HANDFULS HICKORY WOOD CHIPS, PERFORATED GRILL PAN

Incorporating a touch of smoke gives a regular red potato salad a terrific new quality. While the potatoes are hot, toss them with the vinaigrette so that it soaks into the porous flesh. Then enjoy this salad warm or at room temperature.

VINAIGRETTE
¼ cup thinly sliced fresh basil leaves
2 tablespoons water
1 tablespoon white wine vinegar
2 teaspoons country-style
  Dijon mustard

  Extra-virgin olive oil
  Kosher salt
  Freshly ground black pepper
2 pounds baby red potatoes, each about
  1¼ inches in diameter, cut in half
1 medium red onion, cut into
  ¼-inch-thick half-moons,
  broken apart
2 medium ribs celery, cut into
  medium dice
  Fresh basil leaves

1 Soak the wood chips in water for at least 30 minutes.

2 Prepare the grill for indirect cooking over medium-high heat (400° to 450°F) and preheat a perforated grill pan.

3 Whisk the vinaigrette ingredients, including ¼ cup oil, ½ teaspoon salt, and ¼ teaspoon pepper, until emulsified.

4 Put the potato halves in a large saucepan and cover them by about 2 inches with cold, salted water. Cover the pan and bring to a boil over high heat on the stove, and then remove the lid and cook for 5 minutes. Drain the potatoes well and transfer them to a bowl. Add the onion, 2 tablespoons oil, ¾ teaspoon salt, and ¼ teaspoon pepper and toss to coat evenly.

5 Drain and add half of the wood chips to the charcoal or to the smoker box of a gas grill, following manufacturer's instructions, and close the lid. When smoke appears, add the potatoes and onion to the grill pan, close the lid, and cook over **indirect medium-high heat** until tender, about 40 minutes, stirring once or twice. After 20 minutes, drain and add the remaining wood chips to the charcoal or smoker box.

6 Transfer the potato and onion mixture to a bowl, and then add the celery. Whisk the dressing again and add just enough of it to coat the ingredients lightly. Serve warm or at room temperature, garnished with basil.

BARBECUE CROSSROADS IN KANSAS CITY

Kansas City earned its reputation in the early 1800s as a crossroads town at the confluence of the Kansas River, the Missouri River, and the Santa Fe Trail. As our country's border pushed westward, Kansas City transformed itself from a fur trading outpost on the frontier to a perfectly centered national marketplace, as well as a magnet for an interesting mix of people, merchandise, music (primarily blues and jazz), and meat. Livestock ranchers from all over the central and western U.S. quickly recognized Kansas City's commercial importance and, within decades, hundreds of thousands of animals (cows, pigs, and sheep) had arrived at Kansas City's stockyards by boat, cattle drive, railway, truck, and water.

Kansas City's expansive barbecue menu mirrors the inclusiveness of its stockyards, and unlike other barbecue hot spots around the country, Kansas Citians are not devoted to barbecuing one particular meat in one particular way. Beef, chicken, fish, mutton, and pork, cooked using a variety of woods and techniques, all belong on the city's barbecue plate.

Tradition is a key ingredient in Kansas City barbecue, and legendary restaurants like Arthur Bryant's Barbeque, Gates Bar-B-Q, and Rosedale Bar-B-Q still bring smiles to the city's longtime residents who take pride in their city's pork spareribs and "burnt ends" (succulent cubes of fat-crowned meat chopped off the charred end of a beef brisket). Recently the barbecue competition circuit has pushed the restaurant culture to greater heights thanks, in part, to the stratospheric growth of the Kansas City Barbecue Society (KCBS). With its numerous contests held around the country and its annual American Royal World Series of Barbecue, held right in Kansas City, the KCBS has inspired a number of successful competitors to open restaurants. At these trophy-decorated destinations, diners munch on superlative barbecue from a core menu that tracks the KCBS competition categories. Joe's Kansas City Bar-B-Que (formerly Oklahoma Joe's) was started inside a gas station by the highly decorated Slaughterhouse Five competition team, and it may be the best example of this trend.

Chef Rob Magee, the creative force behind the Q39 restaurant, is a Culinary Institute of America graduate who cooked in upscale hotels before entering the barbecue competition circuit. Chef Magee is convinced that his hotel training gives him a decided edge in taking barbecue "to the next level." Talk with Chef Magee about his signature barbecue sauces, and your conversation will be peppered with technique-drenched words like sweating, simmering, straining, pureeing, and flavor profiles. "My sauce doesn't taste like anybody else's sauce," Magee says. "It's more complex; it's more layered in flavors ... it's not just one note." Magee separates Q39 from local barbecue joints by insisting on scratch cooking for the entire evolving menu and a full staff of waiters and bartenders because he senses that customers today are looking for "something new and special."

Could that "something special," and possibly the future of barbecue, be a plate piled high with vegetables? The folks at Char Bar Smoked Meats & Amusements think so, and so they use fire creatively to flavor fruits and vegetables. Their cooks char brussels sprouts, eggplant, and grapefruit; blister grapes; roast beets; and smoke corn and tropical jackfruit. The smoked jackfruit anchors the restaurant's sandwich "The JackKnife"—this flavorful selection comes with an eclectic mix of provolone cheese, sliced avocado, and fried jalapeño chile peppers that will make you forget, albeit temporarily, about meat.

Today, Kansas City is a "melting pit" of traditional, experimental, and innovative approaches to barbecue. I'd expect nothing less from a crossroads town.

MANGO-RADISH-JICAMA SLAW
WITH CILANTRO-LIME DRESSING

Making beautiful, moist matchsticks from a gnarly root of jicama does require a few steps. Use a sharp knife or vegetable peeler to remove the brownish skin. Cut the jicama in half. Lay the flat (cut) sides down so they don't wobble on the board. Then make thin slices. Stack a few slices in a pile and cut them into skinny matchsticks.

SERVES: 6 TO 8
PREP TIME: 1 HOUR

This refreshing anytime slaw is a great alternative to cabbage-based slaws. The sweetness of the mango balances wonderfully with the tanginess of the lime and the pepperiness of the radishes. Jicama lends a great crunch. Feel free to prep the ingredients hours ahead, but don't toss them all together until you are ready to serve.

DRESSING
½ cup mayonnaise
2 teaspoons finely grated lime zest
¼ cup fresh lime juice
¼ cup finely chopped fresh
   cilantro leaves
2 tablespoons granulated sugar
1½ teaspoons kosher salt

2 medium, ripe mangoes, peeled and
   cut into matchsticks
1 jicama, about 1 pound, peeled and
   cut into matchsticks
10 large radishes, cut into matchsticks
3 scallions (white and light green parts
   only), thinly sliced

1 In a large serving bowl whisk the dressing ingredients until smooth.

2 Add the mangoes, jicama, radishes, and scallions to the serving bowl with the dressing and stir until well combined. Let stand for 10 minutes before serving.

FENNEL AND CABBAGE COLESLAW
WITH BLUE CHEESE

SERVES: 4 TO 6
PREP TIME: 25 MINUTES

This unorthodox slaw manages to deliciously upend most of the standard assumptions about coleslaw. Red and green cabbage join up with fennel in a tart, vinegar-centric dressing with only a little mayo, and a sprinkling of blue cheese adds a rich, tangy finish.

DRESSING
- ¼ cup extra-virgin olive oil
- ¼ cup cider vinegar
- 2 tablespoons mayonnaise
- 1 tablespoon Dijon mustard
- 1 teaspoon kosher salt
- ½ teaspoon freshly ground black pepper
- ½ teaspoon granulated sugar

- 1 medium fennel bulb
- 2½ cups shredded green cabbage
- 2 cups shredded red cabbage
- 1 cup roughly chopped fresh Italian parsley leaves
- 1½ ounces crumbled blue cheese

1   In a large serving bowl whisk the dressing ingredients until smooth.

2   Trim the stalks of the fennel down to the bulb, reserve and chop the fronds, and discard the stalks. Cut the bulb into quarters, remove the thick triangular-shaped core, and then cut the fennel crosswise as thinly as possible.

3   Add the fennel, green and red cabbage, and parsley to the dressing in the serving bowl and toss to mix evenly. Let stand at room temperature for 5 minutes, toss again, and then top with the blue cheese. Serve right away.

CRUNCHY, TANGY COLESLAW

SERVES: 8 TO 10 (MAKES ABOUT 10 CUPS) | **PREP TIME:** 30 MINUTES
STANDING TIME: 45 MINUTES

Coleslaw might just be barbecue's best accompaniment. The fresh, tangy, and crunchy combination plays well against tender meat cooked for hours. It works every time. Well, actually, it doesn't work when the slaw turns watery because the dressing forces the vegetables to leach their natural moisture. The secret to perfectly crunchy coleslaw is to first salt the cabbage to remove excess water, and then rinse off any excess salt so the dressing isn't overwhelmed.

1 head green cabbage, about 3 pounds
2 tablespoons kosher salt
3 medium carrots

DRESSING
¼ cup white balsamic vinegar
2 tablespoons whole-grain
   Dijon mustard
2 tablespoons mayonnaise
2 tablespoons granulated sugar
1 teaspoon Worcestershire sauce
½ teaspoon freshly ground black pepper

1 Cut the cabbage through the core into quarters. Cut out and remove the hard, white core from each section. Set the quarters, cut side down, on a cutting board and cut crosswise into very thin strips. Place the cabbage in a very large bowl, add the salt, and toss well. Set aside at room temperature for 45 minutes.

2 To remove the excess salt, add cool water to completely cover the cabbage. Stir well, and then drain in a colander set in the sink. Repeat this process two times to remove all the salt, and then squeeze the cabbage dry one handful at a time.

3 Using the grater blade of a food processor or the large holes of a box grater, grate the carrots.

4 In a large bowl whisk the dressing ingredients. Add the cabbage and carrots and toss to coat evenly. Serve right away.

BROCCOLI SLAW

For a colorful alternative to broccoli, use purple or yellow cauliflower. Combine it with the grated carrot, thin strips of red bell pepper, golden raisins, and toasted slivered almonds. Add some curry powder and/or mango chutney to the dressing.

SERVES: 4 TO 6 | **PREP TIME:** 20 MINUTES
CHILLING TIME: 1 TO 3 HOURS

Don't throw away tough broccoli stems. Run them through the grater attachment of a food processor, along with some carrots, and toss them in a tangy dressing. Add roasted almonds for a nice, salty crunch. A handful of dried cranberries is good for sweetness. Set the colorful mixture aside a few hours before your barbecue and you are good to go with a fresh new slaw that has nothing to do with cabbage.

DRESSING
- 1 small sweet yellow onion
- 3 tablespoons cider vinegar
- ⅓ cup mayonnaise
- 1 teaspoon Dijon mustard
- 1 teaspoon prepared horseradish
- 1 teaspoon granulated sugar
- 1 teaspoon kosher salt
- ½ teaspoon freshly ground black pepper

- 1 pound broccoli stems, outer layer peeled
- 2 medium carrots
- 1 cup roasted, salted almonds, coarsely chopped
- ⅓ cup dried cranberries

1 Using the grater blade of a food processor or the large holes of a box grater, grate the onion, and then put it and all its juice in a large bowl. Add the vinegar, stir to combine, and let stand for a few minutes. Then add the remaining dressing ingredients and mix well.

2 Using the grater blade of a food processor or the large holes of a box grater, grate the broccoli stems and carrots. To the bowl with the dressing add the broccoli, carrots, almonds, and cranberries. Mix well. Refrigerate for at least 1 hour or up to 3 hours to allow the flavors to develop.

MACARONI AND CHEESE
WITH PARMESAN CRUMBS

SERVES: 6 TO 8 | **PREP TIME:** 25 MINUTES | **GRILLING TIME:** 20 TO 25 MINUTES
SPECIAL EQUIPMENT: 12-INCH CAST-IRON SKILLET

¼ cup (½ stick) unsalted butter
¼ cup unbleached all-purpose flour
2 teaspoons mustard powder
1½ teaspoons onion powder
3½ cups whole milk
4 ounces sharp cheddar cheese, coarsely grated
4 ounces pasteurized cheese product, such as Velveeta®, diced
8 ounces Monterey Jack or Muenster cheese, coarsely grated
1 teaspoon kosher salt
½ teaspoon freshly ground black pepper
1 pound dried elbow macaroni

TOPPING

¾ cup panko bread crumbs
3 ounces Parmigiano-Reggiano® cheese, finely grated
3 tablespoons unsalted butter, melted

With lots of crunchy, cheesy topping, this recipe is purposely on the mild side so that kids of all ages can enjoy it. If you prefer a bit more of a kick, use jalapeño jack cheese. You may also like one cup of grated Gruyère cheese in place of one cup of cheddar. One final tip: If your main course is not heavily smoked, try adding apple wood chips to the grill to work some subtle smokiness into this comforting side dish.

1   Prepare the grill for indirect cooking over medium-low heat (350° to 400°F).

2   In a 12-inch cast-iron skillet over medium heat on the stove, melt the butter. Whisk in the flour and let the mixture bubble for about 1 minute without browning (it should smell like baked piecrust). Whisk in the mustard powder and onion powder. Gradually whisk in the milk and bring to a boil, whisking often until the sauce is smooth. Reduce the heat to low and simmer until all of the raw flour taste is gone, about 3 minutes, whisking often. Remove the sauce from the heat. Add the cheeses all at once and whisk until they have melted. Season with the salt and pepper.

3   Meanwhile, bring a large pot of salted water to a boil for the macaroni, and cook according to package directions, removing the pasta when it is al dente (do not overcook the macaroni, as it will cook more in the sauce). Drain the macaroni well and add it to the skillet. Stir into the sauce and mix well.

4   Combine the topping ingredients, and then distribute the topping evenly over the macaroni.

5   Place the skillet with the macaroni and cheese over ***indirect medium-low heat***, close the lid, and cook until the sauce is bubbling and the crumbs are lightly browned, 20 to 25 minutes. Remove from the grill and let rest for 5 minutes. Serve warm.

CREAMY CHIPOTLE MACARONI SALAD
WITH GRILLED CORN AND TOMATOES

SERVES: 8 TO 10 | **PREP TIME:** 20 MINUTES
GRILLING TIME: 8 TO 10 MINUTES

You can serve this colorful salad right after you make it, but chilling it overnight will allow the spicy, smoky flavors to permeate the macaroni. Slice the basil and add it just before serving because American basil turns black on the edges a few minutes after it is cut.

DRESSING
½ cup mayonnaise
½ cup sour cream
2 canned chipotle chile peppers in
   adobo sauce, seeded and minced
2 teaspoons adobo sauce (from the can)
1½ teaspoons kosher salt

12 ounces dried elbow macaroni
4 ears fresh corn, husked
2 teaspoons extra-virgin olive oil
2 bell peppers, 1 red and 1 green,
   finely chopped
12 ounces grape tomatoes, each
   cut in half
3 scallions (white and light green parts
   only), thinly sliced
½ cup thinly sliced fresh basil leaves

1 Prepare the grill for direct cooking over high heat (450° to 550°F).

2 In a large serving bowl combine the dressing ingredients.

3 Bring a large pot of salted water to a boil. Add the macaroni and cook according to package directions until al dente; drain, rinse under cold water, and drain again. Transfer the macaroni to the serving bowl with the dressing and toss to combine.

4 Brush the corn all over with the oil, and then grill over ***direct high heat***, with the lid closed, until browned in spots and tender, 8 to 10 minutes, turning occasionally. Remove from the grill and, when cool enough to handle, cut the kernels off the cobs. Add the corn, bell peppers, tomatoes, and scallions to the bowl with the macaroni and mix well. Refrigerate until ready to serve. Just before serving, gently mix in the basil.

SESAME-PEANUT NOODLE SALAD
WITH ROASTED LEMON JUICE

SERVES: 6 TO 8 | **PREP TIME:** 20 MINUTES
GRILLING TIME: 10 TO 15 MINUTES | **CHILLING TIME:** 2 TO 8 HOURS

This is for those barbecue days when you want to make a noodle salad ahead of time and know that you have a winner waiting in the wings. Grilling the lemons helps to release a lot of tangy, fragrant juice.

2 lemons, each cut crosswise in half
   Vegetable oil
1 box (13 ounces) Chinese egg noodles, soba, or dried whole-wheat spaghetti pasta
½ cup creamy peanut butter
¼ cup soy sauce
2 tablespoons toasted sesame oil
2 tablespoons minced shallot
1 tablespoon peeled, grated fresh ginger
2 teaspoons honey
½ teaspoon hot chili-garlic sauce, such as Sriracha
3 large scallions (white and light green parts only), thinly sliced
3 tablespoons finely chopped fresh cilantro leaves
1 tablespoons toasted sesame seeds

1 Prepare the grill for indirect cooking over medium heat (350° to 450°F).

2 Lightly brush the cut side of the lemons with oil, and then grill, cut side down, over **indirect medium heat**, with the lid closed, until fragrant and marked by the grill, 10 to 15 minutes (do not turn). Remove from the grill and let cool.

3 Bring a large pot of salted water to a boil. Add the noodles and cook according to package directions until al dente; drain, rinse under cold water, and drain again.

4 In a large bowl combine the peanut butter, soy sauce, sesame oil, shallot, ginger, honey, and chili-garlic sauce. Squeeze the roasted lemon through a fine-mesh strainer into the peanut butter mixture and whisk until smooth. Add the noodles and mix gently with tongs until all the noodles are coated.

5 Cover and refrigerate until chilled, at least 2 hours or up to 8 hours. Serve chilled or at room temperature, garnished with the scallions, cilantro, and sesame seeds.

ZUCCHINI-PEA PAPPARDELLE
WITH GRILLED ONION AND FETA

SERVES: 4 TO 6 | **PREP TIME:** 25 MINUTES
GRILLING TIME: 10 TO 12 MINUTES

⅓ cup fresh dill sprigs, finely chopped
⅓ cup fresh basil leaves, finely chopped
2 tablespoons fresh lemon juice
2 teaspoons Dijon mustard
¼ teaspoon crushed red pepper flakes
  Kosher salt
  Freshly ground black pepper
  Extra-virgin olive oil
2 green zucchini, 1 to 1¼ pounds total,
  ends trimmed
2 yellow squash, 1 to 1¼ pounds total,
  ends trimmed
1 medium red onion, cut crosswise
  into ⅓-inch slices
½ pound dried pappardelle pasta
⅔ cup frozen petite peas, thawed
3 tablespoons crumbled feta

Grilled onion imparts a sweet, earthy quality to this colorful, summery pasta that could easily hold its own as a main course or live happily alongside barbecued chicken or ribs.

1 In a very large serving bowl combine the dill, basil, lemon juice, mustard, red pepper flakes, ½ teaspoon salt, and ½ teaspoon pepper. Slowly whisk in ¾ cup oil to make a vinaigrette.

2 Prepare the grill for direct cooking over medium-high heat (400° to 450°F).

3 Using a sharp vegetable peeler, shave the zucchini lengthwise into long, thin strips. Once you reach the seedy core, stop, and leave the core whole. Turn over and repeat with the other side, again stopping at the seedy core. Repeat with the squash, leaving its seedy core whole as well. Transfer the strips to the serving bowl with the vinaigrette and toss. Discard the cores.

4 Lightly brush the onion slices with oil and generously season with salt and pepper. Grill the onion over **direct medium-high heat**, with the lid closed, until softened and nicely charred, 10 to 12 minutes, turning once or twice.

5 Meanwhile, cook the pasta according to package instructions until al dente. Drain the pasta well, reserving ½ cup of the pasta water, and set aside.

6 Roughly chop the onion slices and add to the serving bowl. Add the pasta and toss well to combine, adding a little pasta water if needed. Top with the peas and feta, season with salt and pepper, and gently toss. Serve right away.

To mimic the shape of the pasta, trim off the ends, and then shave the zucchini and squash with a vegetable peeler. Run the blade lengthwise down each vegetable until you see lots of little seeds. Then turn the vegetable over and do the same on the other side.

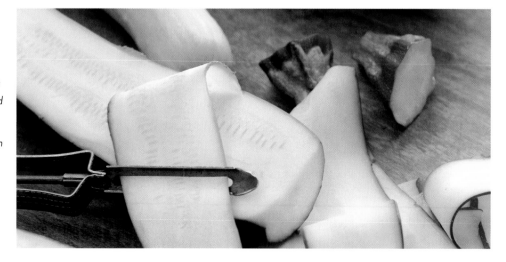

NOT YOUR GRANDMA'S SUCCOTASH

SERVES: 6 | **PREP TIME:** 25 MINUTES | **GRILLING TIME:** ABOUT 25 MINUTES
SPECIAL EQUIPMENT: LARGE GRILL-PROOF SKILLET

In its purest form, succotash is a simple corn and shell bean combination that originated with the Native Americans of the Northeast. This version brings succotash up to date by adding ripe tomatoes, fragrant basil, and umami-rich cheese. Edamame stand in for the usual lima beans. If you wish, the zucchini, corn, and bell pepper could be grilled and prepped a few hours before the final cooking in a skillet.

2 zucchini, 10 to 12 ounces total, ends trimmed, each cut lengthwise in half
Extra-virgin olive oil
2 ears fresh corn, husked
1 red bell pepper, about 8 ounces
2 tablespoons unsalted butter
1¾ cups chopped yellow onion
2 tablespoons finely chopped jalapeño chile pepper
2 garlic cloves, minced
1½ cups frozen shelled edamame, thawed
2 ripe plum tomatoes, about 9 ounces total, cored, seeded, and cut into ¾-inch dice
1 teaspoon kosher salt
¼ teaspoon freshly ground black pepper
2 ounces Parmigiano-Reggiano® cheese, finely grated
2 tablespoons finely chopped fresh basil leaves
2 tablespoons fresh lemon juice

1 Prepare the grill for direct cooking over medium-high heat (425° to 475°F).

2 Lightly brush the zucchini with oil. Grill the zucchini, corn, and bell pepper over ***direct medium-high heat***, with the lid closed, until the zucchini is crisp-tender, the corn is browned in spots and tender, and the bell pepper is blackened and blistered all over, turning as needed. The zucchini will take 5 to 7 minutes, and the corn and bell pepper will take 10 to 12 minutes. Remove from the grill as they are done. Place the bell pepper in a bowl and cover with plastic wrap to trap the steam. Let stand for about 10 minutes.

3 Adjust the temperature of the grill to medium-low heat (350° to 400°F).

4 Remove the bell pepper from the bowl and discard the charred skin, stem, and seeds. Cut the pepper and zucchini into ¾-inch pieces. Cut the corn kernels from the cobs.

5 In a large grill-proof skillet over ***direct medium-low heat***, melt the butter. Add the onion and cook, with the lid closed, until golden and tender, 8 to 9 minutes, stirring occasionally. Stir in the jalapeño and garlic and cook until fragrant, about 1 minute. Add the zucchini, corn, and bell pepper and mix well. Add the edamame, tomatoes, salt, and pepper and cook, with the lid closed, until heated through, about 5 minutes, stirring occasionally. Remove from the grill. Stir in the cheese, basil, and lemon juice. Serve warm.

BORRACHO BEANS

SERVES: 6 TO 8 | **PREP TIME:** 15 MINUTES | **GRILLING TIME:** 1 TO 1½ HOURS | **SPECIAL EQUIPMENT:** CHARCOAL GRILL, LARGE (6-QUART) GRILL-PROOF DUTCH OVEN, 2 LARGE HANDFULS HICKORY OR OAK WOOD CHUNKS

At Texas barbecue restaurants you'll sometimes find a big pot of beans like this simmering on the pit alongside the meat, picking up traces of aromatic smoke. So called because they're cooked with so much beer (the word borracho means "drunken" in Spanish), these beans make a nice alternative to traditional baked beans. I think you will call them some of the most flavorful beans you've ever eaten.

6 slices bacon, cut into ½-inch pieces
1 white onion, about 12 ounces, finely chopped
2 garlic cloves, minced
2 teaspoons prepared chili powder
1 teaspoon ground cumin
¾ cup water
1 bottle (12 ounces) pilsner
3 cans (each 14 ounces) pinto beans, rinsed and drained
2 cans (each 14 ounces) diced tomatoes in juice
1 teaspoon kosher salt
¼ cup coarsely chopped fresh cilantro leaves
3 tablespoons pure maple syrup
1 teaspoon cider vinegar

1 Prepare the charcoal grill for direct and indirect cooking over medium heat (350° to 450°F).

2 In a large grill-proof Dutch oven over **direct medium heat**, fry the bacon, with the grill lid closed, until browned and crisp, 5 to 7 minutes, stirring occasionally. Add the onion and cook until golden, about 5 minutes, stirring occasionally. Add the garlic, chili powder, and cumin and cook for 1 minute, stirring frequently. Add the water, pilsner, beans, tomatoes, and salt and stir well. Close the grill lid and bring the mixture to a boil, which should take about 15 minutes.

3 Add the wood chunks to the charcoal. When smoke appears, slide the Dutch oven over **indirect medium heat** and simmer the beans, uncovered, with the grill lid closed, until the cooking liquid is reduced by about half, 40 minutes to 1 hour, stirring occasionally. Remove from the grill and stir in the cilantro, syrup, and vinegar. Serve warm.

SWEET AND STICKY BBQ BEANS

SERVES: 8 | **PREP TIME:** 30 MINUTES | **GRILLING TIME:** 35 TO 45 MINUTES
SPECIAL EQUIPMENT: 2 LARGE HANDFULS HICKORY, APPLE, OR CHERRY WOOD CHIPS; LARGE (6-QUART) GRILL-PROOF DUTCH OVEN

These bacon-flavored beans dripping with molasses are a great side for hot dogs, hamburgers, or smoked meat. If you want to gild the lily, sprinkle about two cups chopped brisket (preferably the burnt ends) over the beans during the last five minutes or so of cooking time. While the brisket makes this is a very rich side dish, barbecue lovers will go weak in the knees at every bite.

4 slices thick-cut bacon,
  coarsely chopped
1 tablespoon vegetable oil
2 cups chopped yellow onion
2 garlic cloves, chopped
1 cup ketchup-style chili sauce
⅔ cup ketchup
⅓ cup unsulfured molasses
  (not blackstrap)
¼ cup packed light brown sugar
2 tablespoons spicy brown mustard
2 tablespoons Worcestershire sauce
1 tablespoon cider vinegar
1 teaspoon hot pepper sauce
2 cans (each 14 ounces) small white
  beans, rinsed and drained
2 cans (each 14 ounces) pinto beans,
  rinsed and drained

1 Soak the wood chips in water for at least 30 minutes.

2 Prepare the grill for indirect cooking over medium-low heat (325° to 375°F).

3 In a large grill-proof Dutch oven over medium heat on the stove, fry the bacon in the oil until browned and crisp, 8 to 10 minutes, stirring occasionally. Using a slotted spoon, transfer the bacon to paper towels to drain, leaving the drippings in the pan. Add the onion to the drippings and cook until golden brown, 8 to 10 minutes, stirring occasionally. Add the garlic and stir until fragrant, about 30 seconds. Add the remaining ingredients, except the beans, and mix well with a wooden spatula. Scrape up any browned bits on the bottom of the Dutch oven and bring the mixture to a simmer. Stir in the beans and bring to a boil.

4 Drain and add half of the wood chips to the charcoal or to the smoker box of a gas grill, following manufacturer's instructions, and close the lid. When smoke appears, place the Dutch oven, uncovered, over **indirect medium-low heat**, close the grill lid, and cook the beans for 15 minutes. Drain and add the remaining wood chips to the charcoal or smoker box, and continue cooking, with the grill lid closed, until the sauce is thickened and the top of the beans is glazed, 20 to 30 minutes more. Remove from the grill and let stand for 5 minutes. Garnish the beans with the reserved bacon pieces and serve warm.

GREEK WHITE BEANS

SERVES: 6 TO 8 | **PREP TIME:** 15 MINUTES | **GRILLING TIME:** 40 TO 50 MINUTES
SPECIAL EQUIPMENT: 1½- TO 2-QUART GRILL-PROOF GRATIN DISH OR 8-INCH CAST-IRON SKILLET

Instead of the usual sweet profile of American baked beans, this dish is tangy and tomato-y, too. With the feta cheese, oregano, and fresh dill, there is a certain Greek feeling here that makes this a welcome accompaniment to a leg of lamb or smoked beef ribs.

1 large yellow onion, cut crosswise into ⅓-inch slices
2 medium, ripe tomatoes, cored and cut lengthwise in half
    Extra-virgin olive oil
    Kosher salt
    Freshly ground black pepper
6 scallions, ends trimmed
2 cans (each 14 ounces) large white beans, rinsed and drained
4 ounces crumbled feta cheese
1 teaspoon dried oregano
⅓ cup plus 2 tablespoons chopped fresh dill, divided
½ cup panko bread crumbs

1 Prepare the grill for direct and indirect cooking over medium-high heat (400° to 450°F).

2 Lightly brush the onion slices and tomato halves with oil and season liberally with salt and pepper. Grill the onion and the tomatoes over **direct medium-high heat**, with the lid closed, until softened and nicely charred, 10 to 15 minutes, turning once or twice. Remove the onion and tomatoes from the grill and, when cool enough to handle, roughly chop.

    Finely chop the scallions and set aside 2 tablespoons for the bread crumb topping. Combine the remaining scallions, onion, tomatoes, beans, feta, oregano, ⅓ cup of the dill, 1 teaspoon salt, and ½ teaspoon pepper. Mix well and transfer to a 1½- to 2-quart grill-proof gratin dish.

3 Combine the bread crumbs with the reserved 2 tablespoons scallions, the remaining 2 tablespoons dill, 2 tablespoons oil, and a pinch of salt. Distribute the dill crumbs on top of the bean mixture.

4 Place the gratin over **indirect medium-high heat**, close the lid, and cook until warmed through and golden, 30 to 35 minutes. Remove from the grill and let rest for 10 minutes before serving.

GRILL-ROASTED LEEKS
WITH HAZELNUT CHIMICHURRI

SERVES: 4 | **PREP TIME:** 25 MINUTES
GRILLING TIME: 16 TO 20 MINUTES

CHIMICHURRI
- ¼ cup hazelnuts, toasted
- 1 cup loosely packed fresh Italian parsley leaves
- ¼ cup loosely packed fresh oregano leaves
- 2 tablespoons red wine vinegar
- 1 garlic clove, chopped

- Extra-virgin olive oil
- Kosher salt
- Freshly ground black pepper
- 8 leeks, each about 1 inch thick, tough outer leaves discarded
- 6 ounces yellow cherry or grape tomatoes, each cut in half

Sometimes it's fun to live on the edge. Charring leeks right up to the point where they turn black is exciting because there is always a chance that you will completely burn them. No worries. If that happens, you can peel away the burnt leaves and eat the rest. The biggest payoff here is that the interiors of the leeks will soften and turn smoky, especially if you are cooking over charcoal. The nutty and slightly tart chimichurri adds texture and vibrancy to the sweet leeks, making a remarkable side dish.

1 In the bowl of a food processor pulse the hazelnuts to coarsely chop. Add the remaining chimichurri ingredients, including ⅓ cup oil, ½ teaspoon salt, and ⅛ teaspoon pepper, and process until almost smooth (some texture will still remain). Transfer to a small bowl.

2 Prepare the grill for direct and indirect cooking over medium heat (350° to 450°F).

3 Remove the dark green tops from the leeks, cutting about 2 inches above the point where the leaves begin to darken. Trim just enough of each root end to remove the stringy parts, but leave enough of each root end so that the layers remain attached. Cut each leek lengthwise in half. Rinse the leeks under water, opening up the layers to remove any dirt. Pat dry, and then lightly coat with oil and season with ¾ teaspoon salt and ½ teaspoon pepper.

4 Grill the leeks over **direct medium heat**, with the lid closed, until charred on all sides, 4 to 6 minutes, turning as needed. Then move the leeks over **indirect medium heat** and continue grilling, with the lid closed, until tender, 12 to 14 minutes more, turning once or twice and peeling away any burnt leaves. Transfer the leeks to a serving platter. Spread the chimichurri over the leeks and top with the tomatoes. Serve warm.

POT LIKKER COLLARD GREENS

SERVES: 8 | **PREP TIME:** 1 HOUR, PLUS ABOUT 1 HOUR TO COOK THE STOCK
SPECIAL EQUIPMENT: 12- TO 16-QUART STOCKPOT

STOCK

- 1 quart low-sodium chicken broth
- 1½ pounds smoked ham hocks or turkey wings, sawed by the butcher into large pieces
- 1 quart water
- 1¾ cups coarsely chopped yellow onion
- 6 garlic cloves, smashed and peeled

- 1 tablespoon vegetable oil
- 2¼ cups chopped yellow onions
- 3 garlic cloves, minced
- 4 pounds (about 7 bunches) collard greens, thick stems removed
- 2 tablespoons granulated sugar
- 2 teaspoons kosher salt
- ½ teaspoon crushed red pepper flakes
  Hot pepper sauce
  Cider vinegar

Nothing sets off a plate of barbecue more than a heap of tender greens nicely seasoned with smoked meat. Ham is traditional, but smoked turkey has become a new favorite. A tasty cooking liquid makes the difference between good collard greens and those that are truly great, so go ahead and start it beforehand to give the meat extra time to release its flavor. The final broth (called pot likker) is so mouthwatering that it is often served with the greens for sopping up with a hunk of corn bread.

1   In a 4-quart saucepan combine the chicken broth, ham hocks, and water. Bring to a boil over high heat on the stove. Skim off any foam that rises to the top. Add the 1¾ cups coarsely chopped onion, smashed garlic, and additional water, as necessary, to cover the solids. Reduce the heat to medium-low and simmer until the stock is reduced to 6 to 7 cups, about 1 hour. Strain the stock through a fine-mesh strainer placed over a bowl. Discard the onion and garlic and reserve the ham hocks.

2   In a 12- to 16-quart stockpot over medium heat on the stove, warm the oil. Add the 2¼ cups chopped onions and cook until it begins to brown and brown bits form on the bottom of the stockpot, 7 to 8 minutes, stirring occasionally. Add the minced garlic and sauté for 1 minute, stirring frequently. Pour in the stock, add the reserved ham hocks, and bring to a simmer.

3   In the meantime, fill a sink with cold water and add the collard greens. Agitate the greens well to loosen any grit. In batches, lift a handful of greens from the water and shake off the excess water. Roll up the greens into a thick cylinder and, using a large knife, cut the greens crosswise into strips about ½ inch wide. Add them to the stockpot and stir well until the greens wilt. Stir in the sugar, salt, and red pepper flakes. If needed, add enough water to barely cover the ingredients. Bring to a boil over high heat. Reduce the heat to low, cover, and simmer until the greens and the meat on the ham hocks are all very tender, about 30 minutes, stirring occasionally. Transfer the ham hocks to a plate. Remove the stockpot from the heat and cover to keep the greens warm.

4   When the ham hocks are cool enough to handle, but still warm, dice the meat into small pieces, discarding the skin, fat, and bones. Stir the meat into the greens.

5   Using a slotted spoon, transfer the greens to a serving bowl and add enough of the cooking liquid (called pot likker) to moisten the greens without making them soupy. Serve warm, with hot sauce and vinegar for sprinkling on the greens and the remaining pot likker on the side.

If you have a side burner, fire it up to simmer the greens and ham hocks in a large pot while you make the rest of your meal on the grill. These greens are really rich, so one or two spoonfuls will be plenty alongside some barbecued meat and a piece of corn bread.

NAAN
WITH GARLIC-HERB BUTTER

SERVES: 4 TO 8 | **PREP TIME:** 30 MINUTES | **RISING TIME:** ABOUT 45 MINUTES
GRILLING TIME: ABOUT 4 MINUTES PER BATCH | **SPECIAL EQUIPMENT:** PIZZA STONE, SILICONE BASTING BRUSH

¾ cup warm water (105° to 115°F)
1 packet (¼ ounce) rapid-rise instant yeast
Pinch granulated sugar
⅓ cup plain Greek yogurt, at room temperature
Canola oil
Kosher salt
1 teaspoon ground white pepper
2½ cups bread flour, plus more as needed
½ cup (1 stick) unsalted butter
3 tablespoons mixed chopped fresh herbs
2 teaspoons minced garlic

Probably one of the first foods humans cooked over fire (hot stones), about two million years ago, was bread, so this isn't exactly a new thing; but, then again, how many of your neighbors these days are cooking flat bread outside on a pizza stone? It's time to wow the neighborhood with naan hot off the grill. Pick any duo of fresh green herbs you like to season the melted butter seeping into the bread.

1 Pour the warm water into a large, warm bowl and sprinkle with the yeast and a pinch of sugar. Let stand, without stirring, until the yeast dissolves, about 5 minutes. Add the yogurt, 2 tablespoons oil, 1 teaspoon salt, and the pepper; stir to combine. Add 2½ cups flour and stir to form a soft dough (add another ½ cup flour, if needed). Turn onto a clean, dry work surface; knead until smooth, about 8 minutes.

2 Grease the inside of a large bowl with oil. Shape the dough into a ball, set it in the bowl, and turn the dough to coat all sides with oil. Cover with plastic wrap and set aside in a warm, draft-free place until doubled in bulk, about 45 minutes.

3 Prepare the grill for direct cooking over medium heat (350° to 450°F) and preheat a pizza stone for 20 minutes, following manufacturer's instructions.

4 In a small saucepan over low heat on the stove, melt the butter. Stir in the herbs, garlic, and 1 teaspoon salt. Set aside off the heat.

5 Punch down the dough and divide it into four equal balls. On a clean, dry work surface, stretch each ball by hand into an oval about 10 inches long and ⅓ inch thick. If the ovals fail to retain their dimensions once stretched to size, cover the dough with a kitchen towel and let them rest for 10 to 20 minutes before continuing. Transfer the ovals, not touching, to a lightly floured sheet pan.

6 Using a silicone basting brush, brush off any crumbs that may be on the pizza stone. Place two ovals of dough on the pizza stone and lightly brush the tops with some of the herb butter. Grill the naan over **direct medium heat** (as close to 400°F as possible), with the lid closed, for 2 minutes. Turn the naan over, lightly brush with more herb butter, and continue grilling, with the lid closed, until puffy, lightly browned in places, and firm to the touch, about 2 minutes more. Transfer the naan to a basket lined with a napkin and keep covered and warm. When the grill temperature returns to 400°F, continue as above, cooking the remaining pieces of dough in one more batch. Serve warm.

This dough draws nice flavors from yogurt. Take the yogurt out of the refrigerator for 20 minutes before using it so that it's not so cold that it slows down the action of the yeast. Knead and stretch the dough until the surface is smooth. Then let the dough double in size in an oiled bowl. Shape pieces of the risen dough into ovals for buttering and cooking.

BUTTERMILK BISCUITS
WITH HONEY BUTTER

MAKES: 10 TO 12 BISCUITS | **PREP TIME:** 30 MINUTES
GRILLING TIME: 20 TO 25 MINUTES | **SPECIAL EQUIPMENT:** 2½-INCH-ROUND BISCUIT CUTTER

BISCUITS

- 3 cups unbleached all-purpose flour, plus more for rolling the dough
- 1 tablespoon granulated sugar
- 2 teaspoons baking powder
- 1 teaspoon baking soda
- 1 teaspoon kosher salt
- ¾ cup (1½ sticks) cold butter, cut into ½-inch cubes
- 1⅓ cups buttermilk (see caption and photo, page 272)

BUTTER

- ½ cup (1 stick) unsalted butter, softened
- 3 tablespoons honey, preferably clover

Flaky biscuits are delicious icons of American home cooking, including barbecue. Quickly prepared and "baked" on a grill, they are excellent to serve as a barbecue side dish or to sandwich smoked meats. A key to perfect biscuits is gentle handling of the dough, so avoid strong kneading at all costs. Also, when you cut the biscuits from the dough, do not twist the cutter. Pull straight up!

1 Prepare the grill for indirect cooking over medium-high heat (400° to 450°F).

2 Sift 3 cups of the flour, the sugar, baking powder, baking soda, and salt into a large bowl. Add the butter cubes and stir to coat them with the flour mixture. Using a pastry blender or two knives, cut in the butter until the mixture resembles coarse crumbs with some pea-sized pieces of butter. Resist the temptation to use your hands because the colder the butter is, the flakier the biscuits will be. Pour in the buttermilk and, using your hands with your fingers spread apart, gently mix until the dough is moistened. Very lightly knead the dough in the bowl a few times, just until it holds together. If the dough is too moist to knead and it is sticking to your hands, add up to 2 tablespoons more flour, one tablespoon at a time, until the dough is just workable. Do not overwork the dough.

3 Turn the dough out onto a lightly floured work surface and dust the top of the dough with flour. Gently roll or pat the dough into a round ¾ to 1 inch thick. Using a 2½-inch-round biscuit cutter, cut out biscuits, being sure not to twist the cutter. Set the biscuits on an ungreased baking sheet so they are not touching. Repeat the process, but push and pinch the dough scraps into a cohesive mass without kneading for the remaining biscuits. Do this only one time because too much regathering makes tough biscuits.

4 Place the baking sheet with the biscuits over **indirect medium-high heat**, close the lid, and cook until the biscuits rise, are golden brown, and a wooden skewer inserted into the center comes out clean, 20 to 25 minutes.

5 Meanwhile, in a small bowl using an electric mixer on high speed, beat the butter until creamy. Gradually beat in the honey. Cover and let stand at room temperature until the biscuits are ready to eat. Serve the biscuits warm with the honey butter.

MOIST AND TENDER CORN BREAD

SERVES: 8 | **PREP TIME:** 15 MINUTES | **GRILLING TIME:** 20 TO 25 MINUTES
SPECIAL EQUIPMENT: 9-INCH CAST-IRON SKILLET OR GRILL-PROOF ROUND CAKE PAN WITH 1½- TO 1¾-INCH-HIGH SIDES

⅓ cup plus 1 tablespoon unsalted
    butter, divided
1 cup buttermilk (see caption and
    photo below)
1 large egg
1 cup unbleached all-purpose flour
1 cup yellow cornmeal, preferably stone
    ground with not too coarse a grind
⅓ cup granulated sugar
2 teaspoons baking powder
1 teaspoon baking soda
¾ teaspoon kosher salt

Like barbecued meats, corn bread can be prepared in many ways. It isn't unusual to find it thick or thin, sweet or savory, served in wedges or cut into squares, plain or with additions—the variations seem endless. This one, with a moist and sweet crumb, is a real crowd-pleaser, and it can be prepared in minutes. If you prefer a less sweet corn bread, just reduce the sugar to two tablespoons. Change up the recipe a bit by adding small amounts of chopped fresh herbs, such as sage, thyme, or rosemary. Or, for a savory note, stir in some grated cheese, like pepper jack or sharp cheddar, and cooked, crumbled bacon.

1   Prepare the grill for indirect cooking over medium-high heat (400° to 450°F). Grease a 9-inch cast-iron skillet with 1 tablespoon of the butter.

2   Melt the remaining ⅓ cup butter, and then add the buttermilk and egg and whisk until well bended. Sift the remaining ingredients into a separate large bowl. Make a well in the center of the dry ingredients. Pour in the buttermilk mixture and stir with a rubber spatula just until the batter is moistened (the batter may be slightly lumpy). Pour the batter into the prepared skillet and smooth the top.

3   Cook the corn bread over **indirect medium-high heat**, with the lid closed, until golden brown and a wooden toothpick inserted in the center comes out clean, 20 to 25 minutes. Let the corn bread cool for 5 minutes. Cut into wedges and serve warm directly from the skillet. The bread is very tender, and if turned out of the pan, it may break apart. Wrap any leftover corn bread tightly in plastic wrap. Corn bread dries out quickly, so the sooner you wrap it, the longer it will stay moist.

If you don't have buttermilk, mix 1 cup whole or 2% milk with 1 tablespoon cider vinegar or distilled white vinegar, and let stand for 5 minutes.

The corn bread is cooked just right when a toothpick inserted in the center comes out clean with no wet batter attached.

ICED CINNAMON ROLLS

SERVES: 6 TO 12 (MAKES 12 ROLLS) | **PREP TIME:** 40 MINUTES | **RISING TIME:** ABOUT 1½ HOURS
STANDING TIME: 1 HOUR TO OVERNIGHT | **GRILLING TIME:** ABOUT 1 HOUR | **SPECIAL EQUIPMENT:** STAND MIXER WITH PADDLE
AND DOUGH HOOK ATTACHMENTS, 10-INCH CAST-IRON SKILLET OR GRILL-PROOF BAKING PAN

DOUGH

1¼ cups warm whole milk
(100° to 110°F), divided
¼ cup plus 1 tablespoon granulated
sugar, divided
1 packet (¼ ounce) active dry yeast
1 teaspoon kosher salt
3 large eggs, at room temperature
6 cups unbleached all-purpose flour,
divided, plus more for dusting
½ cup (1 stick) unsalted butter, softened

FILLING

1 cup lightly packed light brown sugar
4 teaspoons ground cinnamon
½ cup (1 stick) unsalted butter,
softened, divided

ICING

4 ounces cream cheese, softened
3 tablespoons whole milk
2 cups confectioners' sugar
1 teaspoon pure vanilla extract
⅛ teaspoon kosher salt

Okay, I admit it … including cinnamon rolls in a barbecue book is a stretch. It begs the question, what is barbecue anyway? For a complete answer, read my introduction on pages 5 to 6. You might be surprised by what you learn. You might also be surprised by how amazingly good these cinnamon rolls are. That's another reason they are in this book.

1 In the bowl of a stand mixer whisk ½ cup of the milk, 1 tablespoon of the sugar, and the yeast and let stand until frothy, about 5 minutes. Add the remaining ¾ cup milk, the remaining ¼ cup sugar, the salt, and eggs and, using the paddle attachment with the mixer on low speed, beat for 1 minute. Change to the dough hook and add 5½ cups of the flour. Starting on low speed and working slowly up to medium, mix until the dough is fairly smooth, about 3 minutes. Reduce the speed to medium-low and add ½ cup butter and the remaining ½ cup flour. Transfer the dough to a floured work surface and knead until the dough is soft, smooth, and no longer sticky, about 2 minutes. Transfer the dough to an oiled bowl, cover, and let rise in a warm place until doubled in bulk, about 1½ hours.

2 Combine the brown sugar and cinnamon. Press the dough down, and then turn out onto a lightly floured surface. Knead the dough two to three times, and then roll out into a 24-inch long by 12-inch wide rectangle. Spread the dough all over (do not leave a border) with ¼ cup plus 2 tablespoons of the butter. Sprinkle evenly with the cinnamon sugar. Starting at the long side closest to you, tightly roll up the dough, and then pinch the seam closed. Cut the log of dough into 12 two-inch pieces. Generously grease the bottom and sides of a 10-inch cast-iron skillet with the remaining butter and arrange the rolls, cut side up, in a single layer. Cover with aluminum foil and let stand at room temperature for 1 hour, or refrigerate overnight. (If refrigerating, return to room temperature before proceeding.)

3 Prepare the grill for indirect cooking over medium heat (as close to 375°F as possible).

4 Place the skillet with the rolls covered with foil over ***indirect medium heat***, close the lid, and cook for 25 minutes. Wearing insulated barbecue mitts or gloves, rotate the skillet 180 degrees, close the lid, and cook for 10 minutes. Remove the foil from the skillet and continue cooking until the dough is cooked through and the tops are lightly browned, 20 to 30 minutes more. Remove from the grill, set on a heatproof surface, and let cool for 10 minutes. Meanwhile, make the icing.

5 In a large bowl stir the cream cheese and milk. Sift the confectioners' sugar into the bowl and stir to combine. Add the vanilla and salt and whisk until smooth. Spread the icing over the top of the rolls and let stand for 10 minutes. Using a thin-edged knife, cut between the seams of the rolls and transfer to a platter or cooling rack. Serve warm or at room temperature.

7
SEASONINGS

SAUCES

SWEET CAROLINA MUSTARD SAUCE

MAKES ABOUT 1½ CUPS

In a saucepan mix 1 cup yellow mustard; ¼ cup unsweetened apple juice; 2 tbsp each brown sugar, honey, and unsulfured molasses (not blackstrap); 1½ tsp each granulated garlic, granulated onion, and prepared chili powder; and ½ tsp each ground black pepper and sweet cocoa powder. Simmer for 5 minutes over medium heat, stirring often.

NORTH CAROLINA VINEGAR SAUCE

MAKES ABOUT 3 CUPS

Place a saucepan over medium-high heat and add 2 cups distilled white vinegar, 1 cup ketchup, ¼ cup light brown sugar, 1 tbsp Worcestershire sauce, 2 tsp kosher salt, and ½ tsp ground cayenne pepper. Bring to a boil and cook until the sugar is dissolved and the sauce is reduced to a ketchup-like consistency, 8–10 minutes.

SWEET AND SMOKY KANSAS CITY SAUCE

MAKES ABOUT 2 CUPS

Fry 3 bacon slices in a saucepan over medium heat until most of the fat is rendered out. Eat the bacon. Leave 2 tbsp bacon fat in the pan; add ½ cup finely diced yellow onion and cook until soft, 3–4 minutes, stirring often. Add 3 minced garlic cloves and cook for 1 minute, stirring to prevent burning. Whisk in ½ cup each ketchup, light corn syrup, and cider vinegar; ¼ cup each tomato paste and prepared chili powder; 2 tbsp light brown sugar; 1 tbsp each unsulfured molasses (not blackstrap), liquid smoke, and Worcestershire sauce; 1 tsp celery salt; and ½ tsp kosher salt. Simmer over medium heat for 10–15 minutes, stirring occasionally. Cool. Pour the sauce into a blender and blend until smooth.

ALABAMA WHITE SAUCE

MAKES ABOUT 1¼ CUPS

Whisk 1 cup mayo, ¼ cup white wine vinegar, 2 tsp ground black pepper, ¾ tsp sugar, and ¼ tsp kosher salt until smooth.

CRANBERRY-GINGER BARBECUE SAUCE

MAKES ABOUT 3 CUPS

In a saucepan combine 1 cup ketchup, 1 eight-ounce can jellied cranberry sauce, ½ cup unsweetened apple juice, ⅓ cup each cider vinegar and honey, 2 tbsp unsulfured molasses (not blackstrap), 1 tbsp Worcestershire sauce, 1 tsp each prepared chili powder and ground ginger, and ¼ tsp ground black pepper. Bring to a simmer over medium heat and cook until slightly thickened, about 5 minutes, stirring occasionally.

RED WINE BARBECUE SAUCE

MAKES ABOUT 1½ CUPS

Melt 2 tbsp unsalted butter in a saucepan over medium-low heat. Add ⅓ cup finely chopped shallot and cook until softened, 2–3 minutes, stirring often. Stir in 2 minced garlic cloves and cook until fragrant, about 1 minute. Add ½ cup red wine and increase the heat to medium-high. Boil for 1 minute. Then add 1 cup ketchup, ¼ cup each balsamic vinegar and honey, 1 tbsp each Dijon mustard and soy sauce, 1½ tsp each finely chopped fresh thyme and rosemary leaves, and ¼ tsp crushed red pepper flakes. Bring to a boil, stirring often, and then reduce the heat to low and simmer, uncovered, until the sauce thickens and is reduced to about 1½ cups, 20–25 minutes, stirring occasionally.

PINEAPPLE-HOISIN BBQ SAUCE

MAKES ABOUT 2 CUPS

In a medium saucepan over medium heat, warm 1 tbsp canola oil. Add 1 tbsp finely chopped fresh ginger and 2 tsp finely chopped garlic and cook for 1 minute, stirring often. Add 1 cup pineapple juice, ½ cup each hoisin sauce and ketchup, 2 tbsp each honey and unseasoned rice vinegar, ½ tsp each toasted sesame oil and chipotle chile powder, and ¼ tsp kosher salt. Cook for about 5 minutes, stirring occasionally. If desired, pour the sauce through a fine-mesh strainer to strain out the bits of ginger and garlic.

PEACHY DIPPING SAUCE

MAKES ABOUT 2 CUPS

Put the following ingredients in a large saucepan: 2 cups crushed tomatoes in juice (from a can); 1 cup peach jam; ⅓ cup white wine vinegar; 2 tbsp unsulfured molasses (not blackstrap); 1 tsp mustard powder; ½ tsp each onion powder, ground allspice, and kosher salt; and ¼ tsp each crushed red pepper flakes, garlic powder, and ground mace. Bring to a low boil over medium-high heat, stirring often. Then reduce the heat to low and simmer, uncovered, until thick and reduced to about 2 cups, about 1 hour, stirring often.

KENTUCKY BOURBON BARBECUE SAUCE

MAKES ABOUT 2 CUPS

Cut 2 bacon slices into ½-inch wide strips. Fry in a saucepan with 2 tsp oil over medium heat until crisp, 3 to 5 minutes; transfer to paper towels and keep the bacon fat in the pan. Finely chop a small onion and add to the pan. Reduce the heat to medium-low and cook until soft, 8–10 minutes, stirring occasionally. Stir in 1 minced garlic clove and cook for 1 minute. Then add ¼ cup bourbon, increase the heat to medium-high, and boil to reduce slightly, about 1 minute. Stir in 1 cup ketchup, ¼ cup water, 3 tbsp each cider vinegar and molasses, 2 tbsp steak sauce, 1 tbsp spicy brown mustard, 1 tsp liquid hickory smoke flavoring, and ½ tsp hot sauce. Bring to a boil over medium-high heat, then reduce the heat to low and simmer, uncovered, until the sauce thickens and is reduced to about 2 cups, about 20 minutes, stirring occasionally. Remove from the heat and stir in the bacon.

SAUCES

No matter what you grill or what sort of regional styles you prefer, chances are very good that you will brush, ladle, or drizzle some sort of sauce on your food. Without it, your meal could be missing an essential range of flavor, an important degree of texture, or a beautiful boost of color—or all three. Grilling sauces are usually pretty easy to make. Sometimes the prep is as simple as whisking a handful of ingredients, most of which are probably in your pantry or refrigerator already.

CHARRED POBLANO ROMESCO SAUCE

MAKES ABOUT ½ CUP

- 2 poblano chile peppers, about 8 ounces total
- ½ cup fresh cilantro sprigs
- ¼ cup almonds, toasted
- 1 small jalapeño chile pepper, seeded and chopped
- 3 tablespoons extra-virgin olive oil
- 1 tablespoon fresh lemon juice
- 1 teaspoon kosher salt
- 2 garlic cloves
- ¼ teaspoon freshly ground black pepper
- ⅛ teaspoon granulated sugar

1 Prepare the grill for direct cooking over high heat (450° to 550°F).

2 Grill the poblanos over **direct high heat**, with the lid closed, until blackened and blistered all over, 10 to 12 minutes, turning occasionally. Place in a bowl and cover with plastic wrap to trap the steam. Let stand for about 10 minutes. Remove and discard the charred skins, stems, and seeds, and then coarsely chop the poblanos.

3 In the bowl of a food processor combine the poblanos and the remaining ingredients and process until well blended but some texture still remains.

ESPRESSO BARBECUE SAUCE

MAKES ABOUT 1 CUP

- 1 tablespoon extra-virgin olive oil
- 1 small yellow onion, finely chopped
- 1 garlic clove, finely chopped
- 1 tablespoon prepared chili powder
- 1 teaspoon ground cumin
- ½ teaspoon paprika
- ½ cup ketchup-style chili sauce
- ½ cup drip-brewed espresso or dark roast coffee
- 2 tablespoons packed light brown sugar
- 2 tablespoons balsamic vinegar

1 In a saucepan over medium-low heat, warm the oil. Add the onion and cook until super soft and as dark as possible, about 30 minutes, stirring occasionally. Stir in the garlic and cook until fragrant, about 1 minute. Add the chili powder, cumin, and paprika and stir well. Add the chili sauce, espresso, brown sugar, and vinegar and bring to a boil over medium-high heat. Reduce the heat to low and simmer, uncovered, until the sauce thickens and is reduced to about 1 cup, 15 to 20 minutes, stirring occasionally.

BLACKBERRY-SAGE SAUCE

MAKES ABOUT 1¼ CUPS

- 1 tablespoon unsalted butter
- 2 tablespoons finely chopped shallot
- 12 ounces fresh blackberries (2⅔ cups), divided
- ¼ cup honey
- 2 tablespoons ketchup
- 2 tablespoons balsamic vinegar
- 2 teaspoons minced fresh sage leaves
- 1 teaspoon Worcestershire sauce
- ½ teaspoon freshly ground black pepper
- ⅛ teaspoon kosher salt

1 In a saucepan over medium heat, melt the butter. Add the shallot and cook until lightly browned, about 2 minutes, stirring often. Add 2 cups of the berries, the honey, ketchup, vinegar, sage, Worcestershire sauce, pepper, and salt. Bring to a boil, and then reduce the heat to medium-low. Cook the sauce at a steady simmer until the juices have thickened slightly, about 10 minutes, stirring often and mashing some of the berries to release their juice. Remove from the heat. Puree the sauce in a blender (in batches) with a small opening in the lid to let the steam escape, and return to the saucepan. Stir in the remaining ⅔ cup berries. Let the sauce cool until tepid and slightly thickened.

SWEET MOLASSES BARBECUE SAUCE

MAKES ABOUT 1⅓ CUPS

¾ cup ketchup
½ cup water
¼ cup packed light brown sugar
¼ cup unsulfured molasses (not blackstrap)
1 tablespoon Worcestershire sauce
1 tablespoon prepared chili powder
1 teaspoon kosher salt
½ teaspoon freshly ground black pepper

1 In a saucepan combine the ingredients. Bring to a gentle boil over medium-high heat, stirring frequently. Reduce the heat to medium-low and simmer until the sauce thickens slightly to a light syrupy consistency, 5 to 10 minutes, stirring occasionally.

BLACK CHERRY BARBECUE SAUCE

MAKES ABOUT 1¾ CUPS

1 cup tart black cherry juice
½ cup ketchup
¼ cup yellow mustard
2 tablespoons honey
1½ teaspoons prepared chili powder
1½ teaspoons dried thyme
1 teaspoon Worcestershire sauce
¾ teaspoon freshly ground black pepper
¼ teaspoon paprika
¼ teaspoon kosher salt

1 In a saucepan combine the ingredients. Bring to a simmer over medium heat. Cook for 3 to 5 minutes, stirring occasionally.

HAZELNUT CHIMICHURRI

MAKES ABOUT ¾ CUP

¼ cup hazelnuts, toasted
1 cup loosely packed fresh Italian parsley leaves
⅓ cup extra-virgin olive oil
¼ cup loosely packed fresh oregano leaves
2 tablespoons red wine vinegar
½ teaspoon kosher salt
1 garlic clove, chopped
⅛ teaspoon freshly ground black pepper

1 In the bowl of a food processor pulse the hazelnuts to coarsely chop. Add the remaining ingredients and process until almost smooth (some texture will still remain).

KOGI SAUCE

MAKES ABOUT ¾ CUP

¼ cup *gochujang* (Korean fermented hot pepper paste)
¼ cup soy sauce
3 tablespoons granulated sugar
1 tablespoon toasted sesame oil
2 teaspoons unseasoned rice vinegar

1 Whisk the ingredients.

BUTTERMILK DRESSING

MAKES ABOUT ½ CUP

¼ cup buttermilk
3 tablespoons sour cream
1 tablespoon fresh lemon juice
¼ teaspoon kosher salt
¼ teaspoon freshly ground black pepper

1 Whisk the ingredients until smooth.

BLUE CHEESE DIP

MAKES ABOUT 1½ CUPS

4 ounces crumbled blue cheese
½ cup sour cream
¼ cup mayonnaise
2 tablespoons fresh lemon juice
½ teaspoon celery seed
½ teaspoon kosher salt
Several dashes hot pepper sauce

1 Combine the ingredients and mix well. If you like the dip a little thinner, stir in a little milk.

MARINADES

It's what's inside that counts—and that's flavor, where marinades are concerned. Letting food sit in a mixture of acidic liquid, oil, herbs, and seasonings does wonders to kick-start items that might need a little boost, like leaner cuts of meat and even vegetables, in addition to keeping them moist on the grill. Bold ingredients work best—think garlic, rosemary, or soy sauce—to maximize the marinade's effect, and the right combinations can give your meal a regional or ethnic flair.

KOREAN BBQ MARINADE

6 garlic cloves
1 Granny Smith apple, about 8 ounces, cored and quartered
1 yellow onion, about 6 ounces, quartered
1 piece fresh ginger, about 2 inches long, peeled and coarsely chopped
1 cup soy sauce
½ cup packed light brown sugar
¼ cup Asian rice wine or sherry
2 tablespoons toasted sesame oil
1 teaspoon freshly ground black pepper
½ teaspoon ground cayenne pepper

1 In a food processor combine the garlic, apple, onion, and ginger and process until finely chopped. Add the remaining ingredients and process until pureed and well blended.

JAMAICAN JERK MARINADE

1 Scotch bonnet or habanero chile pepper, seeded and coarsely chopped
6 large scallions (white and light green parts only), coarsely chopped
¼ cup vegetable oil
2 tablespoons soy sauce
2 tablespoons fresh lime juice
2 tablespoons ground allspice berries
2 tablespoons packed light brown sugar
1 tablespoon peeled, minced fresh ginger
1 tablespoon coarsely chopped fresh thyme leaves
1 teaspoon kosher salt
½ teaspoon freshly grated nutmeg
½ teaspoon ground cinnamon
2 garlic cloves, coarsely chopped

1 To avoid burning your skin, wear rubber gloves when you handle the chile. In a blender combine the ingredients. Puree, stopping to scrape down the inside of the jar as needed, and add a little water if the paste is too thick.

LITTLE ITALY MARINADE

1 cup extra-virgin olive oil
¼ cup red wine vinegar
¼ cup fresh lemon juice
¼ cup finely chopped fresh mint leaves
¼ cup finely chopped fresh Italian parsley leaves
2 tablespoons finely chopped fresh dill
1½ teaspoons fennel seed
2 teaspoons minced garlic
2 teaspoons kosher salt
½ teaspoon freshly ground black pepper

HOW LONG?

The right length of time varies, depending on the strength of the marinade and the food you are marinating. If your marinade includes intense ingredients like soy sauce, hard liquor, or hot chiles and strong spices, don't overdo it. A fish fillet should still taste like fish, not like a burning-hot, salt-soaked piece of protein. Also, if an acidic marinade is left on meat or fish too long, it can turn the surface dry or mushy. Here are some guidelines to get you going.

TIME	TYPES OF FOOD
15 to 30 minutes	Small foods, such as shellfish, fish fillets, cubed meat for kabobs, and tender vegetables
1 to 3 hours	Thin cuts of boneless meat, such as chicken breasts, pork tenderloins, chops, steaks, and sturdy vegetables
2 to 6 hours	Thicker cuts of boneless or bone-in meat, such as leg of lamb, whole chickens, and beef roasts
6 to 12 hours	Big or tough cuts of meat, such as racks of ribs, whole hams, pork shoulders, and turkeys

ROSEMARY-LEMON MARINADE

Freshly grated zest and juice of 2 lemons
¼ cup extra-virgin olive oil
2 tablespoons finely chopped fresh rosemary leaves
2 teaspoons kosher salt
4 garlic cloves, minced
1 teaspoon smoked paprika
1 teaspoon freshly ground black pepper

CHINATOWN MARINADE

½ cup hoisin sauce
½ cup bourbon
¼ cup soy sauce
¼ cup honey
2 tablespoons toasted sesame oil
2 tablespoons peeled, minced fresh ginger
1 tablespoon minced garlic
2 teaspoons Chinese five spice
½ teaspoon ground white pepper

MOJO MARINADE

1½ cups fresh orange juice
½ cup fresh lemon juice
½ cup extra-virgin olive oil
1 medium yellow onion, finely chopped in a food processor
20 peeled garlic cloves, finely chopped in a food processor
1 tablespoon dried oregano
1 tablespoon kosher salt

SOUTHEAST ASIAN MARINADE

¼ cup Vietnamese or Thai fish sauce
¼ cup fresh lime juice
2 tablespoons minced shallot
2 tablespoons vegetable oil
1 tablespoon toasted sesame oil
2 garlic cloves, minced

GO-TO FAVORITE MARINADE

1 small yellow onion, grated, with juice (about ½ cup)
¼ cup fresh lemon juice
3 tablespoons extra-virgin olive oil
3 tablespoons soy sauce
2 tablespoons Dijon mustard
1 teaspoon freshly ground black pepper

SWEET AND SIMPLE MARINADE

½ cup soy sauce
¼ cup bourbon or Scotch
¼ cup honey
2 tablespoons ketchup
2 tablespoons Dijon mustard
1 tablespoon cider vinegar
1 tablespoon extra-virgin olive oil
4 garlic cloves, minced

INDIAN MARINADE

½ cup whole-milk yogurt
¼ cup extra-virgin olive oil
2 tablespoons fresh lemon juice
1 tablespoon peeled, finely grated fresh ginger
2 teaspoons ground cardamom
3 large garlic cloves, minced
1 teaspoon ground coriander
1 teaspoon kosher salt
1 teaspoon freshly ground black pepper

FIESTA MARINADE

½ cup fresh orange juice
¼ cup fresh lime juice
¼ cup gold tequila
1 large jalapeño chile pepper, including seeds, finely chopped
3 tablespoons agave nectar
2 tablespoons soy sauce
2 teaspoons ground cumin
4 garlic cloves, minced

SMOKY MARINADE

4 canned chipotle chile peppers in adobo sauce, minced (about ⅓ cup)
¼ cup fresh lime juice
3 tablespoons ketchup
2 tablespoons extra-virgin olive oil
1 tablespoon packed dark brown sugar
4 garlic cloves, minced
2 teaspoons kosher salt
1 teaspoon ground cumin
1 teaspoon prepared chili powder

BRINES

When it comes to making brines, the key is to use the right ratio of salt to water. Too much or too little salt can lead to major disappointments. Begin with ½ to 1 cup of kosher salt for each gallon of water or other liquid. This level of saltiness creates a subtle background of flavor inside the meat. What happens is that the salt penetrates the meat and changes the structure of the protein so that the cells inside the meat are able to trap more moisture and flavor. Nature likes equilibrium, so the saltiness inside the meat rises until it is equal to the saltiness in the brine outside the meat. If you like, you can also add sugar to your brine, about the same amount as the salt, and the sugar will complement the saltiness and also caramelize nicely on the surface of the food. Then you can add whatever other flavors you like, including a variety of herbs and spices.

If your brine includes some acidic liquid, be sure to use a nonreactive container. This is a dish or bowl made of glass, plastic, stainless steel, or ceramic. A container made of aluminum, or some other metals, will react with acids and add a metallic flavor to food.

Whatever you brine should be completely submerged, covered with plastic wrap, and then refrigerated.

APPLE BRINE

2 quarts chilled unsweetened
  apple juice, divided
½ cup kosher salt
½ cup soy sauce
1 three-inch piece fresh ginger, about
  3 ounces, peeled, thinly sliced
1 tablespoon dried rosemary
1 teaspoon black peppercorns
2 lemons, zest removed in wide strips with a
  vegetable peeler
2 bay leaves

1　In a saucepan combine 1 quart of the apple juice, the salt, soy sauce, ginger, rosemary, peppercorns, lemon zest strips, and bay leaves. Bring to a simmer over medium heat, stirring occasionally. Pour into a large heatproof bowl set in a larger bowl of iced water. Let stand until chilled, about 30 minutes, stirring often. Stir the remaining chilled apple juice into the brine.

ITALIAN BRINE

2 cups water
1 orange, quartered
1 lemon, quartered
1 small yellow onion, quartered
¼ cup granulated sugar
¼ cup kosher salt
4 sprigs fresh oregano or thyme
2 teaspoons black peppercorns
4 fresh sage leaves
2 garlic cloves, smashed and peeled
2 bay leaves
2 cups dry white wine

1　Pour the water into a saucepan, and then add the orange and lemon quarters, simultaneously squeezing the juice into the water. Add the remaining ingredients except the wine. Cook over medium-low heat, stirring to dissolve the sugar and salt. Remove from the heat and add the wine. Cool completely.

NORMANDY BRINE

2 cups apple cider
⅓ cup packed dark brown sugar
⅓ cup kosher salt
4 fresh thyme sprigs
6 whole cloves, smashed and peeled
1 tablespoon yellow mustard seed
2 teaspoons black peppercorns
2 bay leaves, torn
2 cups water

1　In a saucepan over medium-low heat, combine all of the ingredients, except the water, whisking to dissolve the sugar and salt. Remove from the heat and add the water. Cool completely.

TURBINADO SUGAR BRINE

1 quart water
3 cups turbinado sugar
1½ cups kosher salt
1 tablespoon celery seed
1 tablespoon coriander seed
1 tablespoon cumin seed
1 tablespoon yellow mustard seed
1 quart ice cubes

1 In a saucepan combine all of the
ingredients except the ice cubes. Cook
over high heat until the salt and sugar are
dissolved, whisking constantly. Remove
from the heat and add the ice cubes.

BLACK CHERRY BRINE

1 quart water
2 cups tart black cherry juice
½ cup kosher salt
½ cup packed brown sugar
2 quarts ice cubes

1 In a saucepan combine all of the ingredients
except the ice cubes. Bring to a boil, mixing
well to dissolve the salt and sugar. Remove
from the heat and add the ice cubes.

BUTTERMILK-HERB BRINE

1½ quarts buttermilk
¼ cup kosher salt
¼ cup granulated sugar
2 tablespoons chopped fresh rosemary leaves
2 tablespoons chopped fresh oregano leaves
1 tablespoon fresh thyme leaves
12 garlic cloves, minced
⅓ cup hot pepper sauce

1 Combine the ingredients and stir until
the salt and sugar are dissolved.

BEER BRINE

4 bottles (each 12 ounces) lager
1 cup packed light brown sugar
¾ cup kosher salt
3 tablespoons smoked paprika
1½ tablespoons dried thyme
1 tablespoon cracked black peppercorns
1 tablespoon granulated garlic
1 tablespoon granulated onion
½ teaspoon ground cayenne pepper
3 quarts ice water

1 Combine all of the ingredients, except
the ice water, and whisk until the salt and
sugar are dissolved. Add the ice water.

BOURBON BRINE

½ cup bourbon
½ cup water
¼ cup packed brown sugar
2 tablespoons kosher salt
½ teaspoon crushed red pepper flakes
1 cup ice cubes

1 In a saucepan over medium heat, combine
the bourbon, water, sugar, salt, and red
pepper flakes. Stir until the sugar and salt
dissolve. Remove from the heat and add
the ice cubes.

ALL-PURPOSE BRINE

2 cups water
½ cup kosher salt
⅓ cup packed light brown sugar
1½ quarts ice cubes

1 In a saucepan combine all of the
ingredients except the ice cubes.
Bring to a boil over high heat and
whisk until the salt is dissolved. Add
the ice cubes and let the brine cool
to room temperature.

HOW LONG?

The most deserving candidates for brining
are big, lean cuts of meat, such as pork loins
and whole turkeys, which you should soak
in a brine for several hours. But even small
items like pork chops, chicken pieces, and
salmon fillets are bound to be juicier and
more flavorful if you brine them for an hour
or two. Here are some guidelines.

TIME	TYPES OF FOOD
Up to 30 minutes	Small foods, such as shellfish, cubed meat for kabobs, and vegetables
30 minutes to 1 hour	Thin cuts of boneless meat, such as chicken breasts, fish fillets, pork tenderloins, chops, and steaks
2 to 4 hours	Thicker cuts of boneless or bone-in meat, such as leg of lamb, whole chickens, and beef roasts
4 to 12 hours	Big or tough cuts of meat, such as racks of ribs, whole hams, pork shoulders, and turkeys

RUBS

A rub is a mixture of spices, herbs, and other seasonings (often including sugar) that can quickly give a boost of flavors to foods before grilling. These two pages provide some mighty good examples, but dare to be different. One of the steps toward developing your own style at the grill is to concoct a signature rub recipe or two. Only you will know exactly what ingredients are blended in your special jar of "magic dust."

A word about freshness: Ground spices lose their aromas in a matter of months (eight to ten months maximum). If you have been holding on to a little jar of coriander for years, waiting to blend the world's finest version of curry powder, forget about it. Dump the old, tired coriander and buy some freshly ground. Better yet, buy whole coriander seeds and grind them yourself. Whatever you do, store your spices and spice rubs in airtight containers away from light and heat, to best preserve their flavors and fragrances.

ALL-PURPOSE RUB

2 tablespoons kosher salt
2 tablespoons packed light brown sugar
2 tablespoons prepared chili powder
1 tablespoon paprika
2 teaspoons granulated onion
1 teaspoon ground cumin
1 teaspoon freshly ground black pepper

PORK RUB

2 teaspoons kosher salt
1 teaspoon ground cumin
½ teaspoon freshly ground black pepper
½ teaspoon dried oregano
½ teaspoon packed light brown sugar
¼ teaspoon chipotle chile powder

BEEF RUB

2 teaspoons kosher salt
1 teaspoon granulated garlic
1 teaspoon freshly ground black pepper
1 teaspoon smoked paprika
½ teaspoon ground coriander
½ teaspoon ground cumin

LAMB RUB

2 teaspoons kosher salt
1 teaspoon paprika
1 teaspoon curry powder
1 teaspoon freshly ground black pepper
½ teaspoon granulated onion
½ teaspoon anise seed

POULTRY RUB

2 teaspoons kosher salt
2 teaspoons dried thyme
1 teaspoon dried oregano
1 teaspoon granulated onion
1 teaspoon ground coriander
1 teaspoon freshly ground black pepper
½ teaspoon prepared chili powder

SEAFOOD RUB

2 teaspoons kosher salt
1 teaspoon prepared chili powder
1 teaspoon granulated garlic
½ teaspoon ground coriander
½ teaspoon celery seed
½ teaspoon freshly ground black pepper

VEGETABLE RUB

1 teaspoon mustard powder
1 teaspoon granulated onion
1 teaspoon paprika
1 teaspoon kosher salt
½ teaspoon granulated garlic
½ teaspoon ground coriander
½ teaspoon ground cumin
½ teaspoon freshly ground black pepper

CAJUN RUB

1 tablespoon paprika
1 tablespoon packed light brown sugar
1 teaspoon garlic powder
1 teaspoon kosher salt
½ teaspoon dried thyme
½ teaspoon dried oregano
½ teaspoon celery salt
½ teaspoon onion powder
½ teaspoon mustard powder

ASIAN RUB

2 tablespoons paprika
2 teaspoons kosher salt
2 teaspoons ground coriander
2 teaspoons Chinese five spice
1 teaspoon ground ginger
½ teaspoon ground allspice
½ teaspoon ground cayenne pepper

KANSAS CITY RUB

½ cup packed light brown sugar
¼ cup smoked paprika
4 teaspoons kosher salt
2½ teaspoons prepared chili powder
2½ teaspoons garlic powder
2½ teaspoons onion powder
1½ teaspoons coarsely ground black pepper
½ teaspoon ground cayenne pepper

CHIPOTLE SPICE RUB

2 teaspoons kosher salt
1 teaspoon packed light brown sugar
1 teaspoon chipotle chile powder
1 teaspoon ground cumin
1 teaspoon smoked paprika
½ teaspoon freshly ground black pepper
¼ teaspoon ground cayenne pepper

TURBINADO RIB RUB

¼ cup turbinado sugar
2 tablespoons paprika
2 tablespoons prepared chili powder
4 teaspoons granulated onion
4 teaspoons kosher salt
2 teaspoons ground ginger
2 teaspoons freshly ground black pepper

MOROCCAN RUB

2 teaspoons pure chile powder
1 teaspoon kosher salt
½ teaspoon freshly ground black pepper
½ teaspoon ground coriander
½ teaspoon ground cumin
½ teaspoon caraway seed
¼ teaspoon garlic powder

GARLIC LOVERS' RUB

1½ teaspoons kosher salt
1½ teaspoons garlic powder
1 teaspoon ground cumin
¾ teaspoon freshly ground black pepper
½ teaspoon prepared chili powder
½ teaspoon ground ginger
⅛ teaspoon ground cinnamon

PASTRAMI RUB

1 tablespoon black peppercorns
1 tablespoon coriander seed
2 teaspoons yellow mustard seed
2 tablespoons packed light brown sugar
1 tablespoon kosher salt
2 teaspoons paprika
1 teaspoon ground cumin

1 In a small skillet over medium heat, stir and shake the peppercorns, coriander seed, and mustard seed until lightly toasted and fragrant, 3 to 4 minutes. Transfer to a small bowl and cool for 5 minutes. Pour into a spice mill and pulse 15 to 20 times until coarsely ground. Transfer back to the small bowl, add the remaining ingredients, and mix well.

SMOKED PAPRIKA RUB

1 teaspoon smoked paprika
1 teaspoon packed light brown sugar
1 teaspoon kosher salt
1 teaspoon granulated onion
½ teaspoon chipotle chile powder

DALMATIAN RUB

¼ cup kosher salt
3 tablespoons freshly ground black pepper
3 tablespoons turbinado sugar (optional)

HOW LONG?

If you leave a rub on for a long time, the seasonings intermix with the juices in the meat and produce more pronounced flavors as well as a crust. This is good to a point, but a rub with a lot of salt or sugar will draw moisture out of the meat over time, making the meat tastier, yes, but also drier. So how long should you use a rub? Here are some guidelines.

TIME	TYPES OF FOOD
Up to 15 minutes	Small foods, such as shellfish, cubed meat for kabobs, and vegetables
15 to 30 minutes	Thin cuts of boneless meat, such as chicken breasts, fish fillets, pork tenderloins, chops, and steaks
30 minutes to 1½ hours	Thicker cuts of boneless or bone-in meat, such as leg of lamb, whole chickens, and beef roasts
2 to 8 hours	Big or tough cuts of meat, such as racks of ribs, whole hams, pork shoulders, and turkeys

8

RESOURCES

GRILLING } GUIDES

The following cuts, thicknesses, weights, and grilling times are meant to be guidelines rather than hard and fast rules. Cooking times are affected by such factors as altitude, wind, outside temperature, and desired doneness. Two rules of thumb: Grill steaks, fish fillets, boneless chicken pieces, and vegetables using the direct method for the time given on the chart or to your desired doneness, turning once. Grill roasts, whole poultry, bone-in chicken pieces, whole fish, and thicker cuts using the indirect method for the time given on the chart or until an instant-read thermometer reaches the desired internal temperature. Cooking times for beef and lamb are for USDA's definition of medium-rare doneness except ground beef and lamb (medium). Let roasts, larger cuts of meat, and thick steaks and chops rest for 5 to 10 minutes before carving (the internal temperature of the meat will rise 5 to 10 degrees during this time).

⊙ PORK

CUT	THICKNESS / WEIGHT	APPROXIMATE GRILLING TIME
Bratwurst, fresh	3-ounce link	20 to 25 minutes **direct medium heat**
Bratwurst, precooked	3-ounce link	10 to 12 minutes **direct medium heat**
	¾ inch thick	6 to 8 minutes **direct medium heat**
Chop, boneless or bone in	1 inch thick	8 to 10 minutes **direct medium heat**
	1¼ to 1½ inches thick	10 to 12 minutes: sear 6 minutes **direct medium heat**, grill 4 to 6 minutes **indirect medium heat**
Ham, smoked, bone in	7 pounds	1½ to 2 hours **indirect medium-low heat**
Loin roast, bone in	3 to 5 pounds	1¼ to 1¾ hours **indirect medium heat**
Loin roast, boneless	3½ pounds	28 to 40 minutes: sear 8 to 10 minutes **direct high heat**, grill 20 to 30 minutes **indirect high heat**
Pork shoulder (Boston butt), boneless	5 to 6 pounds	5 to 7 hours **indirect low heat**
Pork shoulder roast, bone in	6 pounds	8 to 10 hours **indirect very low heat**
Pork, ground	½ inch thick	8 to 10 minutes **direct medium heat**
Ribs, baby back	1½ to 2 pounds	3 to 4 hours **indirect low heat**
Ribs, spareribs	2½ to 3½ pounds	3 to 4 hours **indirect low heat**
Ribs, country-style, bone in	1 inch thick	45 to 50 minutes **indirect medium heat**
Ribs, country-style, boneless	1 inch thick	12 to 15 minutes **direct medium heat**
Tenderloin	1 pound	15 to 20 minutes **direct medium heat**

 # BEEF

CUT	THICKNESS / WEIGHT	APPROXIMATE GRILLING TIME
Beef, ground	¾ inch thick	8 to 10 minutes *direct medium-high heat*
Brisket, whole (untrimmed)	12 to 14 pounds	8 to 10 hours *indirect very low heat*
Flank steak	1½ to 2 pounds, ¾ inch thick	8 to 10 minutes *direct medium heat*
Kabob	1½-inch cubes	6 to 7 minutes *direct high heat*
Rib roast (prime rib), boneless	5 to 6 pounds	1¼ to 1¾ hours *indirect medium heat*
Rib roast (prime rib), with bone	8 pounds	2 to 3 hours: sear 10 minutes *direct medium heat*, grill 2 to 3 hours *indirect low heat*
Short (plate) ribs	4 to 4½ pounds	6 to 7 hours *indirect low heat*
Skirt steak	¼ to ½ inch thick	4 to 6 minutes *direct high heat*
Steak: New York strip, porterhouse, rib eye, T-bone, and filet mignon (tenderloin)	¾ inch thick	4 to 6 minutes *direct high heat*
	1 inch thick	6 to 8 minutes *direct high heat*
	1¼ inches thick	8 to 10 minutes *direct high heat*
Strip loin roast, boneless	4 to 5 pounds	50 minutes to 1 hour: sear 10 minutes *direct medium heat*, grill 40 to 50 minutes *indirect medium heat*
Tenderloin, whole	3½ to 4 pounds	35 to 45 minutes: sear 15 minutes *direct medium heat*, grill 20 to 30 minutes *indirect medium heat*
Top sirloin	1½ inches thick	10 to 14 minutes: sear 6 to 8 minutes *direct high heat*, grill 4 to 6 minutes *indirect high heat*
Tri tip	2 to 2½ pounds	30 to 40 minutes: sear 10 minutes *direct medium heat*, grill 20 to 30 minutes *indirect medium heat*

 # LAMB

CUT	THICKNESS / WEIGHT	APPROXIMATE GRILLING TIME
Chop: loin or rib	¾ inch thick	4 to 6 minutes *direct high heat*
	1 inch thick	6 to 8 minutes *direct high heat*
	1½ inches thick	8 to 10 minutes *direct high heat*
Lamb, ground	¾ inch thick	8 to 10 minutes *direct medium-high heat*
Leg of lamb, boneless, rolled	2½ to 3 pounds	30 to 45 minutes: sear 10 to 15 minutes *direct medium heat*, grill 20 to 30 minutes *indirect medium heat*
Leg of lamb, butterflied	3 to 3½ pounds	30 to 45 minutes: sear 10 to 15 minutes *direct medium heat*, grill 20 to 30 minutes *indirect medium heat*
Rack of lamb	1 to 1½ pounds	15 to 20 minutes: sear 5 minutes *direct medium heat*, grill 10 to 15 minutes *indirect medium heat*

▼ POULTRY

CUT	THICKNESS / WEIGHT	APPROXIMATE GRILLING TIME
Chicken breast, bone in	10 to 12 ounces	23 to 35 minutes: 3 to 5 minutes *direct medium heat*, 20 to 30 minutes *indirect medium heat*
Chicken breast, boneless, skinless	6 to 8 ounces	8 to 12 minutes *direct medium heat*
Chicken drumstick	3 to 4 ounces	26 to 40 minutes: 6 to 10 minutes *direct medium heat*, 20 to 30 minutes *indirect medium heat*
Chicken thigh, bone in	5 to 6 ounces	36 to 40 minutes: 6 to 10 minutes *direct medium heat*, 30 minutes *indirect medium heat*
Chicken thigh, boneless, skinless	4 ounces	8 to 10 minutes *direct medium heat*
Chicken thigh, ground	¾ inch thick	12 to 14 minutes *direct medium heat*
Chicken, whole	4 to 5 pounds	1¼ to 1½ hours *indirect medium heat*
Chicken, whole leg	10 to 12 ounces	48 minutes to 1 hour: 40 to 50 minutes *indirect medium heat*, 8 to 10 minutes *direct medium heat*
Chicken wing	2 to 3 ounces	35 to 43 minutes: 30 to 35 minutes *indirect medium heat*, 5 to 8 minutes *direct medium heat*
Cornish game hen	1½ to 2 pounds	50 minutes to 1 hour *indirect high heat*
Duck breast, boneless	10 to 12 ounces	9 to 12 minutes: 3 to 4 minutes *direct low heat*, 6 to 8 minutes *indirect high heat*
Duck, whole	5½ to 6 pounds	40 minutes *indirect high heat*
Turkey breast, boneless	2½ pounds	1 to 1¼ hours *indirect medium heat*
Turkey, whole, not stuffed	10 to 12 pounds	2½ to 3½ hours *indirect medium-low heat*

USDA AND CHEF STANDARDS FOR DONENESS

> For optimal safety, the United States Department of Agriculture (USDA) recommends cooking red meat to 145°F (final temperature) and ground red meat to 160°F. The USDA believes that 145°F is medium rare, but virtually all chefs today believe medium rare is closer to 130°F. The chart at right compares chef standards with USDA recommendations. Ultimately, doneness decisions are your choice.

DONENESS	CHEF STANDARDS	USDA
PORK	145°F	145°F
RED MEAT: Rare	120° to 125°F	n/a
RED MEAT: Medium rare	125° to 135°F	145°F
RED MEAT: Medium	135° to 145°F	160°F
RED MEAT: Medium well	145° to 155°F	n/a
RED MEAT: Well done	155°F +	170°F
POULTRY	160° to 165°F	165°F

▼ SEAFOOD

CUT	THICKNESS / WEIGHT	APPROXIMATE GRILLING TIME
Clam (discard any that do not open)	2 to 3 ounces	6 to 8 minutes *direct high heat*
Fish, fillet or steak: halibut, red snapper, salmon, sea bass, swordfish, and tuna	½ inch thick	6 to 8 minutes *direct high heat*
	1 inch thick	8 to 10 minutes *direct high heat*
	1 to 1¼ inches thick	10 to 12 minutes *direct high heat*
	1 pound	15 to 20 minutes *indirect medium heat*
Fish, whole	2 to 2½ pounds	20 to 30 minutes *indirect medium heat*
	3 pounds	30 to 45 minutes *indirect medium heat*
Lobster tail	6 ounces	7 to 11 minutes *direct medium heat*
Mussel (discard any that do not open)	1 to 2 ounces	5 to 6 minutes *direct high heat*
Oyster	3 to 4 ounces	5 to 7 minutes *direct high heat*
Scallop	1½ ounces	4 to 6 minutes *direct high heat*
Shrimp	1½ ounces	2 to 4 minutes *direct high heat*

▼ FRUIT

TYPE	THICKNESS	APPROXIMATE GRILLING TIME
Apple	whole	35 to 40 minutes *indirect medium heat*
	½-inch slices	4 to 6 minutes *direct medium heat*
Apricot	halved lengthwise	4 to 6 minutes *direct medium heat*
Banana	halved lengthwise	3 to 5 minutes *direct medium heat*
Peach/Nectarine	halved lengthwise	6 to 8 minutes *direct medium heat*
Pear	halved lengthwise	6 to 8 minutes *direct medium heat*
Pineapple	½-inch slices or 1-inch wedges	5 to 10 minutes *direct medium heat*
Plum	halved lengthwise	6 to 8 minutes *direct medium heat*
Strawberry	whole	4 to 5 minutes *direct medium heat*

⊙ VEGETABLE

TYPE	THICKNESS	APPROXIMATE GRILLING TIME
Artichoke hearts	whole	14 to 18 minutes: boil 10 to 12 minutes; cut in half and grill 4 to 6 minutes *direct medium heat*
Asparagus	½-inch diameter	6 to 8 minutes *direct medium heat*
Beet (6 ounces)	whole	1 to 1½ hours *indirect medium heat*
Bell pepper	whole	10 to 12 minutes *direct medium heat*
Carrot	1-inch diameter	7 to 11 minutes: boil 4 to 6 minutes, grill 3 to 5 minutes *direct high heat*
Corn, husked		10 to 15 minutes *direct medium heat*
Corn, in husk		20 to 30 minutes *direct medium heat*
Eggplant	½-inch slices	8 to 10 minutes *direct medium heat*
Garlic	whole	45 minutes to 1 hour *indirect medium heat*
Mushroom, button or shiitake	whole	8 to 10 minutes *direct medium heat*
Mushroom, portabello	whole	8 to 12 minutes *direct medium heat*
Onion	halved	35 to 40 minutes *indirect medium heat*
	½-inch slices	8 to 12 minutes *direct medium heat*
Potato, new	halved	15 to 20 minutes *direct medium heat*
Potato, russet	whole	45 minutes to 1 hour *indirect medium heat*
	½-inch slices	9 to 11 minutes *direct medium heat*
Potato, sweet	whole	45 minutes to 1 hour *indirect high heat*
	½-inch slices	12 to 15 minutes *direct medium heat*
Scallion	whole	3 to 4 minutes *direct medium heat*
Squash, acorn (1½ pounds)	halved	40 minutes to 1 hour *indirect medium heat*
Tomato, garden or plum	whole	8 to 10 minutes *direct medium heat*
	halved	6 to 8 minutes *direct medium heat*
Zucchini	½-inch slices	4 to 6 minutes *direct medium heat*

ACKNOWLEDGMENTS

There are so many people that made this book what it is. It took total dedication to excellence at stage after stage.

First, there was the idea that sprouted, believe it or not, in Germany (at the Frankfurt Book Fair) from the sharp minds of Stephanie Wenzel, Gabriella Hoffmann, and other wonderful colleagues at Gräfe und Unzer. They saw the potential for a book in Europe about traditional American barbecue. Mike Kempster, Brooke Jones, and Susan Maruyama at Weber broadened that vision to capture the evolving diversity of styles in new American barbecue. Thank you, Mike, Brooke, and Susan, for your compelling ideas and your unwavering trust in me.

Charged with the mission of telling a comprehensive story, I interviewed dozens of pit masters, chefs, food writers, and barbecue fanatics all over the land. I want to thank all of them, especially Doug Adams, Arthur Aguirre, Peter Botcher, Bryan Bracewell, Melissa and Pete Cookston, Steve Cruz, Ardie Davis, Greg and Gabrielle Denton, Ryan Farr, Aaron Franklin, Meathead Goldwyn, Craig and Gay Jones, Ray Lampe, Adam Perry Lang, Edward Lee, Chris Lilly, Amy Mills, Mike Mills, Wayne Mueller, Robert Moss, Sonny Orsini, Steven Raichlen, Barry Sorkin, Norman Van Aken, Daniel Vaughn, Lee Ann Whippen, Carolyn Wells, and Doug Worgul. Each of them is a blazing star in the barbecue universe.

I also want to acknowledge the talented members of the 2015 Danish National Barbecue Team, who allowed me to watch them compete with impressive success at the Memphis in May World Championship Barbecue Cooking Contest. I salute you all: Per Svane Aastradsen, Jim Boland, Peter Bragh, Asger Hvam, Anders Jensen, Mads Bo Kristensen, Claus Hasse Olesen, Stig Pedersen, Michael Dahl Thomsen, and the amazing Anne Jungersen Thomsen.

While working on the recipes and text, I was spoiled by some of the brightest, most creative culinarians in the country. My heartfelt gratitude goes to: Patty Ada, Lynda Balslev, Brigit Binns, Lena Birnbaum, David Bonom, Linda Carucci, Sarah Epstein, Suzy Farnsworth, Heather John Fogarty, Elizabeth Hughes, Allison Kociuruba, Adrian Miller, Marge Perry, Lesley Porcelli, Rick Rodgers, Cheryl Sternman Rule, Mic Stanfield, Kerry Trotter, Bruce Weinstein, and Terri Wuerthner.

When it came time to photograph the recipes and all the techniques so important for making barbecue successfully, I relied on the endlessly skilled Tim Turner and his team. We couldn't have done all this without Brett Bulthuis, Mike Caviani, Ben Leikness, Josh Marrah, Meghan Ross, and Donte Tatum. For the phenomenal food styling, we were fortunate to work with Lynn Gagné and Nina Albazi. The photography of restaurants featured in essays throughout the book was done beautifully by Michael Warren.

Throughout the book-making process, I turned time and again to the barbecue professionals at Weber. I can't thank these people enough for responding every time with genuine collaboration and professionalism: Kim Lefko, Suzanne Brown, Deanna Budnick, Mike Chavez, Marc Colavitti, Neal Conner, Larry Donahue, Kim Durk, Mark Fenne, Lexy Fricano, Heather Herriges, Melanie Hill, Matt Jost, Kevin Kolman, Jennie Lussow, Theresa Stahl, and the man who steers the entire company, Tom Koos.

The main reason this book is such fun to peruse is that Christina Schroeder led a team of creative wizards at rabble+rouser. Thank you, Marsha Capen, for giving every aspect of this book your acute editorial expertise. Shum Prats will forever have my admiration and respect for his brilliant design. Alyx Chapman also worked wonders with the graphics. Tamara McTavish and Teddy Sirotek stepped up whenever they were asked and performed like champions. Becky LaBrum pulled it all together in a clear, thorough index.

This is my first book with Houghton Mifflin Harcourt (HMH) as publisher, and I couldn't be happier with the partnership. Bruce Nichols, Natalie Chapman, and Cindy Kitchel brought tremendous insights and editorial resources to this project. I am confident that the book will be sold far and wide because of dedicated HMH people, especially Laurie Brown, Maire Gorman, Lori Glazer, Brad Parsons, James Phirman, Rebecca Liss, Colleen Murphy, and Allison Renzulli.

At home I am blessed to have a fabulous family that doesn't object when I set off for yet another research trip or when I walk in the front door with yet another immense brisket that will require barbecuing throughout the night. Thank you, Fran, Julia, James, and Peter. I love you all.

AUTHOR
Jamie Purviance

MANAGING EDITOR
Marsha Capen

EDITORIAL, DESIGN, AND PRODUCTION
rabble+rouser, inc.:
Chief Creative Officer: **Christina Schroeder**
Editorial Director: **Marsha Capen**
Creative Director: **Shum Prats**
Graphic Design: **Alyx Chapman**
Senior Producer: **Tamara McTavish**
Producer: **Teddy Sirotek**

FOOD PHOTOGRAPHER
Tim Turner

LIFESTYLE PHOTOGRAPHER
Michael Warren

PHOTOGRAPHY CREDIT
Jamie Purviance, pp. 56, 80, 81, 82, 160, 164, 186

PHOTO ASSISTANTS TO TIM TURNER
**Brett Bulthuis, Mike Caviani, Ben Leikness,
Josh Marrah, Donte Tatum**

LOCATION MANAGER
Meghan Ross

FOOD STYLING
Food Stylist: **Lynn Gagné**
Assistant Food Stylist: **Nina Albazi**

PROP STYLING
Christina Schroeder

COLOR IMAGING AND IN-HOUSE PREPRESS
Weber Creative Services:
Deanna Budnick
Neal Conner
Mike Chavez

CONTRIBUTORS
**Patty Ada, Lynda Balslev, Brigit Binns, Lena Birnbaum,
David Bonom, Linda Carucci, Sarah Epstein, Suzy Farnsworth,
Heather John Fogarty, Elizabeth Hughes, Allison Kociuruba,
Adrian Miller, Marge Perry, Lesley Porcelli, Rick Rodgers,
Cheryl Sternman Rule, Mic Stanfield, Kerry Trotter,
Bruce Weinstein, Terri Wuerthner**

INDEXER
Becky LaBrum

ROUND MOUNTAIN MEDIA
Consulting Global Publishing Director: **Susan J. Maruyama**

WEBER-STEPHEN PRODUCTS LLC
Executive Board Director: **Mike Kempster**
Chief Marketing Officer: **Kim Lefko**
Vice President Marketing, Global Marketing: **Brooke Jones**

HOUGHTON MIFFLIN HARCOURT
Vice President, Publisher: **Natalie Chapman**
Editorial Director: **Cindy Kitchel**
Managing Editor: **Marina Padakis Lowry**
Production Director: **Thomas Hyland**

www.hmhco.com
www.weber.com®
www.rabbleandrouser.com

Library of Congress Cataloging-in-Publication Data is available.
ISBN 978-0-544-71527-1 (pbk)
ISBN 978-0-544-71530-1 (ebk)

Printed in the United States of America

1421   10 9 8 7 6 5 4 3 2 1

4500589591

SOURCES
The following books and websites were excellent sources of
information for this book.

Cookston, Melissa. *Smokin' in the Boys' Room: Southern Recipes from
the Winningest Woman in Barbecue.* Andrews McMeel Publishing,
LLC, 2014.

Engelhardt, Elizabeth S. D. *Republic of Barbecue: Stories Beyond
the Brisket.* University of Texas Press, 2009.

Franklin, Aaron, and Jordan Mackay. *Franklin Barbecue:
A Meat-Smoking Manifesto.* Ten Speed Press, 2015.

Goldwyn, Craig. www.amazingribs.com.

López-Alt, J. Kenji. *The Food Lab: Better Home Cooking Through
Science.* W. W. Norton & Company, Inc., 2015.

Moss, Robert F. *Barbecue: The History of an American Institution.*
University Alabama Press, 2010.

Raichlen, Steven. *BBQ USA: 425 Fiery Recipes from All Across
America.* Workman Publishing Company, Inc., 2003.

Vaughn, Daniel. www.tmbbq.com.